Royal Navy Monitors of the First World War

THE END OF ADVENTURE
"Severn's" enemy as she lies today rusting up the Rufiji

Royal Navy Monitors of the First World War

Actions off the Belgian and East African Coasts and Rivers, 1914-18

ILLUSTRATED

"Severn's" Saga

E. Keble Chatterton

The Royal Marines in the East African Campaign

General Sir H.E Blumberg

Royal Navy Monitors of the First World War
Actions off the Belgian and East African Coasts and Rivers, 1914-18
"Severn's" Saga
By E. Keble Chatterton
The Royal Marines in the East African Campaign
By General Sir H.E Blumberg

ILLUSTRATED

First published in the titles
"Severn's" Saga
and
Britain's Sea Soldiers-A record of the Royal Marines during the war 1914-19
(extract)

Leonaur is an imprint of Oakpast Ltd
Copyright in this form © 2025 Oakpast Ltd

ISBN: 978-1-917666-48-0 (hardcover)
ISBN: 978-1-917666-49-7 (softcover)

http://www.leonaur.com

Publisher's Notes
The views expressed in this book are not necessarily those of the publisher.

Contents

The Monitors	7
Sea Surprise	17
Belgian Coast	25
The Bombarders	34
North Sea	46
Mystery Voyage	56
The Raider Puts to Sea	68
Dangerous Adventure	79
Blockade	88
In the Red Sea	100
Tropical Arrival	108
Preparing For Battle	117
Secret Plans	128
The Great Occasion	136
The Result	152
Dash Into Tanga	165
The River Hazard	174
Yambe Island	188
Narrow Waters	196

Glorious Adventure	205
Advance Begins	215
Bagamoyo and Dar-Es-Salaam	222
Down South	234
The Royal Marines in the East African Campaign	247

Chapter 1

The Monitors

August 4, 1914.

War imminent, Great Britain in a state of tension, France in a condition of alarm; the Grand Fleet already somewhere in the North Sea, the French Mediterranean Fleet under way in the Middle Sea, and the British Government about to send Germany an ultimatum that would expire at midnight. A few hours later, telegraph cables in the English Channel connecting Berlin with the outward world would be cut by Admiralty orders, and in that final act would be the severance from an old era. Thereafter the whole of civilisation must begin a strange new epoch.

Excited London crowds were thronging Whitehall, army officers were seeking interviews at the War Office, whilst across the road naval officers not lucky enough to be serving with the Grand Fleet were hurrying into the Admiralty buildings asking for jobs. Captains and commanders still on the active list; others long since retired, but now roused from country home or comfortable club chair, surged down the corridors till they formed a veritable blockade outside the room of the Second Sea Lord's private secretary. And each applicant arrived with the same request.

Command of a sea-going ship, or at least some appointment afloat, ere it was too late: for the expectation of only a short, sharp sea campaign, which might be over before Christmas and end without their own personal participation, added acuteness to enthusiasm.

But this sudden gathering of sailors had awakened happy memories; old shipmates, separated for years by time and place, now resumed contact.

"Well! Well! If it isn't 'Ginger' Brown! We haven't met since...."

"Recognised you at once—though you've put on a little weight. And when did you leave the Service? Oh! Fruit-farming in Devonshire? But does it pay?"

"Came up by the milk train. Wonder what they'll offer me. Oh, no! Not a shore job: if you please. Eyesight as good as ever, fit as the youngest. I'd like one of those new destroyers."

"M'dear fellow, don't you realise? These people in the Admiralty always get first choice. The last of the new destroyers yesterday was allotted to Captain...."

"Well, s'long. And good luck!"

The office door opened, and he disappeared within.

So, the anxious day passed into dusk, and still the stream of callers seemed unending. On the morrow many of the same unsatisfied mustered again, peering round the door, buttonholing anyone in authority who might be able to short-circuit urgent request. But presently the numbers swelled considerably: the morning's newspapers had electrified the Kingdom's remotest corners.

"*Britain Joins France. War With Germany Declared.*"

Senior lieut.-commanders, junior commanders, post-captains promoted so recently as last June, were jostling each other in suspenseful expectation, when once more the solid door swung open and a contented face emerged. Decisions were being made more rapidly, appointments to ships needed now the fewest minutes, gradually little groups dissolved and vanished; the corridors thinned noticeably as speedy departures to Portsmouth, Chatham, Devonport, shipbuilding yards or some Scottish port, synchronised with that sudden twist which was to alter completely many a naval career.

Out of that throng strode Commander Eric J. A. Fullerton R.N., appointed in charge of the Monitor Squadron, and across his course at this moment an old friend passed—Lieut.-Commander R. Amcotts Wilson R.N.

"Hallo, Wilson! Would you like to come in a monitor?"

"Monitor! What the deuce is a monitor?"

The question was natural enough, for the very word suggested a sea-heresy of our forefathers; but the "Blue Water" school had years since educated opinion to think in terms of battle-squadrons and attack, rather than to await the enemy. Men-of-war should be active rather than passive, and monitors surely belonged to the obsolete "Coast Defence" theory; which was dead as crinolines, antimacassars, and Mr. Gladstone.

True, indeed, half a century ago, the historic frigate *Merrimac* during the American Civil War had been cut down almost to the waterline and armoured with two thicknesses of plating; then, to outrival her, Captain Ericsson had designed an iron ship of 614 tons, whose hull was visible only a couple of feet above the sea. Intended primarily for defence of the coast, this low-lying vessel with her couple of centrally mounted cannon, was really little more than a mobile gun-platform. Speed did not enter into the question, and inconspicuousness was more desirable than seagoing ability.

Named the *Monitor*, she played her destined part and exercised some influence over the conservative British Navy who adopted both the name and the idea. After the *Royal Sovereign* had been cut down from being a lofty three-decker to a ship of only 6 feet freeboard, and a further stage in development was reached in the *Monarch*, monitors still persisted a while and then went to be broken up.

All this belonged so entirely to the dim past, that for the present generation of naval officers the term was meaningless: not one person in the corridor had ever beheld such a ship.

"A monitor," Commander Fullerton began to explain, "is a ship with a flat bottom, draws very little water, and . . . anyway, come and have lunch at my club."

So, out of Whitehall the two walked round the corner into Pall Mall, and were joined by Commander A. L. Snagge R.N. What did a monitor look like? Speed? Guns? Many questions were asked, much laughter took the place of solid information, nor could conjecture provide any satisfying picture. She was neither battleship nor cruiser, neither destroyer not submarine; but that summed up all knowledge. Lunch being over, these officers returned to the Admiralty, formal instructions were typed out, and at 11.30 that same night Commander Fullerton, Commander Snagge, Lieut.-Commander Wilson, left Euston in a hot, stuffy, north-bound train overfilled with naval ranks and ratings. Next morning at Bartow-in-Furness the trio gazed down at three extraordinary craft lying alongside Messrs Vickers' quay.

Actually, the firm had completed building these modern monitors for the Brazilian Government when the European crisis ripened, but, before delivery could be made, in stepped the British Government who promptly took them over. Designed for river work, having not more than 3¼ feet of freeboard for'ard and aft, they seemed at first glance all right for the Amazon's upper reaches but all wrong for the treacherous waters that wash England, Scotland, and Ireland. Single-funnelled, with an 80-ft. mast amidships, possessing excessive beam and not a sweet line anywhere; each monitor measured 265 ft. long,

49 ft. wide, and suggested not so much a ship as some squat floating fort with a citadel in the centre.

It was learned that the draught, when loaded, was quite ridiculously slight: no more than 6½ feet, yet this connoted a whole heap of future trouble: for, if they could be navigated in little more than a heavy dew, the slender grip on the water would make them slippery creatures except during a flat calm. With anything of a beam wind, they would be like motorcars skidding across a frozen street. And one glance at those low decks sufficed. Butting into a head sea, or running before an autumn gale, monitors would be as wet as a half-tide rock.

Their reputed tonnage was about 1,260, their alleged speed 12 knots; though as to the latter someone must have been exaggerating. Perhaps for a few minutes' spurt on a smooth tideless river, that rate might be possible, but obviously a monitor had never been designed for fast steaming. She carried only 187 tons of coal plus 90 tons of shale oil, and her radius would scarcely allow her to be away from port long. And in what capacity did the Lords of the Admiralty propose employing these freaks? Were such craft destined to go up England's canal system to protect grazing cattle?

Altogether the monitors seemed a poor sort of joke, and utterly useless against Germany's efficient forces.

The three newly appointed captains stepped aboard, and found the *Solomos*, *Madeira*, *Javery*, still in caretakers' hands. The tour of inspection began. National customs, of course differ, but the Brazilian standards of comfort for commanding officers was astonishingly high: nothing like their cabins had been experienced except aboard a millionaire's yacht. Such beautiful oak panelling, such wonderful Turkey carpets, such luxurious curtains, were beyond all belief. Then, too, the blue tablecloths ornamented with red anchors, the marvellous chairs with interchangeable seats to suit the weather, the resplendent brasswork against a multi-coloured background, fairly stunned seafaring minds. No picture could be less suggestive of war.

All these charming superfluities would have to come out at once and be thrust into store, every bit of bright work other than the working parts of guns would have to be painted over before going to sea, the white hulls would be transformed into a dark navy grey, and anything reminiscent of pleasure cruising must be altered completely.

At least one officer made a mental resolution. If peace should ever return, he would by no means refuse command of a monitor in some picturesque sunny corner of the Mediterranean, say among colourful islands of the Aegean or Adriatic, nosing up creeks and *calanques* away from stress and turmoil. But with the Great War barely two days old, such pleasant contemplation could not be indulged.

Meanwhile there was a vast amount of detail to get through ere these untried monitors were ready for sea, but on August 8 they were formally commissioned, the names being altered respectively to *Severn, Mersey, Humber*, Commander Fullerton taking the first, Lieut.-Commander Wilson the second, and Commander Snagge the third. Of the personnel to serve under them, some officers belonged to the active list, others had rejoined from the emergency list, whilst some had come from the Royal Naval Reserve; one, indeed, having already forsaken the sea for the stage, and he trusted the war might soon be over to allow him to play a leading part in *The Diamond King*. A schoolmaster, who had been teaching modern languages to Dartmouth cadets, came aboard as interpreter with a commission in the Royal Naval Volunteer Reserve, whilst two of the squadron's three surgeons had temporarily laid aside professional ambition for routine afloat.

As to the ships' companies, these consisted entirely of men from reserves, who either had become accustomed to shore life in steady jobs or, till a few days since, had been serving in the Merchant Service. Most of them needed considerable training and attention, but many were both raw and inexperienced.

For everybody life began afresh, and all sorts of new things had to be learned. Although Bartow happened to be part of Lancashire, it seemed to share a certain similarity with the perils of France's front line. Indeed, the eccentric zeal of Lancashire Territorial sentries round the docks quite astounded the sailors fitting out the squadron at the quay. As part of her equipment each monitor had been assigned one motorboat, and in a later chapter we shall observe the remarkable duties which these small open craft were to perform: but many of us have not forgotten that right from the earliest days of hostilities till long after armistice British naval motorboats of this type were notoriously unreliable, with a curious reluctance to start when required.

Even whilst the *Severn* and her sisters were still at Bartow, this trouble with the starting-handle manifested itself, wherefore a special mechanic from some motor works up the town had been employed to put matters right. One day he set off in the boat, together with a petty officer as coxswain in the stern and a seaman in the bows. It had been arranged that she should run her trials within the shipyard precincts so far as the caisson and back. This had been going on throughout the

BRITISH MONITORS, MERSEY, HUMBER, AND SEVERN.

forenoon, and gradually the unwilling engine yielded to treatment. Then, about mid-day, just as the boat approached the caisson and the coxswain standing up put his helm over to return, he noticed a bullet strike the water at surprisingly close range.

Forthwith a regular fusillade followed, bullets flying over his head and under his arm so plentifully that he ordered "all hands lie down and take cover". Luckily the motor never stopped, but having withdrawn from the danger zone and gained the monitor's side, sure enough a bullet hole in the brand-new wooden boat told its own story; which so impressed the mechanic that he threw on his coat, picked up his tool-bag, and departed. A protest from the navy to the colonel resulted in a new order that henceforth blank cartridges were to be served out to recruits, and only old soldiers were to have ball.

The real comedy of monitor life was inaugurated on the day when "acceptance trials" took place preparatory to the ships being finally handed over from the builders. Normally during peace times these formalities are quite enjoyable occasions, with the contractors' men doing all the work but naval officers and crew as interested spectators. Everything having passed off satisfactorily, corks fly, healths are drunk (at the firm's expense), and the ship enters her career under favourable auspices.

But this August life was different, routine was different, and monitors were different from normal men-of-war. If old customs needed to be cut out, a lot of new tricks required to be learnt quickly, and time pressed. The day arrived when all three monitors should go out through the lock in turn at hourly intervals and demonstrate capabilities off Walney Island, with a representative of the builders to show each captain sundry special idiosyncrasies. Right from the first it was a cause of surprise that the local expert deemed three tugs indispensable for a vessel of only 1,500 tons having twin propellers. But the man acted with sound prudence: one tug ahead, one astern, and another standing by for emergency, turned out to be essential in narrow passages.

It had been hinted that monitors were slow and unhandy, but the full truth came with a shock after tugs were slipped and a course was set down river. The wash from the propellers, very moderately submerged, might have impressed some minds, but a glance towards a near-by buoy indicated the most leisurely progress. Perhaps the tide was still flooding?

Not a bit! The ebb had already set in, and the monitor ought to

Monitor being towed at sea to operational area

be doing far better, yet even as the favourable stream strengthened, she just sidled slowly across the channel, so that when a steamer approached it became urgently requisite to get out of the way.

The pilot rang down engine-telegraphs to 'Stop': then to 'Full Astern'.

But nothing happened, and the wayward warship persisted slowly on, which amazed even the cautious pilot who, visibly agitated, walked uneasily up and down the bridge. Then suddenly he halted.

"Hell! The flap!", he recollected, and running across the bridge pulled over a lever.

"What's that for?", inquired the naval commanding officer.:

"Jump aft, someone please, and see if the flap's down."

This piece of steel had to be dropped over the tunnel before reversing engines, or the monitor would not go astern, and thus another peculiarity presented itself. None the less, whatever might happen in the future, the flap appeared to make so little difference that captain and pilot decided to summon the tug alongside and call it a day.

The nett result of that initial trip proved quite definitely not merely that these river gunboats were ridiculously slow, but that they were practically uncontrollable with the wind at right angles to the hull. Dangerous to themselves in restricted waters, and a source of anxiety to other vessels, the demand for ample sea-room became obvious.

THE "MONITOR" ENTIRELY CASED IN WITH STEEL PLATES READY FOR OCEAN TRANSPORT. PART REMOVED TO SHOW INTERIOR.

"MONITOR IN ACTION. CASING REMOVED. FUNNEL MAST AND SUPER STRUCTURE HAVING BEEN RE ERECTED.

CHAPTER 2

Sea Surprise

Even a casual examination of *Severn's* photograph will enable the reader to appreciate the unseaworthiness of low-lying decks, and it was during the night of August 22 when the *Mersey*, lying at anchor as guardship to Barrow's approaches in comparatively sheltered water, gave practical proof of this undesirable feature.

The wind increased, anchor dragged, and by daylight it was necessary to weigh; but ere this could be effected, waves kept breaking over the foc'sle, deluging the first lieutenant and his men as if they were surf-bathing. Two days later *Humber* was sent away independently, then on the night of August 25 at 10-30 *Severn* with *Mersey* steamed off from Barrow under orders to make for Dover "with despatch", not even delaying in order to practise their guns.

The start was accompanied by perfect weather, and good wishes signalled from the local military. Such encouragement at the first could do no harm, for the Irish Sea has a nasty habit of changing its temperament and making itself objectionable with too little warning. Sure enough, not six hours had elapsed when a "fresh breeze" sprang up, and both monitors were badly caught. As daylight returned, so did wind and waves get more ferocious, hatches had to be battened down, mess-decks were flooded, sleep out of the question, feeding quite a problem, and the crew must be accommodated in officers' wardroom as well as captain's cabin, which alone were free of water.

Throughout this initial day at sea the monitors fulfilled the worst suspicions. Wet? They seemed to spend most of their time in submergence, and the pounding waves broke over them mercilessly. Darkness brought weather viler still, so that it was unsafe for anyone to tread the foc'sle, but the gale's climax occurred as they were endeavouring to round St. David's Head about midnight. Very slowly *Severn* succeeded in forging ahead, making slightly better progress, though *Mersey's* speed against wind and tide dropped to 3 miles over the ground and finally to a one-mile gait.

A desperate fight ensued as wind plus tide were driving her shoreward, and Welsh rocks loomed up unpleasantly near. To make the situation less bearable, she now carried away her foc'sle hatch, and the ship would have presented an easy opening to be filled up had not Commander Wilson stopped engines, while men waded forward and jammed up the aperture. The Pembrokeshire coast throughout the centuries has been so entirely at the mercy of southwest gales that portions of the county have broken away into a series of islets, including the Bishop and Clerks, the Smalls, Skomar, Skokham, Grassholm, but on each of the first two a lighthouse aids navigation.

A full hour's fight was needed to get the Bishop's radiance astern, and now *Mersey* steadily seemed to be losing her steam, which remained inexplicable till the engineer-lieutenant mounted the bridge to announce that the Leading Stoker on watch, in charge of the stokehold, had made a bad mistake. He had been spraying on the fires *cold* oil-fuel, which tended to extinguish instead of increase good burning; but the incident was expressive of the prevailing naval precipitancy. Having come so recently from the "beach", he had now for the first time been shipmates with fluid fuel.

The error having been discovered in time, furnaces were cleaned, a fresh effort made, and the tide turned so as to set the monitors away from the shore. This somewhat eased the suspense, though a more atrocious disturbance developed through the stream being opposed to southwest gale. Down below the sweating stokers were toiling to coax all the possible knots out of a shallow hull, and a weird spectacle the two ships presented in the black night, as flames shot higher and higher almost to the masthead. For this flagrant belching from funnel was another tiresome trick which the monitors displayed quite early, and it was going to cause no little anxiety later. Just now, what the signal stations on land thought of these two blazing factories beyond St. Bride's Bay, and what sort of reports were being transmitted, could only be conjectured.

At length the lonely Smalls light drew nearer, but on the wrong side. It should have been rounded on its west (or seaward) approach, but nothing would induce the wayward monitors to hold such a course, and the only alternative was to up-helm, bring the wind more on the beam and trust that after the Smalls had been left on the east side, neither monitor would strike the unlit Skokham island, where

H.M.S. MERSEY.

the tides rush by at most of 3 knots. One danger at a time! Each problem in its turn! When clear of the Smalls, the ships were rolling heavily, yet they had freed their wind and thus attained better speed. Milford Haven was just round the corner, and a weak glimmer of the moon sufficiently illumined Skokham at the right moment.

Now Milford Haven, with the Pembroke Dockyard well inside, was destined during the war to lose much of its old-world sleepiness and become a busy naval base. The haven's entrance happens to be wide, and affords plenty of water. Well buoyed and lit, the navigation needs merely normal care even during the dark hours.

For the monitors the certainty of a safe anchorage, a short spell to allow of hatches being unscrewed, ventilation fore and aft, the drying of personal gear, and the chance of tired men catching up with sleep, made the mention of Milford sound more than attractive. Perhaps, however, not one officer to-night realised that for shallow vessels the Haven mouth is thoroughly dangerous during a southwest gale, as was to be proved in the following December twelve months. It was a night that some of us remember vividly nearly twenty-five years after.

Caught in a Christmas blow, the Milford patrol drifters were running for home, but the *Ferndale* foundered in the jobble at the mouth, and the *Ladysmith* was driven on to Skokham island: in both cases all hands were lost. Yet these vessels drew 2½ feet more than the monitors, and possessed greater seaworthiness. What finally prevented *Severn* and *Mersey*? from turning into this natural harbour was the thought of a very different possibility. The sight of two unusual hulls, suddenly coming up towards the forts at dead of night, would almost certainly start something. Soldiers would switch on searchlights, signals might be misunderstood, a gun might be loosed off prematurely, and then a torrent of shells from every land battery would have to be borne disastrously.

No: better to face this August gale than risk the attentions of well-meaning friends. Wherefore, course was altered for Land's End, the weather shewed signs of improvement, and neither the Bristol Channel nor the rugged Cornish coast appeared so boisterous as it can be. Other vessels came into sight; a large armoured cruiser flying the Stars and Stripes, a British destroyer steaming at full speed, went past; and as the English Channel opened, so the meteorological change became complete. Summer had returned.

Then was due another touch of comedy.

So gracious and calm was the sea on reaching the Isle of Wight, that

H.M.S. "Severn"

this would be a good opportunity for testing the manoeuvring powers of monitors in ample space long before reaching the narrow entrance of Dover harbour. More especially it was required to see again if these awkward vessels could be persuaded to go astern properly.

Alas! Neither of them would obey their masters, preferring to rotate in wild circles and perform strange antics, which so puzzled the Isle of Wight gunners that they kept their sights trained on such suspicious ships. News was telephoned through to the naval Commander-in-Chief Portsmouth that two men-of-war, unlike anything inside the book of British silhouettes, were behaving off the coast in a most astounding manner, and might they be fired on?

Happily, one of the admiral's staff knew that monitors were on passage, inquired as to their appearance, and promptly forbade the requested permission.

"The ships are all right, and bound east up Channel."

"No", denied the gunner down the telephone. "That's just it. They're not steaming east at all: they're coming west, and stern first."

With some final reluctance was the soldier appeased, and the voyage continued past the Sussex chalk cliffs, beyond Dungeness, and at last the solid breakwaters. of Dover were abreast.

Signalling between *Severn* and shore began.

"What ship?"

Permission to enter was not forthcoming. The secret recognition-signal, though made correctly, failed to satisfy the authorities: in fact, the Examination Service were thoroughly incredulous. Never had they set eyes on such ugly ships, and, notwithstanding the White Ensigns aft, these squat hulls could not be British. Some fancy trick on the enemy's part, no doubt: but it wouldn't work.

So, the unfortunate monitors were kept out in the strong Dover tide till further inquiries could be made, and that wasted about two hours. Even after identification had been effected and crisis averted, a chilly welcome awaited them. The Examination Steamer still didn't like the look of this breed, and was convinced they had been built in Germany. "Where have you come from? Did you capture them?"

The harbour seemed alive with shipping, but every man on deck stopped work to watch these "flat-irons" come slowly to anchor.

"'Strewth! But what *are* they?"

Soon everybody afloat and in the coastal signal stations would learn what was a monitor, for photographs were now sent far and wide. Meanwhile, having taken 3½ days to steam only 610 miles, *Severn* and

Mersey began filling up each with 60 tons of coal. A day later arrived also the *Humber*, and now the squadron again was complete.

Beyond the Dover Straits terribly serious developments had been fashioning history. The British Army had been compelled to retreat from Mons, the French from Charleroi. Dunkirk, Calais, Boulogne looked like falling into the Germans' hands as bases threatening Dover's very existence from three points. On the very night that the two monitors left Barrow, orders had been sent out for three battalions of Marines to leave for Ostend with the object of creating a diversion against the German western flank, and some of the older British battleships including the *Vengeance* were to co-operate.

Ostend was indeed successfully occupied, then immediately ensued the naval action off Heligoland on August 28, the day preceding *Severn* and *Mersey's* arrival at Dover. But events were chasing each other so closely that a fresh phase ripened almost every hour. Although the transportation of the British Expeditionary Force had not yet been completed, its port of entry into France could no longer be on the north but the northwest: well down the Bay of Biscay at St. Nazaire, where the Loire flows by from Nantes. This important resolve was being made as the monitors neared the Dover cliffs.

Then at midnight of August 30-31 came the sudden order for the Marines to be re-embarked from Ostend, and at once there would be an opportunity for this little squadron to operate among the shallows off the Flemish coast, even entering Ostend harbour, where cruisers and battleships might be thwarted for lack of water. Actually, the monitors were ready by 8 p.m. on the 30th, but it will be recollected that though each mounted a couple of 6-inch and two 4.7-in guns, there had been no time for firing these. That was why departure had to be postponed till 6 a.m. on the 31st, when the squadron went out of Dover by the northern entrance and made towards the Varne shoal. There the trials took place, to the extent of two rounds being fired from each gun at a bit of bunting on a pole, which caused such a sensation ashore that local correspondents telegraphed their editors in London:

"*Heavy Firing in the Channel. Action With German Ships.*"

On the whole this trial was satisfactory, although the Brazilian cartridges for the 4.7-in howitzers did not fit the guns, which necessitated the advent of workmen to file half an inch off each brass cartridge-cylinder. At 3.30 p.m. away the monitors steamed in the direction of Ostend, passing eight cruisers and two destroyers which escorted the Queen of the Belgians with her children bound for England. Next arrived a wireless from H.M.S. *Vengeance* saying that monitors would not be required after all, for by 8.30 p.m. Ostend had been evacuated and the Marines taken on board the battleships who were already hurrying home. One and a half hours later the monitors anchored in the outer roads off Ostend awaiting further orders, and at midnight to their great disappointment another wireless signal told them to make for the Medway. They had been cheated of their chance at the very last.

Once again were monitors subjected to rude buffetings, and the sand-laden shoals of the Flemish banks with their short steep seas are notoriously unkind to ships. During the middle watch (12.4 a.m.) it piped up, the fore hatch aboard *Mersey* had to be battened down; moreover, when it was time the relief men should come on deck at four o'clock, the captain must needs put ship stern on to wind ere the hatch were lifted. The new watch tumbled out into the damp quick enough, having been starved of ventilation and unable to sleep because of the violent banging about.

Carrying with them the last of the Thames flood, the monitors reached Sheerness by noon, not without having caused many a surprise. As this quaint trio steamed slowly in line-ahead, merchant steamers and men-of-war eyed them with the old suspicion. In those days the Thames estuary lightships marking the navigation were still in place, but here and there an occasional British submarine was on the lookout for enemy units. Today, as the monitors approached towards high water, it was practicable for the light-draught squadron to swerve out of deep water channels and cut across corners, which so alarmed a submarine that she signalled "You are going on to dry land," and so astounded the lightship-keeper that he fired a rocket and began sounding his foghorn.

Six weeks of uninteresting patrol off the Nore were succeeded by an entire change of outlook, and the sequence of military events in Belgium provided these river gunboats with special work for which they were exactly suitable and no one could have foreseen. It was as if history had designed this niche for the monitors to fill, and so fashioned events that the crisis occurred only after the crews had settled down, some improvements been caused by Chatham Dockyard working night and day to put armoured plates over the magazines; and even the least experienced rating had been made efficient by constant drill.

CHAPTER 3

Belgian Coast

Now in Belgium a land race between the Allies on one side and the Germans on the other with the Channel ports as prize, had become an amazing competition before September was ended. The vast hordes of unlimited German soldiery pouring across the flat country, the possibility of the Belgian Army being cut off, and the probability of Antwerp being captured, were of such seriousness in themselves that it was impossible to foretell the immediate effect. Collectively, however, these were likely to bring about a result which would alter the whole future of European history.

Something had to be done about it, and quickly; wherefore British reinforcements numbering 20,000 troops, were rushed across the English Channel into Belgium by October 7. But three days later Antwerp capitulated, the Royal Naval Division were retiring towards Ostend, and thither likewise the Belgian Government was withdrawing. The situation scarcely encouraged an optimistic view under any circumstance. If the reinforcements had arrived too late and in too little strength to sustain Antwerp, at least they did hinder the enemy from cutting off the Belgians, and thereafter continued as additional aid to the hard-pressed Allies. But the realisation that the German right was rapidly stretching out towards the sea-dunes, and might fall upon Ostend whilst transports were being filled, roused unpleasant fears.

There were over 5,000 men of the Royal Naval Division to be carried back to England, more than twice that number of Belgian recruits destined for one of the French ports, to say nothing of wounded and stores. In some form—by land, or from sea—the enemy might spring a surprise during these embarkations, but in order to ward off such an attack definite naval cover was now afforded by the British Admiralty. The selected force was the Monitor Squadron who rendezvoused in the Downs and left there at 7.30 a.m. on October 11 escorted by destroyers. Notwithstanding that *Severn* broke down six hours later, and had to be taken in tow by *Humber*, the trio reached their destination by six the same evening and anchored outside Ostend piers.

Next day they moved closer in towards the beach, and again anchored, each ship being a couple of miles apart. Careful bearings were taken of shore objects, the terrain examined through glasses, in readiness for shelling the first signs of Germans. One after another the transports were loaded and sent off, with some hours to spare. Information came that the enemy would not reach Ostend till the 14th, so on the afternoon of the 13th a wireless message from the Admiralty recalled all three monitors, the Belgian Government having already left by steamer at 6 a.m. bound for Havre.

Whilst *Severn* and *Humber* went off direct for the Downs, *Mersey* was detailed to call at Dunkirk on the way and, having brought up temporarily by the harbour entrance, Commander Wilson proceeded ashore during the afternoon in *Mersey's* not too reliable motor-boat. This was the period when German U-boats had begun to cause no little anxiety, and already on September 22 off the Dutch coast U-9 had sent the three cruisers *Aboukir, Cressy, Hogue* to the bottom, whilst five days later in the Dover Straits H.M.S. *Attentive* had been attacked by U-18, and another submarine was sighted near the Goodwins on October 2. Judge, then, of Commander Wilson's uneasiness when the French general in Dunkirk announced that a submarine was lying in wait just outside this harbour.

Off sped the monitor's anxious captain back to his boat in dread that *Mersey* might have succumbed. The miserable autumn day was drawing to a close, the rain streamed down in torrents and—of course—the boat's engine definitely refused to start. Half an hour passed without result, wherefore relying on a pair of oars they drearily endeavoured to row until by good fortune a small French steamboat near the mouth took compassion on them and towed the craft outside. Not without thankfulness was *Mersey* found afloat, anchor was weighed, and through the night she steamed in the direction of Dover.

Now at the beginning of October the Admiralty had laid a minefield in a certain area between the Goodwins and the neighbourhood of Ostend, which on this thirteenth day of the month performed a certain service of its own. At four o'clock that afternoon whilst *Severn* was leading, she sighted 300 yards away on the port beam a U-boat which had just fired at the monitor a torpedo, and then had risen to the surface expecting to find the ship sinking: but the enemy had failed to appreciate the shallowness of a monitor's draught, and the missile passed harmlessly below the hull. Thus disappointed, the German dived out of sight, yet the danger continued. In those early days submarines were slow, but neither did monitors have much speed, and sunset was due in about an hour. More than likely the U-boat, taking advantage of the failing light, might decide to follow in the monitor's wake and attack after dusk. She would have no difficult target since, even when the *Severn* was steaming at 7 knots, a tell-tale flame poured out high above the funnel.

What then could Commander Fullerton under these circumstances do?

He replied with his machine-guns, immediately altered course, worked up to his best speed, and dashed into the minefield well knowing that his own draught might or might not make *Severn* immune, but would imperil the much deeper submarine. Of course, it is impossible to guarantee that mines will always preserve their intended depth below the surface, and I myself on several occasions discovered German mines revealing themselves to a ground swell when they should have been invisible by several feet. But the early British mines composing the Goodwins-Ostend parallelogram were notoriously inefficient, acted uncertainly, drifted up the North Sea, and accounted for the loss of a British submarine during November.

Fortunately, both *Severn* and *Humber* emerged safely, anchored that night in the Downs, and before morning were rejoined by *Mersey*, when the squadron proceeded into Dover. Less lucky was the 4,590 tons French S.S. *Amiral Ganteaume* only a fortnight later. Whilst on passage through the Straits, carrying Belgian refugees, she became victim on October 26 to U-24, off Cape Gris Nez, but was towed into Boulogne. Such incidents were to make all communications by sea between Dover and the Continent one perpetual risk, and they must very shortly become still more perilous; for on October 15 the Germans marched into Ostend, Zeebrugge with its mammoth breakwater and canal (that led inland to Bruges) fell most readily into enemy control, which enabled a U-boat base to be established throughout the next four years. The first submarine to enter Zeebrugge was U-12 on November 9, to be followed by U-11 and many others.

Thus began the famous Flanders Flotilla, the "Suicide Club" of sea dare-devils that was to suffer heavy losses but not without inflicting appalling punishment on the Allies' shipping. History is marked by curious coincidences, and quite minor events sometimes completely alter the trend of time. Looking back on the past, with present omniscience, we can perceive that had Germany sent round every available submarine into Zeebrugge or Ostend within a couple of days after acquiring these invaluable Belgian ports, it is very doubtful if anything could have stopped her armies before capturing Dunkirk, Calais, Boulogne. And that would have meant ruination for France no less than England. A handful of U-boats during the latter half of October doing their damnedest between Ostend and Dunkirk might have made our activities off that coast impossible, but November 9 was too late: the climax, as we shall presently observe, had just passed.

From the moment the three monitors made fast in Dover harbour on October 14 they were to have little respite for many a day. At once they began coaling, filling up with water and stores, preparing for their first big show which came upon them unexpectedly. The position across the Channel was thus: the Belgian Army had fallen back to the Yser, and was trying to hold on inland from the sea at Nieuport through Dixmude and beyond, but the line lacked strength and might break at any hour. This tattered remnant of King Albert formed the frail barrier that obstructed the Duke of Wurtemberg now making his sweep through Flanders in the direction of Calais.

The Belgians asked help of the British Navy, the French requested this assistance. If men-of-war would approach the coast and bombard the German right, this might enormously relieve the pressure and save the defenders (already short of field-gun ammunition) from being overwhelmed. Rear-Admiral the Hon. H. L. A. Hood had just been appointed in command of the Dover forces which comprised, not merely the light cruisers *Attentive*, *Adventure*, *Foresight*, *Sapphire*, but two dozen destroyers, and other vessels including the Monitor Squadron.

It was this trio which seemed peculiarly fitted for the work of shelling the German flank: three pairs of 6-inch and three pairs of 4.7-inch guns ought to make some effect, and the monitors' hulls could float inside banks or within a few yards of the dunes where other ships would hesitate. Willingly had the Admiralty acceded to the Franco-Belgian desires, and without delay the descendant of that illustrious flag-officer who had vanquished the eighteenth-century French, now made ready his force. When on October 16 he signalled "Monitors to raise steam for full speed", and presently ordered them to proceed, many a mind wondered whither they were bound.

But the autumn gales had set in, a heavy sea was running outside and conditions were considered too bad for this type of vessel, so the signal had to be negatived; at once thereby showing that lightly-constructed units of restricted seaworthiness may become a serious disappointment in a crisis. Next day at 3 p.m. the weather had somewhat moderated, so off they went with an escort of destroyers to screen them against submarines, Admiral Hood flying his flag in *Attentive*.

Less than eleven hours later the monitors anchored off the small Belgian Nieuport, which was about to gain a worldwide significance out of all proportion to its commercial value. The town itself is a little way inland, approached by a very narrow channel, and at low water Springs not more than a foot of water covered the bar. Like Ostend, Dunkirk, Calais, the entrance to the harbour lay between two piers, but unlike all three ports the channel dried out. Nieuport in peace time possessed a unique value by reason of its canal systems which permitted waterborne traffic to pass along to Ostend, Bruges, Furnes, Dunkirk, Calais: in fact linking up with that vast mesh which enables barges from the Low Countries to reach the Scheldt, Rhine, Rhône, Seine, Mediterranean, and Black Sea.

On this Sunday, October 18, the position of Nieuport ten miles southwest from Ostend; its proximity to the Yser; and the centre from which roads, canals, railways radiated to such places as Mannekensvere, Lombartzyde, Westende, Slype, Lovie, St. Pierre Capelle, Ramscappelle; had a rare magnetic attraction, created partly by its unusual geographical characteristics but partly because Germans, Belgians, French, and British during the next few weeks must here find the peak of battle.

To change the metaphor, we may liken the Nieuport-Dixmude line stretching south-eastwards at right angles to the sea as a door hanging on weak hinges. On its northern side the Germans were battering impatiently, on its south side the Belgian troops wearily awaited the worst. And if this door should collapse, then nothing could withstand the enemy's onrush. The role of naval ships thus became twofold: first to prevent any disembarkation of German troops near Nieuport's harbour mouth; second, to fire against the enemy and keep him from any further advance on Nieuport. At this date there existed no little fear that the Germans contemplated landing a force further down the coast at La Panne, where also was King Albert: it would be part of the monitors' duties to see that no such enterprise succeeded.

BELGIAN COAST
Sphere of Naval Bombardments.

At daybreak on Sunday monitors weighed anchor and stood in towards the pier, near which stood the small seaside resort of Nieuport Bains, with its houses, villas, and hotels along the front; its seven-hundred-years old church, townhall, markets, and modern tramway. Rudely had the summer season been terminated, tourists had scurried away home just as their vacation commenced, and the staple industry of shrimp fishing from horseback had become a mere memory.

For the purpose of maintaining communication between ships and shore, a wireless operator was landed from *Humber* at the pier whence a car quickly drove him to Furnes; whilst two signal ratings from *Severn* and *Mersey* bringing their flags and lamp now established themselves at the pierhead. By 10 a.m. the Belgian Army thus was able to flash to *Attentive* a request that the squadron would open fire on the village of Lovie, 4 kilometres E.N.E. of Nieuport, and Blokhuis Farm some 600 metres north from Lovie. So began a terrible bombardment as monitors closed still nearer the shore, until the German batteries opened a rapid reply fire with shrapnel which burst over the ships steaming about 2,000 yards distant from the beach. *Humber* had one man severely wounded, and *Mersey* three men slightly wounded in ten hot minutes.

At last, then, had these river gunboats from Barrow begun their usefulness in the pea-green shallows of Flanders. It seemed likely they had at the outset done considerable damage to the enemy, for the latter now ceased fire. Nothing could have been more annoying to the Germans than the sight this morning of Admiral Hood's *Attentive*, four anti-submarine destroyers, and the three monitors off the coast. Just at stage when the Nieuport-Dixmude door seemed certain to yield, these confounded Englishmen must come across from Dover and interfere.

But the monitors showing up against the horizon were pretty easy targets; at 10.45 a.m. the admiral made them lengthen their range to 10,000 yards and resume the bombardment, which incited the enemy to transfer attention again to the squadron. German shells were now falling short of the ships, but pouring down on the wireless station at Nieuport Bains. Soon after half-past one the ships' fire was concentrated against Westende, the little watering-place immediately north of Nieuport Bains, where German howitzers could be seen half-concealed on the beach. A party of soldiers were espied with a range-finder obtaining the squadron's distance, when *Severn's* 4.7-in. gun from aft made an excellent shot and scattered them. An exciting first day ended at seven o'clock, the nett result being that whilst the enemy had made some advance, they had been robbed of success in regard to Lombartzyde, which lay two miles to the north of Nieuport.

It would be difficult to overestimate the value of this first day's naval assistance. Not merely had it checked German progress, but it had put new heart into the Belgian troops whose morale was overstrained. The monitors' arrival had encouraged them and they could now hold out a little longer.

Next day the Duke of Wurtemberg, having been reinforced, made a new effort against Lombartzyde. An hour before sunrise the monitors left their night anchorage, and proceeded to the firing ground. Today the orders were for one ship to fire at a time with two guns, and the international competition quickly got fierce. A German captive balloon was sent up for spotting purpose, and began making signals by small dark flags, whose number corresponded with the ships' range; for as the latter approached or left the shore, so the flags were taken off or added to.

An incessant fire the enemy maintained against Nieuport pier, and British sailors expected any minute to see it blown away with their friends the signalmen as well. Every moment, too, the ships believed that torpedo attacks might peremptorily bring disaster, and at 10.30 *Severn* thought a submarine had aimed at her. But little more than an hour later this monitor was vouchsafed a wonderful opportunity. One kilometre southeast of a road in a line with Westende and Slype could be perceived something which we now know to have been an ammunition waggon. The ship fired, waited, and then up went a magnificent explosion followed by smoke.

Meanwhile the Belgians were hard pressed, suffering heavy losses, and requested urgently that shelling might be directed on the Westende-Middelkirke road; in the neighbourhood of Blokhuis Farm; as well as on German batteries 400 yards southeast of Slype. Already German and Belgian infantry were separated by only a thousand yards, and care was required to avoid hitting the latter.

With good effect did the naval guns do their job. Enemy batteries under the influence of lyddite shells became quietened, and just before one o'clock large masses of troops were sighted near Leffinghe as well as by St. Pierre Cappelle. The *Severn* got on to both targets and wiped them off the earth. That afternoon some Belgian officers came off from the shore, who brought information that yesterday's bombardment had been magnificent, monitors' shots pitching exactly right, putting out of action a battery of six guns. The ships had killed off 1,600 Germans (including General von Tripp with his Staff), and generally imposed such a retribution as could not be borne.

The *Attentive* had been sent back to Dover, and Admiral Hood with his flag in the destroyer *Amazon* was still on the spot in command of the monitors with a handful of destroyers. Sunday and Monday had certainly put a brake on the German advance, brought about an invaluable delay, yet all this prodigious expenditure of naval shells was about to create a minor crisis which matured on the third day. Economy of ammunition most regrettably must be stressed, and the admiral wondered if Commander Fullerton's trio could continue bombarding till tomorrow night even with one ship firing at a time.

This restraint would be doubly unfortunate, since the monitors were doing such excellent work and the Belgian Army required not less but increased support. Yet there existed shortage in two other quite different respects. The irritated duke, thwarted at the most telling stage by sea power, might all very well ask Berlin to send round a few U-boats from German to Belgian waters, but that could scarcely be complied with: she possessed too few, because not till after the *Cressy* cruisers were sunk did she realise fully what submarines were capable of accomplishing.

This new branch of the *Kaiser's* Navy was being overworked and could not be everywhere simultaneously. The essential localities at present were (*a*) in the upper North Sea, where they hoped to assault the Grand Fleet units, (*b*) in the Dover Straits and off Havre, with a view to sinking transports from England for France. Even in the following February, though Germany owned 23 U-boats, yet only 4 were available to inaugurate the Submarine Blockade. Why? Because underwater craft are very delicate beings, need constant and lengthy overhauls after each voyage, take a long time on passage to and from their operating area. In truth the German Admiralty could not send to the duke's aid that which she failed to have in hand. The most which could be effected (until overhauls freed U-12 and U-11 for Ostend) was to let an occasional U-boat look in among the Flemish banks on her way home from the Dover area: but she could not stop long, and submarine officers would be none too happy dodging about among shoals that hindered them from diving.

Similarly, whilst the British Navy equally was short of submarines it lacked anti-submarine vessels. Both Commodore Tyrwhitt at Harwich, and Admiral Jellicoe among the Northern mists, required every destroyer that Whitehall would assign: other parts of the British Isles had to get along with a few older types.

But, if the monitors were to be kept afloat, they must be assured of destroyer protection, and the solution could be found only by French co-operation. It was at seven o'clock on this Tuesday morning that the bombarding squadron had the satisfaction to see the first French destroyers arrive and assist the handful of British destroyers off the Nieuport coast. This anti-submarine mobility, these sharp steel stems and quick-firers, would surely make any U-boat captain think twice before attacking.

CHAPTER 4

The Bombarders

Encouraging was the report which informed monitors that the Belgians not only held their positions, but had made a slight advance. Provided they could continue thus throughout the next forty-eight hours, there remained a good hope; for tomorrow night they were expecting to be strengthened by a French Army Division.

Too much optimism at present was scarcely justified, and the enemy still exerted a pressure so violent that the door might even now be broken down. Indeed, the Belgians this Tuesday began by asking of the monitors additional aid in the shape of machine-guns, which immediately were forthcoming. The monitors provided also from among themselves a party comprising a sergeant, corporal and eleven Marines, together with several ratings, all under Lieut. E. S. Wise R.N. of H.M.S. *Severn*. At 8 a.m. they were landed on Nieuport pier, and then streaked inland towards Slype, against which the enemy was hammering mightily.

In order that the monitors' big guns should not waste shells at wrong targets, Belgian officers came aboard and pointed out the enemy's positions, but despite reasonable economy the shortage soon became pronounced; which was all the more aggravating when so many German batteries manifested themselves. Each monitor, however, was keeping in reserve 50 rounds of shrapnel lest sudden onslaught should assail by sea or sky. If, signalled the admiral, submarines arrived, then the monitors must seek the shelter of very shallow water.

Ashore the battle for Lombartzyde waged fiercely throughout the morning, and the roar of British naval guns preceded destruction of some farm wherein a German detachment had taken occupation, or trenches were blown to dust. Then the brief dramatic calm on sea, whilst *Severn* listened-in to an important message being wirelessed from Furnes, asking guns to concentrate with all their strength on

Slype.

Once more a ponderous banging, followed by the earnest message from shore to *Severn*:

> Inform admiral situation critical. Heavy fire should be opened on Blokhuis Farm. A secondary objective Westende Bains where there are German troops.

With good results the monitors complied, and the enemy relinquished these spots. As fast as shells could be inserted and loosed off, the guns thundered away until they developed undue heat. But this appeared to be the moment of supreme test, the most essential of all crises, when the German duke must be checked. So, the admiral signalled monitors to use the whole of their ammunition in this tremendous effort.

The drama intensified, suspense waxed keener, the enemy in his annoyance turned batteries seawards on to ships, but his shells failed to reach, though they dropped dangerously close. Shortly afterwards, as if this fierce British answer had not been enough, the Belgian Headquarters requested increased fire forasmuch as German batteries were devastating the Belgian Army's batteries. That was about 2 p.m., and urgently again they pleaded for the heaviest possible blows on positions indicated, "Your assistance most necessary. Shooting has been good", they added.

Alas! All three monitors had just expended the last available shells, and then the signalman on Nieuport pier began flag-waving. It was a sad message on the top of the shortage dilemma.

> Lieut. Wise and party of marines sent to Slype this morning have suffered heavy loss. Lieut. Wise killed, and several wounded.

The survivors had made their way back to the canal, and so down to Nieuport Bains pier, from which they were now fetched after Belgian officers went ashore. Then followed one of those naval occasions, which form the high-lights of history and the inspiration of subsequent fiction-writers: one of those incidents, sudden in occurrence yet proceeding from character long schooled and richly endowed by naval inheritance.

There is a passage in Admiral Beatty's report on the Battle of Jutland which Admiral Jellicoe incorporated in his official despatch, relating how on that memorable May 31, 1916, Rear-Admiral Hood was destined to play a gallant part when his flag flew in command of the Third Battle Cruiser Squadron. Sir David Beatty wrote:

> I ordered them to take station ahead, which was carried out magnificently, Rear-Admiral Hood bringing his squadron into action ahead in a most inspiring manner, worthy of his great naval ancestors.

Yet, ten minutes later, Admiral Hood with his battle cruiser *Invincible* was blown up. How many readers know that the same gallant Hood, in the same inspiring manner "worthy of his great naval ancestors", distinguished himself this October 20, 1914?

His flag was flying aboard the destroyer *Amazon*, and since monitors had used up their projectiles, he dashed in with his other destroyers close to the shore, pouring out a terrific fire from 4-inch and 12-pounder guns, along the three-mile coastline, that extended between Westende and Middelkerke. This picture of *Amazon* leading the flotilla through a shell-swept area, altering course and formation in the most perfect manner, receiving punishment but giving the German batteries more than the destroyers were given, impressed every onlooker.

Commander Wilson of the *Mersey*, even years later, recalled it as "the finest exhibition I ever witnessed." That this cannonade reached the right targets was proved by the subsequent silence of German batteries. The diversion had nobly answered the Belgians' request, but *Amazon* suffered a shell through her bows which necessitated her being sent, not immediately but later, across to England for repairs. The wonder is that no other casualties had been inflicted.

So, this exciting afternoon ended with the monitors steaming towards Dunkirk, and the admiral telegraphing home for another shipload of shells. It was no happy withdrawal. Besides the wounded, *Severn*, *Mersey*, *Humber* took off all their men from Nieuport pier and under shell fire the whole time. In defending the last few miles of King Albert's territory, the squadron had not spared itself, but now came news that tonight the Belgian Army would have to evacuate Lombartzyde: they were retiring to Nieuport.

Trafalgar Day for the monitors consisted of toiling strenuously, coaling from the shore, and then filling up with ammunition that had just arrived in the S.S. *Victoria*. Then, shortly before midnight, they anchored outside Dunkirk but in less than five hours were weighing anchor, steaming once more to their old firing ground. "You have done very well to get back here so soon", the admiral signalled his congratulations. He, realising that the situation demanded more and more naval guns—no matter how ancient and obsolete the hull—had telegraphed the Admiralty to send what they could.

Thus, besides the light cruiser *Foresight* and four additional destroyers, there began to arrive a motley collection, such as the 1,000-tons gunboat *Hazard* which mounted a couple of 4.7-inch. Anything but a valuable unit, she had been acting as a depot ship for submarines; but the funniest surprise occurred when H.M.S. *Bustard* joined up off Nieuport on October 22. She was a tiny gunboat of 254 tons, but what mattered was her 6-inch weapon. Likewise, presently came the 980 tons *Rinaldo* with a schooner bow and generally resembling a steam yacht; yet her four 4-inch guns could not be despised. Nor could the *Vestal*, of similar tonnage and armament though she drew 13 feet; nor even the *Wildfire*. These three were classed officially as "sloops"—a term which the Admiralty used to employ for odd, difficult-to-define, vessels. So also, that old-fashioned light cruiser *Sirius*, 3,600 tons, though unable to stand much knocking about, would at least serve as a useful gun platform.

The arrival of *Foresight* enabled Admiral Hood temporarily to shift his flag from *Amazon*, and this October 22 the monitors began by shelling Slype, as well as Lovie, where enemy batteries were active. Soon after 9 a.m. a fog settled down and somewhat interfered with proceedings, yet with *Bustard's* help they had done enormous damage and enabled the Belgians once more to enter Lombartzyde. In the afternoon Admiral Hood handed over charge of operations to Commander Fullerton, whilst the former went in *Amazon* to Dunkirk that he might consult with Admiral Favereau (commanding the French naval force in the Channel), and learn what were the Belgians' future intentions. Next morning the British admiral was back on the firing ground.

His first instructions revealed that the expected French Army Division had got into place, would be moving out of Nieuport after 9 a.m. in a northeasterly direction, with the hope of winning back Ostend; and Admiral Hood's fleet were to support the French soldiers. At 10 a.m. *Severn*, *Humber*, *Bustard*, and *Vestal* began firing on Slype, Blokhuis Farm, Lovie, Westende, and Westende Bains. *Wildfire* followed, and believed she had just been attacked by a submarine's torpedoes.

Before 12.30 both *Humber* and *Vestal* had run out of ammunition, whilst the Germans were putting up a considerable artillery assault from the road that runs north of Nieuport in the direction of Ostend; and just before 3 o'clock the French Division asked the Fleet to aim at the steeple of Westende, which the enemy was using as observation-post for his batteries 100 metres further northeast. Accordingly, *Severn* got on to the target, fired five lyddite shells, and with the second brought the steeple tumbling down. It had stood well above the sand dunes in an ideal position for surveying sea and land, but its loss meant much. So pleased was Commander Fullerton that he congratulated his chief gunner's mate heartily, and sent a bottle of champagne to be divided among the gun's crew.

Now all this daily bombardment from sunrise to sunset, besides putting a great strain on ships' companies, was also wearing out the guns. Yesterday *Severn's* left 6-inch was found badly scored in the muzzle, and today she had to stop firing a while. Those one-time raw reserves had become such fast workers, and loosed off so many shells in quick succession, that the guns became red hot, though not one man in the perspiring crowd was sorry for an easy spell. Information flashed from shore that prisoners stated the fleet's firing had caused enormous havoc, and everything went to confirm this.

Thanks to the fleet's deadly accuracy and persistent shelling, the French this afternoon were advancing splendidly to Westende, when the Belgians further inland around St. Georges passed under such severe pressure that part of the French Division had to come for their rescue. Of course this made fresh demands on the ships, but empty guns are not much use, so *Severn*, *Humber* (who was also having trouble with her boilers), were ordered into Dunkirk for more supplies of shells.

It was the same old routine in harbour, with little enough rest for anyone. Heavy ammunition was being consumed in an amazing manner, the S.S. *Invicta* hurried across from the Medway with another 60 tons; and one after the other *Severn*, *Humber*, *Mersey*, *Bustard*, *Vestal*, *Wildfire*, went alongside to complete. Ships' companies toiled late, as the admiral was particularly anxious for all ships to be on their bombarding station by 5 a.m. on the 25th, yet this was not possible. The above last-mentioned three got away, but someone up the Medway had made a mistake, and the right sort of ammunition for monitors had to be awaited.

That night seemed just one link in an unlucky chain of trouble. The ugly autumn weather changed from thickness into heavy rain, and then a gale came on. Sloops were sent back into Dunkirk, whilst monitors brought up outside. Then, before 11 a.m., news signalled from the shore indicated that things were not going too well with the Belgians: whilst the French were holding the bridgehead half a mile north of Lombartzyde, the remainder of the Allies' line eastwards from the sea was giving way, except at Dixmude. Five minutes later came further tidings that the Germans had occupied Westende Bains; Westende; Mannekensvere; and the river zone in that vicinity. The situation definitely was most critical.

For the enemy had made a supreme push, and today we know from no less an authority than the late Belgian King Albert himself (who in 1926 sent a notable letter on the subject to Marshal Foch) that on this October 26 the Belgian Headquarters actually contemplated falling back to a rear position, had not the king firmly disapproved. With nearly all the troops behind the Yser, retirement from Furnes was being considered, which would be a serious matter for the fleet since that was the wireless station connecting Allies with the ships.

The admiral accordingly wasted no time, and all ships—destroyers, sloops, monitors—set forth before midday up the coast. The latter were rolling about in the very heavy sea, making bad weather, not more than 5 knots, and considerable leeway. What would they be able to do in action?

Since a beam wind caused them to drift excessively, it would be dangerous for the monitors if they got near the shore. Plenty of sea-room was essential today, so, having arrived north of their usual operational area just after 1 p.m., they prepared to engage Westende and Westende Bains. The German batteries were effecting excellent shooting on the sloops, had got the range of an adjacent buoy to a nicety, but today the monitors could do little or nothing. By reason of their light draught, flat bottom design, and central tophamper, they rolled madly and became impossible as gun-platforms. Shooting was a farce, a mere waste of shells, wherefore at 3.45 p.m. the admiral ordered them to cease fire, and sent them back to Dunkirk plunging atrociously through those vicious hollow seas for which the coast of Flanders is notorious.

The Franco-Belgian troops now were contending in a final struggle to save the Channel ports, when fortunately, on the 27th weather conditions allowed monitors to begin a mighty cannonade at dawn against Lombartzyde and, presently, Blokhuis Farm. On this occasion *Mersey* had to cease action for half an hour to allow her guns a chance of cooling, which was scarcely to be marvelled at: since between 6 a.m.

and 2 p.m. *Severn, Humber,* and *Mersey* had used up nearly 300 rounds. Next day the last mentioned was not long in developing some trouble with her gun-turret, and into Dunkirk for repairs she steamed back.

For the others it was just one more fatiguing day, varied only by submarine scares. Middelkerke, Lovie, Slype, Westende Bains, and German batteries were the targets. Houses along the sea-front, suspected of being used for observation purposes, were all being treated to exploding steel, and an unsuccessful effort was being made to locate a certain tennis court where an enemy battery had been thought to exist. A large hotel, also facing the sea, received the monitors' attention, but it must have been of fire-proof construction, for demolition followed without conflagration.

A call to engage Lombartzyde at noon gave French destroyers their first opportunity of bombardment. Steaming close to the shore at great speed, they fired rapidly, and the nett result by dusk confirmed that Belgian soldiers ashore were able to hold on to their positions merely because during the hours of daylight the Anglo-French Fleet maintained incessant shell showers over German artillery positions. But these sea operations had now been going on for eleven days, and a new phase could not be far distant. More and more enemy guns, and now of heavy calibre, had arrived on land seriously menacing the ships. Submarine scares apart, definite U-boat attacks against this Flanders Fleet might be expected at any time.

In fact, as a reply to the Duke of Wurtemberg's expressed wish, there should have been—not later than October 26—a genuine fox among the poultry and might have caused on that boisterous day a series of calamities outrivalling the loss of three *Cressys*. And here, yet again, do we perceive the strange vagaries of history. A few days previously Lieut.-Commander Kolbe had left Germany in U-19 bound for Zeebrugge, but on the night of October 24, when still off the Dutch coast this submarine was rammed by the British destroyer *Badger* and narrowly escaped being sunk.

Throughout her adventurous life U-19 had the most surprising good luck, and on this occasion, she managed to reach Germany for repairs. So, it chanced that not she but U-12; and not till November 9, was the first German submarine to enter Zeebrugge. As we shall presently observe, the latter began torpedoing with great promptness. Had only a couple of the bombarding ships been sent to the bottom, we may be sure that these Belgian coast operations would have been immediately stopped to the great detriment of the army inland. Let it be further stressed that those conditions of rough seas favoured, rather than hindered, any lurking U-boat.

For protection against submarines, the Fleet were relying on destroyers who maintained an active patrol, but when the monitors at the end of October 28 came fatigued into Dunkirk harbour, they had not long to wait for proof that their fast protectors lacked immunity. Crews watched the British destroyer *Falcon* arrive flying the signal "Require hospital treatment immediately." Her captain, Lieut.-Commander H. O. Wauton, together with seven of his men were dead, and nineteen more had been wounded. A working party was now sent to moor her alongside a hospital ship, and found the sight akin to that of a slaughter house. One German shell, perfectly directed, had hit her forward.

How much longer could this fleet of unarmoured vessels keep afloat against well-hidden powerful artillery?

Dunkirk's docks were a scene of pathetic animation, motor ambulances rushing down to hospital ships with wounded soldiery arriving from the vicinity of Nieuport. Likewise, there had arrived H.M.S. *Venerable* a 15,000 tons battleship, no longer in her first flush of youth, but she mounted four 12-inch, a dozen 6-inch guns, and of these much was expected. True, she might be a first-class target for U-boats, and that would demand increased vigilance by the destroyer flotilla; yet at least the 12-inch weapons would be a match for the Germans' bludgeoning.

On the night of October 29-30 this battleship with *Severn* and *Mersey* reached Nieuport area and from 2-10 a.m. for a whole thunderous hour shelled enemy positions. First all the starboard guns fired, then the ships turned round and fired from the other side. It was one of those impenetrably black nights, and the gun-flashes were alarming even to the oldest seamen, blinding every eye for a while, although handkerchiefs were raised to the forehead till after each shell had left the muzzle. Nothing could be seen of the land, nor could the enemy perceive so much as the outline of ships: consequently, no reply came, yet if the havoc materially could not be exaggerated, the moral effect on tired German combatants and their nerves was something beyond estimation. "I bet the Germans had no sleep tonight", remarked *Severn's* Yeoman of Signals in his diary; and this surprise assault will be remembered as one of the finest efforts during the autumn.

After the monitors had got back into Dunkirk, other ships resumed the attack during daylight. Lacking the cover of darkness, they could not entirely escape injury, and that morning the *Venerable* before 10.30 was wirelessing *Severn* to have ambulances ready for the arrival of *Vestal*. Two-and-a-half hours later, with ensign at half-mast, this sloop rounded Dunkirk piers for, like *Falcon*, she had been hit on the foc'sle, one man being killed and four others wounded. Again, were the *Severn's* men busy landing their fleet-mates, and next arrived *Rinaldo* with foremast splintered, her top riddled from bursting shell, and eight men injured.

Not without justice did Admiral Hood today make the following signal received from Mr Winston Churchill, First Lord of the Admiralty:—

> The Inshore Flotilla and Squadron have played an appreciable part in the great battle now proceeding. You have shown the Germans that in this case there is a flank they cannot turn.

That characteristic message by no means overstated the truth, and today as we look back with all the facts before us, one thing becomes crystal clear: except for the timely arrival of these shallow-draught monitors, the Belgian Army would have collapsed and German artillery would have soon been firmly established at Dunkirk, Calais, Boulogne. What might have resulted during the next four years with these three harbours denied our transports, but all the port facilities at the service of U-boats and enemy destroyers, does not bear contemplation. The Dover Straits would have become impossible for traffic, Dover itself subject to daily raids, the English Channel just one perilous corridor for Allied no less than neutral, shipping. With the North Sea's southern gateway denied, trade-tracks must necessarily have been lengthened by compulsory routes up the west coast and round north Scotland with its unrelenting weather.

It would have made for the German small torpedo craft all the difference in the world if their base had been not Zeebrugge but Boulogne. Less exposed to weather as well as sudden surprise from attackers, the latter's situation west of Gris Nez well beyond the Dover Straits' narrowest section could not fail to give at once security and greater opportunities. That which German submarine captains always hated, both outward-bound and homecoming, was the defile between Dover and the Dyck lightship (west of Dunkirk). By having to hang about off Sandettie lightship, sit on the bottom till midnight and a fair tide coincided; dodge the nets and patrol line; their endeavours were cramped and their anxieties increased. If, however, circumstances had given them Boulogne, they could have avoided the Straits and enjoyed enviable freedom to the westwards. Moreover, though Dover's flotilla might essay mining Boulogne's approaches, this could barely have succeeded in opposition to German guns overlooking that port.

Having performed their special duties, the monitors on the last day of October could do little more. Whilst *Vestal* came out of Dunkirk and committed to the sea what remained of the man killed yesterday, *Severn* with *Mersey* and *Humber* as well as *Bustard* proceeded towards Nieuport pier. There, backed up by *Venerable's* guns they made a final bombardment against Slype, Lombartzyde, and Westende. Plenty of virulence still animated the Germans' fire as it poured down on Nieuport, whilst their 'heavies' sought to blow up the monitors. Remarkable it was that these latter always escaped, yet today two shells fell so close to *Severn* that those on board imagined she had been hit.

Glorious to note how the *Venerable's* 12-inch projectiles were devastating Middelkerke, and to see houses torn up as if made of paper; but *Humber* almost succumbed when a big shell from the land, perfectly aimed at her foc'sle, luckily fell a few yards before reaching her. It was quite obvious that the monitor squadron's role had just about finished, for they could no longer stand up against the recently arrived big calibres: in fact, the *Humber's* 6-inch guns so badly were worn that their range had become from 2,000 to 4,000 yards short. To continue this unequal duel would mean the certain loss of all three units: it was only a question of time.

This same day, too, afforded a good instance of what might have happened during any of these bombarding occasions. Steaming always on the move among the sands, *Severn* almost got ashore—that is to say she was standing into 8 feet of water—and might have become for the land batteries an easy fixed target, with calamitous results at that distance. The off-shore soundings among so many shifting sands were not always accurately marked on the chart, nor can one be surprised that tides and gales should have wrought alterations. The *Venerable* herself had recently got stuck on a bank, but fortunately beyond enemy's gun range, and she floated when the flood came.

Yes: it was time that modification was made in these operations off the Belgian coast. The monitors' arrival back in Dunkirk immediately preceded that of the light cruiser *Brilliant* (3,600 tons) who came in with one man killed, but much worse was the news concerning H.M.S. *Hermes*. This ex-cruiser had been transformed into a seaplane carrier and at dawn of October 31 had started from Dunkirk bound for Dover. She had got to Lat. 51.4 N, Long. 1.42 E (that is to say 8 miles WNW of Calais), but U-27 waylaid her and fired two torpedoes.

★★★★★★★★★★

U-27 was commanded by Lieut.-Commander Wegener. An able officer, he had already on October 18 encountered off Borkum the British submarine E-3 and blown her in two. On the following March 11 he sank the armed merchant cruiser *Bayano*. But on August 19, 1915, Wegener met his match and U-27 with all hands perished during the historic action when the Q-ship *Baralong* sank her at the time Wegener was about to sink the S.S. *Nicosian*.

★★★★★★★★★★

It was about 9.30 a.m. when *Hermes* foundered, and with her loss went 22 lives, but the undeniable and inevitable effect on the British mind found expression in a greater caution.

Thus, by November 2, a curious synchronisation of events achieved one end. The monitors had worn out their guns, and the enemy now outranged them. The squadron had held up the German advance throughout the important critical period, but now the front became stabilised behind the Yser, for sluices were opened to let the North Sea pour across the Flemish flats and make a natural barrier.

The increasing activities of U-boats emphasised the risk which vessels off this coast must expect, yet the great inundation made monitors no longer essential. Wherefore on this second night of the new month *Severn* with *Mersey* came out of Dunkirk bound for Sheerness to the unfeigned joy of everyone aboard; yet who could guarantee them a safe passage? Who could deny that some enterprising U-boat was waiting off the pierheads, or near the Dyck lightship?

It happened to be one of those very clear nights which afford little enough protection, but monitors could float where submarines would get aground. Cutting off a corner, the former went cautiously across a shoal that carried only 8 feet, and then a destroyer escort took over. With all lights dowsed, the convoy moved off keeping a keen lookout, and speed would have been an advantage on such an occasion; but fast steaming meant also tell-tale flames rushing out of the funnel-tops, advertising too blatantly the passage of warships.

That being out of the question, *Severn* and *Mersey* proceeded leisurely, reached the River Medway in safety where they found *Venerable* already arrived; whose men welcomed with loud cheering these ungainly river gunboats that had been in action so successfully day after day.

Yes: they had been lucky indeed. One week later U-12 put into Zeebrugge on November 9 for a few hours only, then came out, stole past Belgium, cut across towards the Kentish cliffs, and on November 11 sank H.M.S. *Niger* off Deal pier. In those times seafaring was just a gamble and no such condition as certainty existed; nevertheless, *Humber* presently arrived in the Medway and so the squadron could be called upon for fresh duties.

CHAPTER 5

North Sea

And here we cannot help noting the curious naval strategy of our late enemies, together with a hardly less strange sequence of happenings. Why was it that Germany permitted a whole fortnight to pass, and a weak squadron to do pretty much as it liked, without one visitation from a raiding force? Yet how easy and effective would have been a sudden incursion off Nieuport by a small body of battle cruisers and light cruisers, remaining only long enough to sink at long range every unit that carried a gun!

★★★★★★★★★★

It is true that Germany sent out from the Ems the four destroyers S-115, 117, 118, and 119, but on the afternoon of October 17 these were encountered by the British light cruiser *Undaunted* with the four destroyers *Lance*, *Lennox*, *Loyal*, and *Legion* off the Dutch coast. The whole German quartet was sent to the bottom. The surprising fact is that the attempt to reach Belgium's coast in greater strength was not made during the critical period of bombardment. A subsequent and more formidable attack, which the British Navy certainly expected, would have involved the Harwich Force and might have brought about a notable action ere the raiders could regain German waters.

★★★★★★★★★★

Think of the results that would have ensued: no more British bombardments for days, and probably a complete cessation altogether, with a corresponding freedom for German arms ashore! Did not the miscellaneous collection of gunboats daily on the same firing area invite attack? At a subsequent date, when small units had been annoying U-boats in the Adriatic, Austrian light cruisers for their part never hesitated to swoop down and wreak vengeance.

Now it so chanced that on the very night when *Severn* and *Mersey* were crossing to the Medway, a German squadron of battle-cruisers and light cruisers were actually hurrying from Heligoland Bight towards Norfolk. At dawn they roused Gorleston by a thirty-minutes' shelling and then scurried back home, but the irony was that though this visitation caused no military advantage to the enemy it did him definite harm; for the cruiser *Yorck* on her return fouled a German minefield and sank with heavy casualties.

Yet the same expenditure of effort a few days earlier, outside the Flemish banks, would have been far better rewarded, and the gamble would not have been any greater.

It was in November, too, that the first invasion scare gripped the authorities, and barely had *Severn* today made fast to her buoy, given shore leave to some of her people, than they were immediately recalled; for report had been made that the Gorleston affair was really a feint, but that the German squadron were now heading south in order to meet transports about to land troops.

This rumour having presently been found false, both *Severn* and *Mersey* were allowed into Chatham docks and began replacing old guns for new, but next came a more definite warning that invasion would shortly be attempted in the neighbourhood of the Wash. Here is a bit of inhospitable water characterised by strong tides, shifting sandbanks, and uncertain channels that need very exact buoyage. A nasty sea soon gets up during northeasters, and at all times expert pilotage is required for strangers other than shallow vessels. Between Great Yarmouth and the Humber exists no easy harbour, yet on the Wash's Lincolnshire side a well-marked channel known as the New Cut leads to the port of Boston, though the amount of water is influenced not merely by the moon but by such factors as wind and rains.

Before the war it had been common talk in certain coteries, that when and if German soldiers landed in the United Kingdom, they would be disembarked somewhere in this vicinity: so, during November, the latest alarm suggested monitors as the ideal type for special service alike off Norfolk sand-dunes or Lincolnshire fens. Once again, then, were these gunboats afforded the privilege of particular selection.

They sailed from the Medway on November 19 northward bound, and made little delay in demonstrating their unhandiness. To slip from a buoy during the strong Medway ebb, and get a monitor round with her bows pointing down tide, always was no easy feat of seamanship; for even if the steering gear did not jam, she became so mulish that a tendency to drift broadside could not be mastered. With the "Not under Control" signal flying, she was apt to be carried across the bows of dredgers and battleships in the most crazy manner.

So also, this same date, whilst entering Harwich after dark and with a powerful flood, the monitors provided their captains with plenty of anxious moments in trying to make fast at the assigned buoys. After calling at Great Yarmouth, the squadron with its destroyer escort passed round the sandy shores of East Anglia and anchored in Boston Deep, as dreary a spot as the British coast affords; and of course, the treacherous North Sea weather soon made the monitors' berths uncomfortable. Steam had to be raised, stern-anchors prepared for letting go so as to swing clear of the shoals, and bridge canvas-screens furled to lessen windage. One man was lost overboard from *Humber* and, after some of *Severn's* people returned from afternoon leave along the lonely beach, a second sailor was missing. Searchlights tried to locate him, but the tide rose quickly over the quicksands and his body was not discovered till the following afternoon up a creek.

Curious fate that, having received no casualties off Flanders, the *Severn* should be robbed in this manner! What with the short sunless days, the gloom of leaden sky, the sullen expanse of marshes, the damp-laden atmosphere, and the seals at the shoal's edge as least uninteresting features, this dismal Wash locality brought happiness to no one. Coaling from a small steamer, practising with small-arms ammunition against the elusive seals as targets, scarcely helped the weary hours to fly, and November dragged laggardly into December. Nor did monotony end, as the almost daily gales lashed dull waters into a shabby whiteness.

But this anti-climax after Flemish bustle, this deadly quietude following the daily violence of guns, was an unavoidable interlude. Secret intelligence from Germany left little doubt of what the enemy had planned, and those of us who at that date happened to be based on the Humber received sufficient hints of the impending adventure. Reasonable enough it seemed if the Germans, now finally checked from capturing the English Channel ports, should seek to create panic by sending ship-loads of field-grey troops across the North Sea. Regarded with this knowledge, the Gorleston incident could be comprehended as a preliminary experiment to test the amount of resistance which might be encountered on the voyage.

From the Wash it is no great railway distance to the midland manufacturing cities of Sheffield, Manchester, Birmingham—Coventry; or south through Cambridge to London. But were the enemy likely even at the top of spring tides to risk transports in the tricky furrows leading to the New Cut? Local seafaring opinion believed they would so endeavour, and suspicions were based on the following notable facts. During peace time the only line which carried on a regular shipping service between Boston and Hamburg was run by Germans. For the last five years these vessels had been commanded by officers who had made careful soundings in the channels, and knew the shoals perfectly.

Before the war two of these captains had tried to pass the examination as local pilots, and the amount of knowledge which they displayed had caused no little astonishment: but, for the best of reasons, official qualification was denied them. The tactless remark by one Teuton that someday "the German flag will be flying over Boston church" had not allayed a certain diffidence.

Naturally enough it was assumed that, in the event of a landing being attempted, these steamer captains would be employed to pilot the cavalcade; therefore, in the first week of December some important alterations were made in regard to the Wash buoyage system. But the essence of successful warfare is surprise, and to the average Englishman a Dutch sailor looks much the same as a German.

Suppose the enemy had wished to send his spies during November to acquire the latest information, and compare existing buoys with the chart? Well, was that quite impossible?

A regular line of Dutch-owned steamers still kept running every week with general cargo between Rotterdam and King's Lynn. Could it be guaranteed, absolutely, that some of the crew were not disguised German nationals? Or that no German stowaways had smuggled themselves aboard? Or that they would not be waiting in the Wash region to signal from the shore—perhaps even to act as guides after the soldiers had disembarked?

The raid was expected to occur on December 10, and arrangements had been made for the three monitors to anchor during the afternoon of the 9th near Hunstanton (northeastern side of the Wash) with 25 fathoms of cable out, steam on the engines, and men ready at their guns throughout that night and the next day. A careful watch was being listened on the wireless, and all things were in readiness if the enemy should arrive at any moment round the corner. The squadron of monitors had come out, with pilots on board, and these civilians might have looked forward to one of the most historic incidents in English history. Doubtless the Grand Fleet and Commodore Tyrwhitt's Harwich Force were ready to deal with the High Sea Fleet and escorts; but *Severn*, *Mersey*, and *Humber* would concentrate on the troop-laden transports.

But, all of a sudden, just as suspense attained its peak, there came a complete alteration of plans. Owing to the push by the Russian Army, Teutonic troops that were intended for the east of England were sent off to Germany's eastern front, and the raid never came off; though later on it was hinted that the postponement would be only till February. Monitors might still have the chance of showing their strength on the day of disembarkation.

For the immediate present everything was altered, the trio were required elsewhere, so the pilots were sent back, and on the afternoon of December 10 the monitors in single-line-ahead quitted the Wash for a more southern destination. Four destroyers—*Lookout, Llewellyn, Laertes, Lysander*—appeared on the horizon at 3 o'clock to convoy them, but the seas were too bad for river gunboats and after a couple of hours the latter sought what anchorage they could by the Burnham Flats, whilst destroyers had to bring up outside. Before chilly dawn broke over the North Sea, cables were being wound in, and next sunset saw the ships letting go for the night off Lowestoft.

Here is no reliable anchorage, and the fun began with the advent of darkness. Not too easily ships' postmen and stewards were landed, but presently the gale blew earnestly, a really heavy sea was running and the monitors' position, with the beach not far to leeward, caused no little anxiety. Waves leapt over the bows, men were keeping watch as if under way, and more cable had to be veered out.

Why not have entered Lowestoft and secured alongside?

The answer is that its entrance is very narrow, the tide runs across the mouth with great strength, and the awkward monitors would certainly have fouled the piers. Moreover, the harbour was fairly full of drifters and trawlers already, since this port had during the previous four months developed into a naval base for minesweepers and patrol vessels. I well remember, even a few weeks earlier, how congested was the space with trawlers, drifters, and others.

The officer in charge on shore was Captain A. A. Ellison R.N. (now deceased), a person quick-tempered, apt to explode somewhat easily. About half-past seven this evening the squadron were made uneasy by a signal from him that *Humber's* gig with its crew was missing, and he feared the men must have been drowned.

Ships' searchlights swept here and there, a tug came plunging out with Lowestoft's lifeboat, but back she steamed into harbour after sighting no such thing as a gig. For amid all this quite unnecessary perturbation *Humber*, in reply to *Severn's* question, signalled that her gig had returned and was already hoisted. An unfortunate error from Captain Ellison's office thus added awhile sadness to discomfort. All the same, monitors were in a tighter corner than ever Belgian conditions had afforded them. Captain Ellison's suggestion that the squadron should clear out and make for Corton Roads was not adopted. No lights were burning, even on the buoys, and anyone who navigated this neighbourhood during the war will agree that unhandy gunboats trying to find their way through the swept channel under such conditions of wind most likely would have been lost. Having been badly caught, the only alternative was to ride out the gale where they happened to be.

At daylight things were bad enough, but 8.30 a.m. saw them weighing. It was well realised aboard that had they sought exit by the main, deeper, north, channel the ships must have been driven ashore. Thanks to their draught, however, they might go down the coast *via* the Pakefield Gat which local fishermen and small yachts in fine weather were wont to use: though on a day like this it needed no little nerve. "The next hour or two", recorded *Mersey's'* captain, "was unanimously voted as the worst in the commission." Heavy seas broke over each monitor forward, above the gun, and even so high as the bridge. Pakefield Gat "looked for all the world like Portland Race on a really rough day", but luckily the tide was well up. Heading into this boiling white mass, it took the ships an hour to do less than a mile, and at one time the soundings dropped to 10 feet though the chart indicated half as much again at low water.

Steep and short, the waves threatened to bump the bottoms out of both monitors if their lightly constructed hulls should strike the hard sands. Commander Wilson remarked:

"My greatest difficulty was to keep my ship's head on to sea, and to do this it became necessary several times to ease down one engine. Once broadside on, I'm doubtful of what might have happened, but think we should have foundered. It was out of the question to let go an anchor, since no one could get forward to let it go or weigh again, and a diver's suit would have been the only possible costume."

When once through this tricky swatch-way and out in the deeper fairway, the gunboats forced their progress, and afternoon found them once more in Harwich. Having replenished with coal, they were steaming down harbour before dawn bound for Dover, yet the North Sea gave them no kindly welcome. After the first two hours the conning-tower of a submarine added a new interest, and away dashed destroyer escort only to find she was British. It turned out to be one of those difficult days with much turbulence, wind, rain, and thickness. Out of the murk now suddenly loomed a certain buoy enabling monitors to check their position, but it gave more than a shock to navigators when they were thus confronted; for, in laying off the course, they had allowed 22½ degrees for leeway, which seemed perfectly reasonable, but actually monitors had made 50 degrees!

This was a serious matter when crossing the shoal-infested Thames estuary, where so many vessels have ended their days throughout all ages, but at least such a tiresome experience brought about knowledge which had to be acquired somehow; and as time went on, these officers between them worked out the following table for counteracting a monitor's drift:

Force of Wind	Description	Velocity		Allow
2	light breeze	13 miles per hour		1 point (11¼°)
4	moderate breeze	23 ,, ,,		2 points
5	fresh breeze	28 ,, ,,		3 points
6	strong breeze	34 ,, ,,		4 points

(But with any wind over Force 6, go home: monitors had no right to be out.)

And this afternoon, having reached a position further off from Dover than whence they had started; the weather being far more than a "strong breeze"; the squadron turned round, limped back into Harwich, where *Humber* reported how the seas had so badly buckled her fore mess-deck that she was leaking. Not till December 15 did conditions suffer Commander Fullerton to take his gunboats out again, and this time *Humber* must be detached to Chatham for repairs, but the other two struggled round North Foreland into Dover and after coaling left at 10 p.m. for Dunkirk.

Yes: *Severn* and *Mersey* were again needed on their old firing ground, and General Joffre had severely missed their help, since the Germans during this absence had been able to maintain, unhindered, a violent bombardment. Already Admiral Hood on November 22 was using that ancient battleship *Revenge*, which however mounted four 13.5-inch guns; and various smaller vessels were assisting; yet big ships proved themselves quite unsuitable for this inshore work. On October 28 the *Venerable* had grounded on a bank till a rising tide freed her and now on December 15, as well as following day, *Revenge* suffered such maltreatment that she must be sent into dock.

The hour selected for the monitors' departure certainly favoured their protection against submarines, but to take these wayward creatures through a crowded harbour in the darkness, past the Dover piers into a fast-running east-going tide, needed a special sort of seamanship. Out in the English Channel, whilst passing the Goodwins, there were lived some thrilling moments amongst the buoys, and with one of the latter *Mersey* had a small difference of opinion as well as a brief bumping match; then *Severn*, just ahead, would be set down towards the next buoy and mask its appearance, which caused her next-astern to do some quick work with the helm as the stream seemed determined to set steel hull against moored mark.

Seven and a half hours later the two ships were anchored off Dunkirk, and forthwith the never-ending December gales drove the monitors inside harbour, consigning them to a month's inactivity. There they found their old friend H.M.S. *Bustard*, and the obsolete gunboat *Excellent*, which had just been shelling with good result the enemy's positions at Westende. There were armed trawlers, too, and minesweepers, but the harbour itself emitted no pleasant odour; the streets, with their cobble-stones and slush, seemed dull by night and at day over busy with motor traffic to and from the Front only fifteen miles distant.

It was a strange coincidence that just as the German cruiser squadron had crossed-the North Sea on the night of November 2-3 when *Severn* and *Mersey* were on their way from Dunkirk, so on this night of December 15-16 the enemy had been at sea with the bombarding of Scarborough as their objective.

During this dreary, tempestuous, month many of our smaller patrol vessels were able to do little enough: they were being saved for great expectations following the year's ending. Nor was bad weather the sole reason why two monitors had to spend day after day alongside Dunkirk's dock-wall. Admiral Hood (who did not always see eye-to-eye with Mr Winston Churchill, the First Lord) had formed definite and decided opinions during the recent coastal engagements from which H.M.S. *Revenge* emerged with injury. He was convinced that to resume the routine bombarding methods of October would be in principle wrong, and he meant to emphasise that attitude till the end.

He was fully prepared to bring out the monitors and other gunboats to shell the enemy whenever the allied armies were ready to make a genuine advance towards Ostend, but until such a development he proposed husbanding his units in Dunkirk. The monitors, he argued, were slow, and required the protection of a battleship, but the latter could stay on the coast not indefinitely, and only two or three days at a time. The Germans' big guns were now too formidable for any reply other than from a *Revenge* or *Venerable*; and whilst battleships could be sent for some particular occasion, or occasionally for night-firing at uncertain dates, times, and from different directions; yet to keep them in Nieuport Roads was to invite disaster from mines or submarines.

Experience had shown that a battleship must keep under way in what amounted to a large "puddle", whence she could not withdraw except at high water. And because such a deep-draught man-of-war must keep moving, there existed always the danger of getting aground. What then? The whole flotilla would approach to rescue her crew, and enemy guns would in concentrating on this mass wipe out every unit.

The disadvantage of night-firing consisted in not being able to see targets or results: and even by day no naval bombardment was of real use unless in conjunction with the Allies' heavy artillery and the soldiers' progress. Ships are unable to knock out the shore guns unless the latter can be located and actually hit: in other words, the very dilemma, which a few weeks later would manifest itself at the Dardanelles, now took shape. The most which naval ships could achieve was not to put out of action shore guns, but to produce a moral effect such as by-causing casualties among massed. troops. Otherwise, the squadron was firing at an invisible target, whilst contrariwise the German Army could shell Admiral Hood's force at will.

Years before the war Admiral Mahan in his authoritative work on *Naval Strategy*, had laid it down that:

> .... ships are unequally matched against forts. ... A ship can no more stand up against a fort costing the same money than the fort could run a race with the ship.

Enemy's batteries must therefore first be occupied by troops, and not till then could the squadron be expected to co-operate.

For a whole month the monitors in vain waited within Dunkirk for the armies' beginning of a movement that would send German divisions back along the coast in the direction of Ostend, but the chance never matured. Scarcely a house stood intact between Nieuport and Dixmude, and there could be no sense in cannonading the same places which had been hammered for weeks—and especially now that shell shortage demanded economy. But nothing is so detrimental to the morale of crews as week after week in harbour, with little ahead except uncertainty; and Conrad's *dictum* that "ships and men both rot in port" has been proved thousands of times through history.

For the monitors' officers the difficult task was to keep ships' companies both keen and fit, uninfluenced by boredom; yet the temptation to desert, make their way to fight alongside those in the trenches, became hard to resist. Football matches were arranged, and sing-songs; just before Christmas men were allowed a three-mile walk in the country to bring back those evergreens which sailors delight fashioning into garlands. At masthead, ensign-staff, and jackstaff, the traditional decorations were hoisted; then as news came that the New Yeat's promotions included the name of Commander Fullerton there was a pint of beer for every man to drink his health.

Just when monotony seemed to be settling down like a damp fog, German air-raids enlivened the rain-swept streets of Dunkirk. Luckily neither monitor received damage, though a tugboat lying astern of *Mersey* was sunk by bomb. It appeared, however, not improbable that lock-gates might be destroyed in this fashion, wherefore as a measure of precaution both ships were now brought outside the dock. With the ceaseless rain, the perpetual raids ending each day, the blaze of searchlights sweeping the night sky, the *clatter-clatter-clatter* of monitors' machine-guns and the booming of the forts' guns, freedom ashore became still rarer. Finally, by the Dunkirk Prefect's order, no one was allowed in the darkened streets after 7 p.m. and even the lighthouse was forbidden to display its gleams.

But all things come to an end, and on the evening of January 10 *Severn* with *Mersey* escorted by destroyers at length set out for England. Joy to be going home, with perhaps four days' 'drop of leave' for each watch, very shortly; and the weather actually had changed for the better. Outside the pierheads not a breath of wind, the sea flat calm: in fact those ideal conditions that monitors had a right to expect. Designed for smooth water, not strong enough to endure North Sea battering, they had suffered far harder service than was justified, and even during a windless passage in nothing worse than a moderate swell, steaming at only 54 knots, *Severn* (by reason of her flat bottom) used to come down with such a heavy wallop that her structure shook violently, and her people feared she might shear off the hull's rivets.

By seven o'clock tonight, with *Mersey* astern, she was just reaching the Dyck lightship, when a fairly stiff breeze from southwest began to pipe up, as the barometer firmly commenced to drop down. Four hours later everything seemed to happen at once.

CHAPTER 6

Mystery Voyage

Wind and sea increased, the monitors were scooping up the short steep waves, heavy rain poured down from a black sky, and so a usually stormy passage was assured. Soon enough both *Severn* and *Mersey* could scarce be controlled: they were like wild bulls obedient to nothing save their own freakish wills.

Commander Wilson's ship, whilst turning to port in the rain, during an endeavour to keep astern of *Severn*, lost sight of her leader; and now, with the wind's full force on *Mersey's* starboard bow, the latter was no less than 157 degrees off her course—heading in the direction of Calais though bound for the Downs! All the more annoying, since wireless messages kept arriving with the cheerful news that a U-boat was operating in the Calais neighbourhood.

This was no sort of night to be cast upon the sandy shores of northern France, where many a good ship has left her own ribs, and the bones of her mariners. The tide goes rushing past Gravelines and Calais furiously, whilst a southwester in opposing this stream never fails to make things vilely unpleasant, the deepest water hereabout not exceeding 90 feet. Six times her captain tried to get *Mersey* round on the other tack, away from the approaching beach, and six times he failed. At the risk of advertising his monitor's presence, he whacked her up to full speed, which of course made flames rise high out of funnel, and invited any submarine to come within range.

The gale became angrier, seas were alarmingly high, and though Calais lighthouse is situated right inland amid the town's streets, yet it had become so near that almost the warmth from its lenses could be felt aboard.

Still the ship refused to answer her helm.

With much permission, and all the engines' horsepower, she would come within a point of the wind, only to fall off at once, wallow in the next hollow, and then drive persistently shorewards.

Something desperate had to be done, and imaginations began to picture French gunners suddenly opening fire at a low grey mass that might be taken for a submarine partially visible over the crests. But what could be attempted to aid the steering, and keep ship's head up to wind? Every sailor reader will immediately answer: "Give her some sail set right aft!"

And that is exactly what had to be effected. All hands hurriedly set to work cutting away canvas screens from the bridge, and rigging up an awning vertically aft like to the mizzen of a yawl or a sailing-ship's spanker. Then, and then only, did *Mersey* become docile; she allowed herself to be headed away from Calais and, after a thoroughly dirty night, anchored in the Downs where *Severn* likewise had arrived with difficulty. So successful had this improvised bit of canvas proved, that both monitors shortly afterwards were provided with specially made spankers from the dockyard, and thus it chanced that the most modern built men-of-war borrowed from the olden days of hemp and oak.

But who would ever have expected that steam monitors could come tacking across the English Channel?

✯✯✯✯✯✯✯✯✯✯

It is worthy of record that though the course from Dyck lightship to the Downs is N 60 W, *Mersey* actually steered by compulsion such variations as: N 66 W, N 8 E, S 50 W, and N 20 E. The distance on the chart is 27 miles, and from the Dyck to Dunkirk another 9: total 36 miles from Dunkirk to the South Goodwin lightship, 'This required over 10 hours. A well-reefed small yacht or trawler would have got across tonight not less quickly.

✯✯✯✯✯✯✯✯✯✯

Next afternoon *Severn* and *Mersey* were back in the Medway where *Humber* was already awaiting them. Now began a period of two months preliminary to the monitors' great adventure. Hitherto, they had been employed as improvised stop-gaps, rather than on the special service that their design and light construction intended; but whilst no one in the world —least of all the officers and men—could ever have foreseen their ultimate destination, it was generally supposed in the squadron that if these units were to find their perfect role it would be amid more sheltered waters than off the Belgian coast. Meanwhile, hulls had been so battered about that into dry-dock they must at once go and receive detailed attention: the wonder was that they had survived at all, and Admiral Hood had long ago accepted the probability of all three foundering in Flemish soundings if overtaken by a sudden northerly gale.

First of all, then, Captain Fullerton's ship entered Sheerness dock, and then followed a surprise for all. During the last three months *Severn's* tiller-compartment had always been full of water, but when they pumped the dock dry there was no need to pump out the monitor herself. To walk under flat bottom was like going beneath a heavy shower, and at least ten *per cent* of her rivet-holes were leaking royally. Repairs, alterations, improvements to gun-mountings, drawing stores, adjusting compasses, painting ship, and generally refitting for further duties, brought time well into February: the promised date for a likely invasion drew very near.

Yet week succeeded week, the squadron swung round at their Medway buoys, ships' companies became bored with inactivity, and, just when sailing orders were being expected, another abrupt development matured: ships were told to take out ammunition and go back into dock. More alterations to guns, then back to the buoys, shuffling sideways down the tide like ducks unable to stem the stream! Compasses adjusted again, bunkers filled up anew, a fresh lot of rumours flying about, and thus February passed away.

Still swinging to the Medway tides!

But on March 5 something quite out of the ordinary was foreshadowed. Gangs of dockyard workmen came aboard with heavy baulks of timber and wedges, evidently to shore up the monitors forward and prevent any recurrence of the mess-deck being buckled up. Ah! This looked like going to sea? Then alongside *Severn* arrived Admiral Sir George Callaghan, Commander-in-Chief at the Nore, and took Captain Fullerton off with him to consult the Admiral Superintendent of Sheerness Dockyard. Oh! Yes: something important was in the wind, for these three officers had barely got together than the barge returned and disembarked them aboard *Severn*, bringing also a cluster of dockyard officials. And, having made some inspection forward, taken a few notes, measured both vertically and horizontally, they pronounced their verdict.

For the third time in less than two months monitors were to make into the dockyard, and on this occasion not only were ships to be strengthened below, but a very substantial breakwater was to be built ahead of the foremost 6-inch gun, and another similar obstruction abaft that gun. It was obvious enough that such elaborate preparations were to guarantee protection against something mightier than the Narrow Seas. The squadron was "going foreign", across the ocean: that seemed beyond dispute. They had finished with Belgian or East Anglian "puddles", and were to seek blue water: an assumption that received assurance at noon when Captain Fullerton had his men fallen in, gave them instructions about white clothing, and impressed on them the duty of not giving information away by foolish talk.

From now, in mess and wardroom, began that "buzz" which always pervades a ship when the slightest mystery exists. "Where are they sending us?" No one knew, but everybody made his own guess. Some were betting on the Mediterranean, some believed that their destination was the Suez Canal: flat-bottom monitors would be ideal for that smooth stretch of water. Others thought of the Dardanelles, which seemed likely enough since the campaign to force the Straits had begun only on February 19 when the forts were—bombarded: doubtless the British admiral out there would welcome monitors' guns in his big task.

But so varied were the opinions and rumours aboard that during this week every maritime country on the map had been put forward, and one wag even announced that they were bound for the Antarctic in order to succour Shackleton's expedition.

This was Friday, and orders came that the squadron must be ready to leave England by the following Thursday midnight, wherefore ensued days and nights of intense activity. All portable fittings were dismantled and sent below, all boats were removed, and the funnel top was covered with an iron plate to prevent water getting down. Topmasts were stowed, every part of hull and decks was made watertight, light guns were removed for another purpose, as also signalling gear and searchlights. But each monitor took in her full amount of coal and oil, and those stores for which she had no further space were to be carried otherwise. Thus, by the time hatches had been slammed down, the squadron resembled nothing so much as three plain steel hulks.

For they were not to use their own steam but to be towed out, and if they should founder after all this trouble and sealing up, that would mean without loss of life; for officers and men would not be aboard them. Six ocean tugs—each carrying in her complement a couple of signal ratings—had been selected, and by midnight of March 11-12 the voyage from Medway to Plymouth began. Captain (afterwards Commodore Sir) Frederick W. Young R.N.R. the famous salvage expert, had been responsible for selecting and fitting out the tugs *Blackcock, Danube II, Sarah Jolliffe, Southampton, T. A. Jolliffe, Revenger.*

It was no small undertaking even from the seafaring point of view, and meant considerable organisation, First-class skill, a good deal of patience and tact, and a certain amount of risk were essential. Special towing spans were fitted round each monitor's fore gun turret, and there was plenty of good sound gear available: yet these river gunboats with their flat bottoms and shallow draught might be awkward creatures, when being towed, and inclined to slew about. If they encountered heavy weather, there was no telling what might happen, and at the best a monitor's low foredeck would be under water most of the time. Then, it must be remembered that the German Submarine Blockade had begun from February 18, and the curious cavalcade definitely invited torpedo attack. Add to this the delicate matter of possible human friction between two branches of the sea service, for here were naval units being taken out by the Merchant Service, yet from Plymouth Sound the whole crowd would be under the orders of Captain Fullerton.

Towing is a fine art, and deep-sea towing is a highly developed ability belonging to only a limited number of master mariners, who have made it their career in life, and have nothing to learn on the subject from even the most experienced naval officer. These tug-captains and crews belonging to the Mercantile Marine might resent interference under certain circumstances. Commander Vigers R.N.R., in the *Blackcock* was appointed senior officer of the tugs, and made responsible for setting both the course and speed. He would use the International Code of signals, and the naval signal ratings lent to him would be of great assistance. To each monitor went two tugs, who were to use plenty of oil during bad weather and so create smooth patches.

A tenth vessel had also been selected, the S.S. *Trent* of the Royal Mail Line, which had been in the passenger trade to South America. Her the Admiralty had taken up as mother-ship and depot for the squadron. Whilst she lay near London in the Royal Albert Docks, well-laden lighters with stores and guns came up from the Medway, and these guns she now mounted as anti-submarine protection. Only a handful of naval officers and men joined her by the 11th; she still retained her Mercantile Captain, officers, and crew; but on arrival in Plymouth Sound, she would receive all the other personnel from the three monitors. She also carried, apart from her own boats, the monitors' motorboats together with the *Talawa*, a privately owned motorboat lent by Lieut. Bowle Evans R.N.V.R., who came accompanied by his engineer.

Fortunately the *Trent*, 6 tugs, and 3 battened-down lifeless monitors, all reached Devonport safely by March 14, whither arrived by special train the ships' companies of *Severn*, *Mersey*, *Humber*. By midnight Captain Fullerton, Commander Snagge, Commander Wilson, their officers and men, being all aboard *Trent*; the ten ships with lights out sailed in company for a certain destination, escorted by the two destroyers *Lookout* and *Foyle* who were to take care of them till well clear of the land. Daylight revealed more destroyers, but by 3 p.m. they had seen their charge well beyond the English Channel and could now part company. For as yet the U-boat danger zone did not extend into the Bay of Biscay.

Nevertheless Lieut.-Commander Hersing, one of the very ablest of Germany's submarine officers, had already taken his U-21 down the English Channel, up the Irish Sea; and on January 29 arrived off Walney Island fronting Barrow-in-Furness, the very birthplace of these monitors, where he amused himself awhile bombarding the place. It was this same U-21 which left Wilhelmshaven on April 25, passed down the Bay of Biscay, and became the first German submarine that ever entered Gibraltar Straits. If this successful and ruthless captain had only been a few weeks earlier, he would have sunk monitors, tugs, and mother-ship with the same ease that he sank the British cruiser *Pathfinder*, the British battleship *Triumph*, the British battleship *Majestic*, and the French cruiser *Amiral Charner*.

How the destruction of monitors at this stage might have altered history will be manifested in a subsequent chapter.

It was well, then, that the squadron had left the Thames when it did. Their orders were to keep west of the normal steam track until the Straits of Gibraltar, avoiding headlands as much as possible, not going into harbour except through stress of weather, and then using Portuguese rather than Spanish ports, since the latter contained too many Germanic sympathisers.

For Captain Fullerton's squadron was bound to Lemnos *via* Malta, and without delay. So not for them was the defence of Suez Canal: the monitors were wanted at the Dardanelles, which had begun to change its character from a diversion to a big campaign. Whensoever the Fleet got through past Chanak Narrows into the Sea of Marmora, the Bosphorus and the Black Sea, there might be some interesting work for *Severn* and her sisters. It was known that two new Austrian monitors, *Ems* and *Inn*, were now ready and probably had reached the Danube. Of 440 tons, armed with two guns and 3 howitzers, each ship had

(Top) H.M.S. "Severn"
(Bottom) Bound for East Africa
The tug "Revenger" at sea alongside "Trent" to receive fresh water in casks

a speed of 12 knots, and monitors-versus-monitors would assuredly mean river operations of no ordinary interest.

This contemplation at sea restarted discussions, as the tugs rose and fell to the Bay of Biscay swell, yet the very day they were passing rugged Finisterre was that fatal March 18, when the Anglo-French Fleet made their great attack and proved by their failure that ships would never get through the Dardanelles until soldiers had first captured the land batteries. For the present such a set-back, such a decisive crisis, was withheld from universal knowledge: it sufficed to suppose that the Aegean might be monitors' sphere for the immediate future.

Life aboard the *Trent* just now seemed far from unpleasant. Captain Fullerton's officers occupied the first-class staterooms; chief petty officers lived aft in the second class; whilst the remainder of monitors' crews were berthed forward in temporarily fitted messes. Instead of a bleak British spring, they were enjoying fine weather and the sun getting warmer every mile; but, most important of all, the towage so far had been a great success. The accompanying sketch shows how the column was arranged in line-ahead, with H.M.S. *Trent* (Captain Hayes R.N.R.) on the port beam.

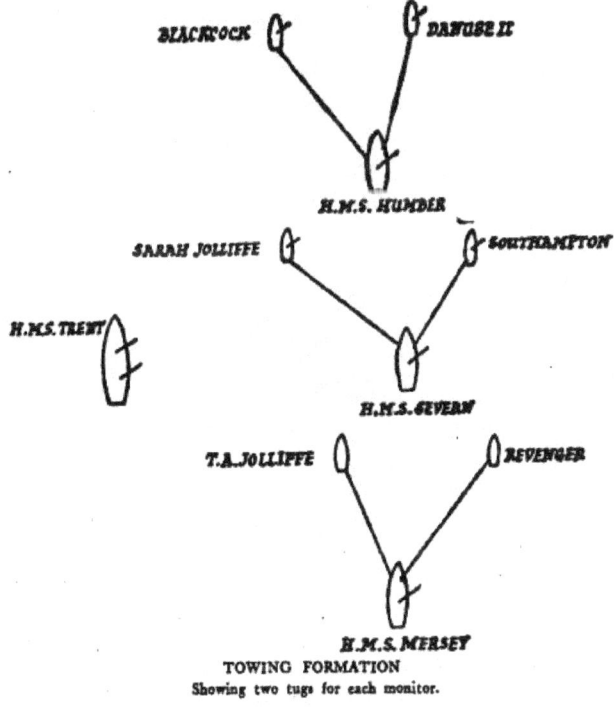

TOWING FORMATION
Showing two tugs for each monitor.

(Top) The German Cruiser "Königsberg"
(Bottom) Tirene Bay, Mafia Island

Jogging along at 6½ knots, sighting only an occasional steamer, the squadron made steady progress past the Iberian Peninsula. The sea kept breaking over the sealed monitors, but tow-ropes never snapped. Aboard the supply ship men were drilling, making boarding nets, being inoculated against enteric, and now came wireless instructions for monitors not to enter Gibraltar. Yet these little tugs possessed no great bunker space, and were getting short of coal: the problem was how to obey the Admiralty, and at the same time replenish with fuel.

Captain Fullerton solved the difficulty quite simply on Monday morning when nearly abreast of "The Rock". At 5.30 a.m. engines were stopped, then without any complication *Danube II* transferred her tow-rope to *Blackcock*, *Southampton* did the same to *Sarah Jolliffe*, and *T. A. Jolliffe* to *Revenger*. This enabled *Danube II*, *Southampton* and *T. A. Jolliffe* to run into Gibraltar, hurry up with their coaling, whilst the squadron with single tows continued towards Malta. A few hours later one trio came back rebunkered, enabling the other three to complete likewise, so that by Wednesday afternoon *Blackcock*, *Sarah Jolliffe*, *Revenger*, rejoined and the pageant could accelerate to its original pace.

Occasionally *Trent* would sight some British steely and exchange semaphore signals, but requested the trader not to report monitors to anyone. "All right, sir", came the reply. Out of Gibraltar *Blackcock* had brought letters and some fresh stores, but it was *Trent's* wireless which acted as news collector and disseminator. The tugs happened to be Liverpool owned with Liverpool crews; and, war or no war, these men could not repress their sporting instincts. Great, therefore, was their joy when *Trent* signalled across the result of the Liverpool Grand National.

By March 29 this fortnight's voyaging from Devonshire brought the ten ships at last into Malta; and if latterly they had been slightly delayed by bad weather, with seas breaking over monitors' quarter-decks, yet it was something to have arrived undamaged. But what next? Were the three monitors really destined for the Dardanelles? In those days Malta was busy with British transports carrying troops to the Aegean; with French battleships, cruisers, destroyers, using the harbour as their base; and an occasional British man-of-war arriving or departing. Hither, also, limped some of those Anglo-French units which had been so badly mauled on that terrible March 18 when the combined fleet was thwarted by Turkish shells and mines. Already the monitors' people saw the French battleship *Suffren* come in after having been holed below water-line, and our battle-cruiser *Inflexible* would soon follow. Both had narrowly escaped destruction.

Now the latter part of March and the early days of April were the preparatory period for the famous landing of the Army which was to take place on April 25 with the hope of capturing Gallipoli peninsula. Already several of the monitors' tugs were being sent off to the Dardanelles with lighters, yet the monitors themselves still remained battened down, so that when His Excellency the Governor of Malta wished to see what manner of ships they might be, he could but walk overt the upper decks.

But on April 3 came sudden orders for *Trent* to raise steam, and the tugs *Blackcock, Danube II* together with the *Rescue* (from Gibraltar) to be ready for taking monitors in tow at ten o'clock next morning. Liberty-men were recalled from shore, drinking water and beef were taken in by the supply ship, and everything was arranged for sailing; but nature decided otherwise. For bad weather had set in, a heavy sea outside was running, and the risk would have been too great. Then, on April 6, an alteration of plans enabled tugs to draw fires and men to have usual leave. What had happened?

The answer is that Admiral de Robeck at the Dardanelles had wished to have these three monitors for the big adventure of April 25, and they must reach Mudros by the 12th. But when he learned that they had been held up by this burst of bad weather; would need five days for their towing; and another fortnight after arrival before being unbattened and fitted for service; he realised that they would not fit into his scheme.

So, monotony dominated monitors' men, painting and fitting bullet-proof plates kept hands and minds partially occupied, but in no sense satisfied the intense longing to be away and doing big things. Just now the tugs seemed to be having most of the fun: *Blackcock, Revenger, Rescue*, went away with more lighters, *Sarah Jolliffe* came back after a very rough trip, with her starboard boat stove in, and upper-deck fittings damaged. Three of the four lighters being towed for Lemnos had foundered in the gale, yet the work must continue, and the tugs fetched out another lot; though *Southampton*, shortly after leaving Malta, put back with one of her lighters in a sinking condition.

But when were Captain Fullerton's gunboats to have their chance again of cooperating with the soldiers? Six months had passed since monitors' guns had barked at the enemy, and great disappointment was being felt that after hurrying south to Malta the squadron seemed to have been slighted by fate. Other ships were coming in with thrilling tales of Dardanelles doings, and even the minesweeping steam trawlers had exciting incidents to relate. Were *Severn* and her sisters to consider their utility at an end?

However, on April 21 it was very obvious that a considerable change of intentions had been made; that *Humber* would remain some time in Malta; but the other two with *Trent* were bound for some distant spot beyond the Mediterranean.

So, again, imaginations started guessing and tongues projected new theories: yet nobody had dared to put forward anything half so daring and original as that which the Admiralty in Whitehall had just arranged.

CHAPTER 7

The Raider Puts to Sea

As the monitors lay in Lazaretto Creek today, *Humber* began taking aboard from *Trent* both stores and ammunition, whilst a fresh activity in *Severn* and *Mersey* indicated that another towing voyage was imminent. But the thick awnings which now were being fitted on *Trent's* bridge and boat-deck surely proved that a warmer climate would soon be experienced. Suez Canal, perhaps, after all

All doubt and speculation were washed away when the new orders burst on them, that *Trent*, *Severn*, *Mersey*; the four tugs *Blackcock*, *Revenger*, *T.A. Jolliffe*, *Sarah Jolliffe*; together with the collier *Kendal Castle*, were shortly to leave for Zanzibar. That would mean a voyage of some 5,000 miles and about 5 weeks, but, by reason of the few ports on the way, the problem of coaling would be otherwise than easy, especially between Aden and Zanzibar.

Then there was the question of whether the smaller units could endure the hard winds and smashing seas. True, the shorter passage from England to Malta had been accomplished with surprising ease, yet this spell of luck had no right to be relied upon further. Down the Red Sea bad conditions were probable, and across the Indian Ocean practically certain. These tugs drew not less than 12 ft. when empty, but in that state would roll pretty badly and might receive damage, so the towing must at times fall to *Trent* and *Kendal Castle*: for this reason, hawsers and special gear were being got ready in Malta Dockyard.

At first consideration, the idea of hauling unseaworthy steel boxes (as were these monitors) all that distance seemed fantastic: surely they would spend most of their time under rather than on the water. But the Admiralty fully realised the risk, and Captain Fullerton was authorised to exercise his own judgment, use any sheltered anchorage, or even turn back from the project should Red Sea weather prove impossible.

On the other hand, at last by an exceptional sequence of events, there had ripened both the opportunity and an immediate need for these gunboats. When Captain Fullerton's father-in-law, that farsighted First Sea Lord, Admiral Lord Fisher, had considered the likely utility of monitors, he visualised employing them up some German river—if such an occasion should mature. They would be able to carry gunpower right up country, whither no other men-of-war could advance. But the trend of hostilities, having robbed them of their proper role in smooth sheltered waterways, they were not even permitted to try their artillery strength in the less exposed Dardanelles area which lies between Europe and Asia; although the *Humber*, after quitting Malta, performed good work this summer in bombarding the Gallipoli peninsula off Anzac. But primarily and essentially the monitors were built for river work, and German East Africa was now to offer them a wonderful delta. Let us see how the demand arose.

On the eve of hostilities, the Cape of Good Hope naval area was of vast extent, including the whole of East Africa with its outlying islands, the important Capetown-Durban section, and the West of Africa so far north as St. Helena; but for this considerable region from Atlantic to Indian Ocean Rear-Admiral Herbert King-Hall possessed responsibility. He had under him a cruiser squadron of three comparatively slow and old-fashioned units comprising the thirteen-years-old *Hyacinth* (flagship), 5,600 tons; the twenty-years-old *Astraea*, 4,360 tons; and the fifteen-years-old *Pegasus*, of only 2,135 tons.

Not one of these had ever been able to steam at better than 21 knots in their prime. By July 27, 1914, one week preceding outbreak of war, the admiral had reached Mauritius but the grave outlook caused him to detach *Astraea* and *Pegasus* for the purpose of watching Dar-es-Salaam, wherein more than likely lay the German cruiser *Königsberg*.

Now Dar-es-Salaam, some fifty miles from Zanzibar, was both a military station and capital of German East Africa. There, too, the *Königsberg* had her base. A fine, modern, ship of 3,400 tons, she had been completed only seven years previously at a cost of £320,000. With her three funnels and ten 4.1-inch guns, the German cruiser had an impressive appearance even to Europeans, but the significant fact was that her speed of 24 knots gave her a clear 3-knot superiority over any of the Cape Squadron.

On July 31 *Königsberg* was engaged in target practice and running her torpedoes, after which she ran into Dar-es-Salaam, got rid of all superfluous gear, and filled up her bunkers whose maximum contents were 850 tons of coal. At 4 p.m. she sailed and, whilst leaving harbour her commanding officer, Captain Max Looff made a speech to his crew assembled on the quarter-deck. He announced that Russia had declared war on Germany, but at present it was not known what France and England intended. If these two powers should become Germany's enemies, *Königsberg* would do all she could in her duty as "overseas cruiser". This peroration ended with patriotic cheers for the *Kaiser*, and the men set about their respective tasks.

That same afternoon Admiral King-Hall was steaming towards Dar-es-Salaam, when a wireless message from *Pegasus* reported that the latter had sighted *Königsberg* coming out of harbour. Actually, the German also perceived her on the horizon, and about dusk increased to full speed. Night fell, the moon rose, *Hyacinth* took up the chase and got within 3,000 yards of the German cruiser; but here, at the very eve of big events, *Königsberg* had no difficulty in widening the distance and, thanks to those priceless 3 knots, quickly disappeared with lights out into the darkness. She had won the first round of what was to be a protracted contest.

There has come into my hands a manuscript translation of the diary kept by Signalman P. Ritter aboard S.M.S. *Königsberg*, and this document is so faithfully filled almost from hour to hour, that we now have a perfect revelation of that adventurous ship's movements for the rest of her life. Thus, for the first time, we are able to set at rest all theory and see the picture as a whole, without any item lacking. And if we begin by placing ourselves on her forebridge, we shall share in the suspense which was Captain Looff's.

Admiral King-Hall having been foiled at the first meeting, and being in need of coal, made for Zanzibar which he entered next morning (August 1). He then hurried south to the Cape of Good Hope, but left *Astraea* with *Pegasus* behind. This was really playing into the hands of a potential enemy, for whilst *Hyacinth's* eleven 6-inch plus eight 3-inch were more than a match for *Königsberg's* ten 41-inch; and there was not much to choose between the latter and *Astraea's* armament of ten guns (two 6-inch and eight 4.7-inch); yet the German could have no excessive fear of *Pegasus*' eight 4-inch. But, apart from other considerations, *Königsberg's* speed enabled her always to choose her own range; and if one day she chanced to meet either of these two British units alone, the result could be foretold.

At present, however, in accordance with German pre-war plans,

Königsberg's duty was to engage on commerce raiding; to reach the trade-routes and sink shipping. It was also a long-standing arrangement that at outbreak of war German liners on voyage should place themselves under the orders of cruiser captains. So away went Captain Looff on his job.

As a feint, he spent most of that initial night going south towards Mafia Island but early on August 1 altered course to the northeast and so continued for several days, thus coming up the Indian Ocean towards Cape Guardafui at the entrance to the Gulf of Aden. Thereabouts he might well expect to find plenty of traffic on the way between the Orient and Red Sea, but his immediate objective was to intercept the Norddeutscher Lloyd S.S. *Zieten*, which had left Colombo for Germany on July 29. For on the China station the German Navy owned the armed surveying vessel *Planet*, to which a relief crew had recently been sent, but the original ratings were now coming home in *Zieten*; it was highly desirable that these naval men should not fall into British hands.

By August 5 *Königsberg* had gained the Guardafui region, when a steamer was sighted on the horizon. A chase began, but the steamer did her best to get away. Captain Looff, on this first day of war against Great Britain, was determined to make an early capture and his speed gradually wore down the intervening distance. The range came down to 20,000 yards, so he fired a shot which had the effect of making the stranger take notice. She now hoisted her national flag and thus gave the chaser a first-class shock: those were German colours, and this was the S.S. *Goldenfels*. The latter had supposed *Königsberg* to be a British cruiser! The meeting turned out for Captain Looff most convenient: he had been steaming five days and his bunkers were getting low, but *Goldenfels* was full of coal.

Still searching for the *Zieten*, whose track should soon be crossed, *Königsberg* by 9 p.m. of the 6th had reached a spot some 280 miles east of Aden when he sighted in the moonlight two steamers: one being a large passenger ship, and the other a fine new vessel of 6601 tons carrying general cargo. The first turned out to be the German S.S. *Zieten*, and the second was the British S.S. *City of Winchester* belonging to the Ellerman Hall Line bound for London at the end of her maiden voyage. On watch was the third officer, and with him on the bridge was an apprentice Mr J. G. Waring who had recently finished his training aboard H.M.S. *Worcester*. The *Königsberg* after crossing from the Ellerman liner's port side to speak *Zieten*, devoted her attention to the *City of Winchester.*

Mr Waring tells me that:

The German cruiser was next seen on our starboard quarter, calling us up on the lamp, asking our name, and then telling us to stop immediately, but we did not obey. She then fired across our bows, and we did stop. A boat was sent across to us with an armed boarding party, who immediately took charge of the ship, disabling our wireless, and remained on board. We were ordered to follow astern of the cruiser.

Next day *Königsberg* with *City of Winchester* anchored in the bay of Makalla, which is a port on the south Arabian coast 300 miles ENE of Aden, and here arrived *Zieten* as well as the Hamburg-Amerika liner *Ostmark*. It will be noted how easily three German steamers, within the first two days since Great Britain's entering the war, were at Captain Looff's disposal, also that he was careful to choose for temporary retirement an anchorage not too far from the shipping tracks, yet in an area less likely to befriend British than Germans. Nor will the reader fail to have noticed that *Zieten*, after clearing Colombo only a few hours earlier than the Ellerman liner, was in a position to shadow *City of Winchester* along the route during those critical early days of August. Wireless communication had its obvious uses.

Whilst anchored off Makalla, the British steamer's navigational instruments and charts were confiscated; at seven o'clock on this same evening of the 7th after a prize crew of forty officers and men had come aboard the Ellerman liner, she with *Königsberg*, *Zieten*, and *Ostmark* got under way. Whither bound? None of the English mariners could guess, though the course seemed to settle down at about NE which would bring them towards the Persian Gulf approaches. Early next morning *Königsberg* and *Ostmark* left them, and a change was foreshadowed when Mr Waring's shipmates were told to pack their belongings. Still following in the wake of *Zieten*, the *City of Winchester* at 3 p.m. of the 9th let go anchor in a secluded bay of the Khorya— Moria, a group of islands situated 500 miles from Makalla at Arabia's southeast corner.

Here were already *Königsberg* and *Goldenfels*, but the former was in the act of coaling from the latter when smoke was reported. Captain Looff became alarmed, stopped refuelling, raised steam, cast off, and prepared for action; but very soon the two blurs shaped themselves into the hulls of the British steamer with *Zieten*. *Ostmark* having been sent away, and the islands affording privacy though not excluding a certain amount of swell, *Zieten* on the 10th lay alongside the *City of Winchester* helped herself to coal and stores, took aboard most of the latter's people excepting the second mate and third engineer. At 2 a.m. on the 11th *Zieten* weighed and departed for a secret destination, but the prisoners observed that throughout today she steered to the southwest, next day and on the 13th to the west, but thereafter the course was again about southwest.

These directions should eventually bring them somewhere down the East African coast, but food began to run short; and, because also the coal was getting scarce, *Zieten* had to economise by slowing down. Finally, having repainted her funnels to make her look like one of the British India Steam Navigation Company's vessels, she hoisted the Red Ensign and entered the neutral port of Mozambique in Portuguese East Africa. This was August 20, and the prisoners were now given their freedom. A week later they took passage in the British India S.S. *Palamcotta* for Delagoa Bay, caught the Union-Castle *Walmer Castle* from Durban, and so reached London early in October. It so happened that two months later Mr Waring, having now joined the S.S. *City of Vienna*, was passing the Yorkshire coast on the morning of December 16 when the German squadron's guns were heard bombarding Scarborough.

As to *Königsberg*, she was in the centre of a coal crisis. All these German liners, having been halted on their respective voyages, needed more rather than less fuel. The *Goldenfels* had yielded all she could to *Königsberg*, but that did not suffice for the cruiser's greedy furnaces. Fourteen hours after *Zieten* had left the Khorya-Mory islands, Captain Looff took his ship alongside the Ellerman liner, extracted the remaining 250 tons of coal, her fresh water, and what provisions had been left; these transhipments needing more than twenty-four hours.

Having no further use for the *City of Winchester*, the *Königsberg* shelled her till she began to sink. The second mate and third engineer, with the rest of the British crew, were taken by *Goldenfels* who landed them at Sabang.

By August 12, with the *Planet's* crew on board, *Königsberg* was able to resume her cruising. So far, she had been not over successful: one prize snatched out of a normally busy Aden Gulf was nothing very wonderful. Now the weakness of these raiders consisted in their necessity for frequent refuelling, and this meant either (*a*) relying on the coal found in captured ships, or (*b*) the prompt arrival at given

"Severn" off the African Coast

rendezvous of the cruiser's supply vessel. Thus (*a*) resolved itself into a gamble, and (*b*) demanded both exact navigation as well as avoiding British patrols.

And here let us introduce the S.S. *Somali* owned by the German East Africa Line. She was of only 2550 tons, had been built at Hamburg a quarter of a century ago, but she was a familiar sight to German colonials, and her name is now recorded in naval history. Captain Looff, in accordance with the pre-war scheme, had arranged for *Somali* to attend him on the Indian Ocean, so she had left Dar-es-Salaam during the first days of August and on the 13th, she had, after coming north, joined him. But our late enemies seem to have been somewhat nervy, for when *Somali* signalled that she had seen searchlights, Captain Looff put to sea followed by this supply vessel, whose cargo would be needed quite soon.

The *Königsberg* steamed about for several days, sighted no British cruiser nor even a British merchantman, so on August 18 made for Ras Hafen, an out-of-the-way spot where she might draw fires and clean her boilers peacefully. This she managed to effect but, when a boat was sent ashore looking for fresh water, the men returned aboard disappointed. Next morning *Somali* steamed in, came alongside, the coaling and provisioning commenced immediately, but were not concluded till 10 p.m. on the 21st.

Seven hours later, thus made independent for another week, Captain Looff put to sea and headed south. His three weeks dedicated to commerce raiding had signally failed, and he must get back to his station for other exploits. Certainly he had been able to keep the world ignorant of the disaster which befell the *City of Winchester*, but by this date the cables from Mozambique must have got busy, the British Admiralty would be sending cruisers along the Gulf of Aden, and he determined to let them find him not. He therefore resolved to make for the northwest side of Madagascar and annoy the French; for almost facing Mozambique is the natural harbour of Majunga, where he might capture a French steamer or release some coal-filled German ship which the French colonial authorities had detained. Meanwhile he sent away *Somali* to meet him at the end of this month in the waters of a British Island, so rarely mentioned that the reader may perhaps never have heard its name.

But, on the third day after quitting Ras Hafen and the *Somali*, there came into *Königsberg's* wireless-room a tiresome item of news, which henceforth and for ever must vitally affect this cruiser's wel-

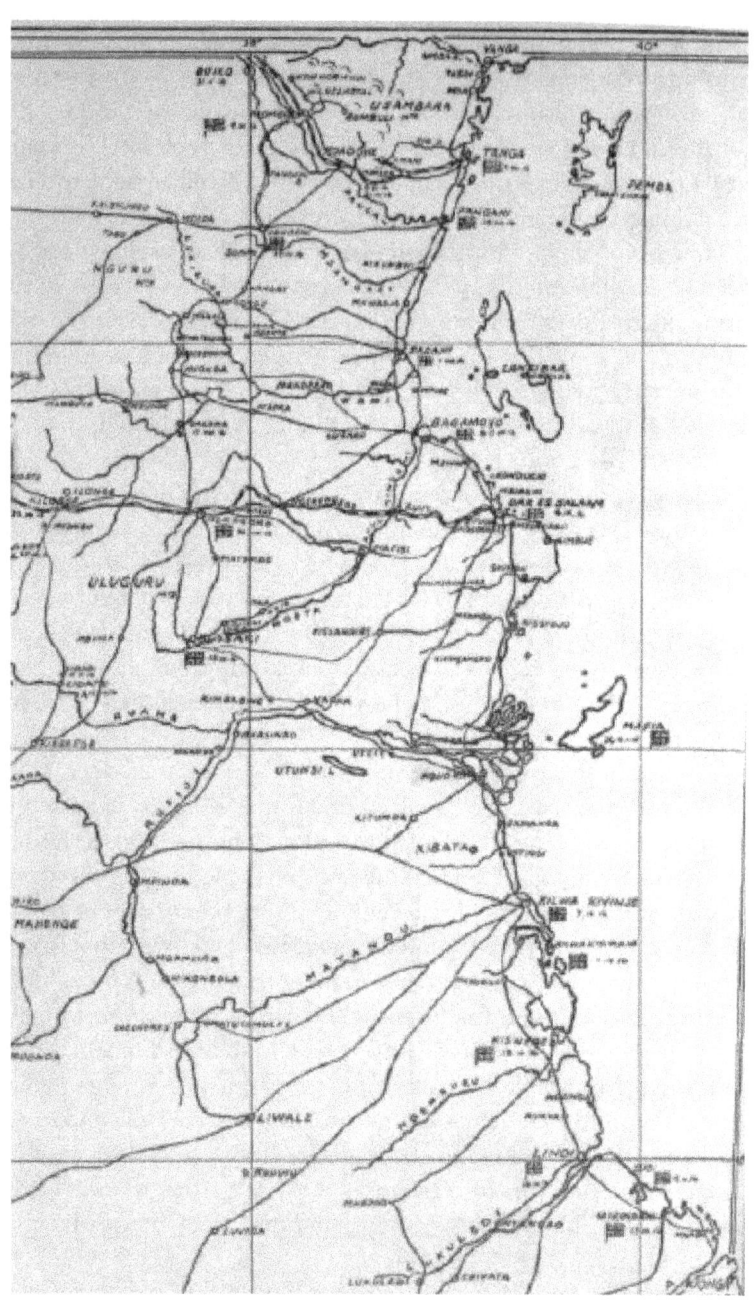

Chart of Naval Operations, East Africa 1914-1919

fare. It is a truism that human imagination cannot always foresee the sequels to every action, but no one entirely appreciated on August 8 the full results that would follow a straightforward incident performed by H.M.S. *Astraea*. Early on this last-mentioned date *Astraea* had arrived off Dar-es-Salaam and shelled the important wireless station to destruction, which had the effect of temporarily cutting out the ordinary means for communication between the one German cruiser and the colonial capital. Yet it did not end at that.

So great was local alarm that the Germans feared a landing, and for their own protection sank a large floating dock across the harbour entrance, thereby imprisoning several of their fine steamers including the 8,000-tons East Africa Company's liner *Tabora*. This multiple-decker had arrived with an aeroplane less than a week before. Like the Company's smaller ship *Somali*, she might have been a useful tender to *Königsberg*, or as an armed merchant cruiser playing the part of decoy. But the dock obstruction had precipitately put a stop to that, which was a pity. For *Tabora's* holds could have carried enough fuel to keep *Königsberg* going for weeks, whereas *Somali's* supply was getting somewhat low.

Later in the month, when contact had been made with East Africa again, Captain Looff had heard something about this *Astraea* visit, and that the Dar-es-Salaam entrance was closed.

★★★★★★★★★★

The Germans had four useful wireless stations inland at Tabora, Muanga, Bukoba, and Mgau Mwania. The first-mentioned was so powerful that it could communicate with Windhock in Southwest Africa. But apart from the four land stations, there was nothing to prevent the S.S. *Tabora* using her *telefunken*.

★★★★★★★★★★

This meant that he was bereft of the one naval base for thousands of miles, his ship without a home, his hope of getting future fuel and food less than slender. It was now August 25, and there seemed all the more reason for gambling a raid on the French.

The intervening days passed without incident, the northern coast of Madagascar approached, and during the night of August 28-29 *Königsberg* cleared for action. Just before daylight she crept into Majunga Bay, unexpected and unseen. Taking up a suitable position, she waited for dawn to reveal anchored shipping but, recorded Signalman Ritter, "we were greatly disappointed. There was not a single ship in the harbour." So, they came out again, after a completely profitless enterprise. The outlook had now become serious; not only had they no dock, no port, but very little beer, meat or coal.

Never had the modern mechanical man-of-war so plainly shown her essential weakness, and attachment to conditions ashore. How different from the old self-contained sailing vessel with enough salt beef and biscuits to last her for months; no engines or boilers to demand overhaul; but just once in a long while some snug lagoon for careening ship and tarring her bottom!

The *Königsberg* looked like lurching heavily into a dilemma so real, that it would call for all Captain Looff's ability, plus a large measure of luck: unless he were about to intern himself.

CHAPTER 8

Dangerous Adventure

Right out on the Indian Ocean, 400 miles due east of Lindi and about the same distance north from Madagascar's Majunga (or precisely Lat. 9.25 N, Long. 46.20 E), lies the lonely island of Aldabra, a remote outpost of the British Empire where the advent of any ship is a real event. At this date the manager of the settlement was a Mr Mein, who on August 30 observed the unwonted picture of a merchant steamer come at anchor. Not unnaturally he went off in a boat to call on her captain.

He noticed her name *Somali*, but to mount aboard was denied him; the excuse proffered being that the ship had some cases of small-pox. That might have been accepted as possible, but the vessel next day still remained, and at night fired several rockets which surely must be with the intention of attracting some other vessel. Sure enough, about eight o'clock on the following morning (September 1) there steamed in a grey, lithe, lean warship with three funnels but showing no flag. She proceeded alongside *Somali*, spent the whole day coaling, and departed at 6 p.m., having completely emptied the supply vessel.

This was the last occasion that *Königsberg* refreshed herself at sea, though she had indeed by now accustomed officers and men to unusual anchorages. Her course next lay to the northwest but, in order to throw off any pursuers, she steered first southeast till dark, and then headed for Mafia Island which was sighted by nine on the morning of September 3. Now Mafia is situated opposite the complicated delta of the River Rufiji, and the many-mouthed stream deposits its mud so far out that the sea is shallow for a long way off the mainland: even at four miles from the delta less than 18 feet could be obtained.

This tropical course rises to the northeast of Lake Nyasa and flows through "Darkest Africa" past native settlements, casuarina trees, coconut palms, mangrove swamps, till its final fifteen miles are just a network of interconnecting intricate waterways with islands of dense forest everywhere. Inhabited by crocodiles and hippopotamus families, the stream rushes by at 3 to 5 knots. Lions, elephants, monkeys, people the higher reaches, but all the banks are mosquito-infested and the country fever-breeding.

Reading from north to south there are three principal mouths: Kikunja, Simba Urange, Kiomboni, but only the first and second need concern us: and, because some ten miles inland they join to form a wish-bone shaped way, it is possible for vessels of a certain draught to enter by one mouth then emerge seaward by the other. The trouble was that whilst small coasters in peace time were known to come up and load wood for Zanzibar, British charts were very indifferent: and if the Germans possessed private knowledge from secret surveys, not even the latter could wholly be relied upon. What with shifting shoals and bad holding-ground, the Rufiji branches were reputed too risky for any except shallow-draught craft: the area was in fact "No Mariner's Region".

But that made it exactly suitable for Captain Looff, with a little difficulty and careful pilotage, to bring his cruiser where she would be hidden by mangroves from the civilised world. He chose the Simba Urange entrance, but since the channel approach outside in places drops to 10 feet at low water (Springs); and whereas the *Königsberg* drew 17½ feet when fully loaded; he would have to work his tides, come in slowly, and keep sounding all the time. Being sore pressed, he could even afford to take some risks and force her through slight patches of mud.

It is obvious that he would need at least 7½ feet more than existed during low water. Doubtless the reader is well aware that every fortnight, with the advent of new or full moon, tides rise higher, when they are known as Springs: they also are greater still towards the time of the equinoxes, *i.e.* March 21 and September 23. On September 3 the tides were getting big and approaching Springs, which here rise 14¾ feet, but, if he kept rigidly to the channel about 11.30 a.m. (or after half-flood) he would have not less than 18 feet until well within the river. Moreover, should *Königsberg's* keel just touch the mud, she would soon come off with the rising tide; for high water was due about 2.15 p.m.

The *Königsberg* steamed safely into the Simba Urange, turned sharp to port past the Kiomboni peninsula, then worked herself up river till she anchored off a village named Salale. "On either side", wrote Ritter, "nothing but mangroves." It was a pretty dull, dismal, place for 350 sailors to accustom themselves, away from any sort of civilisation, and boredom would be just one of the ever-pressing enemies which must occupy Captain Looff's mind; but for him the great accomplishment lay in having obtained stealthily a temporary resting-place close to the ocean, yet unseen by the British. He had every reason to suppose that, however many cruisers the Allies might care to send, not one would find *Königsberg's* concealment.

An atrocious rough road of seventy-five miles, partly through jungle, led northwards to Dar-es-Salaam, and besides, this captain had his wireless; so now he could keep himself in touch with current news, no less than with the extensive German spy system established along the coast as well as on the outlying islands. As to the Rufiji natives, these were treated with no little severity, but they had been marvellously impressed when they watched the 360-feet cruiser coming up with the tide, winding in and out of the twisting reaches. And, very shortly, there came also the *Somali* which had left Aldabra two hours after *Königsberg*, though with empty holds.

For working her auxiliary engines, Captain Looff still kept up steam; but for purposes of economy the furnaces now burnt wood. Ten days after his arrival he received coal and provisions by the small steamers *Gertrude* and *Rovuma*; then on the 15th more coal was on its way in lighters, being towed by the tug *Hedwig* from Lindi to Salale. The whole of this fuel had come from the SS. *Präsident*, which was at Lindi.

But the first two satisfied his wants for a certain immediate purpose, which was to avenge being shut out from Dar-es-Salaam; and, having obtained from the very efficient East African secret service news that one of Admiral King-Hall's ships at this moment lay off Zanzibar in no condition for battle, Captain Looff found every condition suitable for a short quick raid. On September 20 it would be Spring tides, practically equinoctials, with high water off the Rufiji at 4 a.m. and 4.15 p.m. Wherefore on the 19th at 1.30 p.m. he put to sea with a rising tide and ample water for getting over the shoal patches, and at 11 p.m. passed at sea the *Hedwig* bringing more coal.

It was only on September 18 that H.M.S. *Pegasus* had reached Zanzibar for a necessary overhaul of engines and cleaning of boilers. The risk of being for some time in no fighting condition had to be accepted, but *Königsberg* had not been heard of since July 31 except for the *City of Winchester* affair, and this incident suggested that the enemy had moved himself a long way from the Central African coast. As a measure of precaution *Pegasus* kept up steam on one engine, and the armed tug *Helmuth* (Sub-Lieut. C. J. Charlewood R.N.R.) was patrolling Zanzibar's South Channel.

Of course, it was easy enough in a port like Zanzibar for everyone to know of *Pegasus* inactivity, but Captain Looff acted on the news with great promptness. By 4 a.m. on September 20 he picked up the lights of Zanzibar, an hour later he cleared for action and went full speed ahead; but at 5.30 a.m., before *Helmuth* could get a warning signal through to the British cruiser, the stranger from 11,000 yards opened fire, her first shot falling 200 yards short of the British cruiser.

Creeping up to about 7,500 yards, Captain Looff let off his first salvo, and with his second got the range perfectly, taking *Pegasus* completely by surprise, so that the latter did not reply till after *Königsberg's* seventh salvo. The British man-of-war burst into flames, her bridge was carried away, she began to heel over and to be down by the head. After ten minutes' hot action, *Königsberg* ceased attacking during the period of five minutes whilst turning round, but then resumed with her other broadside. Altogether the German fired 276 4.1-inch shells, with such accuracy and at such a rate, that the *Pegasus* was instantly doomed. Before the latter could make a hit, *Königsberg*, quite untouched, had finished the morning's raid, and at 6 a.m. was rushing out again seawards: she had, by the element of surprise and superior guns, scored a definite victory. With eighty casualties, the *Pegasus* had been wiped quickly off the list, and at 2 p.m., turning over, went down to the sea-bed.

Southward the three-funnel enemy sped, past Dar-es-Salaam now avenged, then back to the Rufiji with plenty of water to get over the shallows. Entering again by the Simba Urange mouth, she came up river on the flood, negotiated the sharp bends, and by 3 p.m. was safely moored off Salale village 1¼ hours before high tide.

Yes: it had been a brilliant adventure, perfectly conceived and admirably executed. Yet here was *Königsberg* once more in hiding, compelled to act on the defensive, still lacking a safe or efficient base. Moreover, she had at last revealed her presence, and Captain Looff knew that the British Navy would rest neither day nor night till they should find him.

The news cabled to Whitehall concerning *Pegasus* was sensational enough, but no time was wasted in despatching the cruiser *Chatham* to strengthen the station and seek out the elusive raider. The former, being only two years old, armed with eight 6-inch guns, having a speed of 26 knots and a displacement of 5,400 tons, would be more than a match for the enemy. Happening to be in the Red Sea on September 21, H.M.S. *Chatham* (Captain Sidney R. Drury-Lowe R.N.) was able to reach Zanzibar a week later, and within twenty-four hours had begun to examine the coast southwards.

Apart from rumours and some coded German signals intercepted by wireless, there were no very definite data on which to work; but, proceeding on the assumption that the enemy was concealed up one of the many rivers or creeks, Captain Drury-Lowe began a thorough combing of harbours, islands, bays, reefs, inlets between Mafia Island and Portuguese territory. By October 6 three more cruisers—*Dartmouth, Weymouth*, and *Fox*—had reached the station, the hunt became intensive and extended over 1700 miles of coast, so far south as even to Delagoa Bay. It was a considerable and wearisome undertaking and not devoid of navigational dangers, so that *Chatham* on one occasion struck a reef with resulting minor injury.

But during October 10 the *Dartmouth*, near to Mozambique, captured the German tug *Adjutant* (250 tons) bound from Beira on her way to reach *Königsberg* at Salale. (*Adjutant* drew only 11 feet, so would have been able to get into Simba Urange with but little rise of tide. Moreover, this draught would have enabled her to reach the Kikunja by a connecting channel.) Nine days later *Chatham* arrived off the German port of Lindi, where she sent in one of her steamboats which discovered upriver the German S.S. *Präsident*, and aboard the latter were found documents proving that on September 15 so much coal out of this liner had been despatched in lighters to Salale. This was most valuable information, but not until October 30 did *Chatham* actually sight the masts of *Königsberg* and *Somali*: yet the Germans were too far off to be shelled today. Captain Drury-Lowe's vessel was drawing about 18 ft, and he could not get within effective range until Spring tides, which again were due on November 3: wherefore he contented himself with shelling the enemy's signal station at the south end of Mafia Island.

Meanwhile the Germans appreciated that if *Königsberg* was to retain her safety, the several delta entrances must be defended by some land forces, suitably entrenched and concealed by the mangrove trees at the Kikunja and Simba Urange mouths. Troops recruited from settlers were got together up country at Tabora, brought by land till reaching the Upper Rufiji, then put aboard the small river steamer

Rovuma which called at *Königsberg* on September 26. It seemed none too soon, for three days later off the delta was sighted the first British cruiser, and now Captain Looff mistakenly supposed his own lair had been revealed. This alarm put him still more on the defensive, and a plan was inaugurated for launching torpedoes from a *dhow* which happened to be here in the river; but such missiles are not rarely erratic, and the first rehearsal caused such an irregular run that Lieut. Angel, the torpedo-officer had to spring overboard after the wayward silver fish.

By mid-October existence aboard *Königsberg* had already become unpleasant. "A very dreary life", records Ritter; "no more decent meals, and nothing more to smoke."Thus, within six weeks the cancer of monotony had started, but the sailors might have been worse off, for the ship was in direct wireless touch with Dar-es-Salaam whence she received her daily news bulletin, and by road therefrom most of the desired provisions could be carried in less than a week. Less fortunate seemed the likely lot of the 60 soldiers with rifles, one machine-gun and three field-guns between them, now shot over at the river mouths; for these men might be starved out or shelled into death if the British were to make a proper campaign against the Rufiji.

There can be no question that Captain Looff was a very fine commanding officer, and his people trusted him implicitly. Place yourself in his position and consider all his anxiety of every sort. He knew that the British must be planning some surprise, and it might come at any moment. Nor could he dismiss from his mind the truth that naval mutiny often is born of monotonous inactivity; but that the only way to maintain morale is to keep men's minds and bodies always busy towards some new adventure. To let the ship's company moodily brood and grouse in the tropical heat, daily cursing the dull Salale swamps and all the time developing a bitter nostalgia; meant the gradual transforming of a splendid fighting unit into a mob of sullen murmurers. Best would he be fulfilling his duty towards ship and Emperor, if a raiding excursion out to sea and in the cooling fresh breezes of the open were attempted, but he must needs synchronise his plans with the approach of spring tides.

By October 29 the long-awaited provisions came alongside *Königsberg*, and today the cruiser got ready for fuelling. These two items taken collectively afforded the crew sufficient hint of what was impending, and gloom gave way to great joy. She still had 200 tons of coal in her bunkers, and another 200 were being taken aboard, which would thus give her less than half her maximum amount: yet it should suffice for a tip-and-run trip, and to be of slightly inferior draught would be advantageous for getting over the Simba Urange bar. Every day it was becoming deeper at high water, and November 3 would provide the top of spring tides about 4 o'clock.

But this phenomenon of nature was at the service of German and British equally: both could make use of the same augmented depth, for Captain Drury-Lowe might take advantage of the identical aid on which Captain Looff relied. Thus, the best laid schemes afloat may receive their check quite unexpectedly, hopes be suddenly banished by surprise, rival minds be animated by the same idea.

Ritter noted in his diary at the beginning of November:

> First of all, it happened differently. Secondly, as one thought it would, the Englishman is coming to pay us his visit. Yesterday an English cruiser tried to come in here but, owing to her large draught, failed. Today he tried again. On the horizon there were two more cruisers.

Actually, on November 1 *Chatham* fired her 6-inch guns against *Somali*, but could not hit her. Although the better tide this afternoon enabled the former to get within 4½ miles of the mouth, *Somali* was still 14,500 yards away, which happened to be *Chatham's* maximum long range. But *Königsberg* was distant 16,250 yards (or about another land mile above her supply ship) and could not be reached. Conversely, *Königsberg* would have only wasted shells, had she tried to reply, for the range of her 4.1-inch guns was but 12,760 yards.

It was next day that the other "Town"-class cruisers, *Dartmouth* and *Weymouth* joined *Chatham*. Thanks to the improving tide, and (being short of coal) to her own moderate draught, the first-mentioned worked her way into 164 feet and stood within 2 miles of the mouth for a short while at high water, but could not get into the river. All three then bombarded both banks, and *Chatham's* steam cutter dashed in to make a reconnaissance. She returned with news that Simba Urange's entrance was strongly held with trenches, rifles, machine-guns, and that a telephone had been laid on also. The enemy had made excellent use of thick mangroves for concealment; in fact, what with shoals and defences, the task of getting up to *Königsberg* seemed impossible.

Captain Looff, however, regarded the matter differently and felt certain one of the British cruisers would force her way in, which caused him now to send another of his machine-guns down to the mouth. He had lowered his topmasts and, in their stead, had lashed great branches of trees for further concealment, making the British gunners' job still more difficult. On November 3 they made their supreme effort with the afternoon tide when Captain Drury-Lowe, having reached a spot 2 miles from the shore, listed his ship five degrees and thus obtained a range of 14,800 yards. This bombardment could not continue for long after high water, and with the falling tide *Chatham* withdrew.

Today, however, over twenty years after, (as at date of publication 1938) we know that though *Königsberg* on the 3rd was not hit, she had a very narrow escape. One shell flew over her and fell into the mangroves a hundred yards away. Ritter adds:

"Then followed salvo after salvo from the 23.4-centimetre guns of *Chatham*. We could only sit idle and watch, as our guns were no use at this distance. The shelling continued an hour without our receiving one hit, which was an absolute wonder, as the shells fell close in front and behind us the whole time."

And according to another German sailor, Diaz y Rodriguez, (who became a prisoner, later on, aboard H.M.S. *Severn,* see chapter 16), one of *Chatham's* shells burst so near that pieces of it fell aboard *Königsberg.*

Now that was quite close enough, and the German man-of-war had never been so near to destruction: any shell onward from this moment might have settled her fate. Captain Looff next day accordingly weighed anchor to get further up river beyond danger, but he had left it rather late and his ship ran on to the mud, nor did she float off till high water (about 6 a.m.) on the 5th: he was indeed lucky that *Königsberg* had not been neaped during the ensuing fortnight till spring tides should return. Less fortunate, however, became *Somali*, which had been left with bows towards shore below Salale as of no further utility. *Chatham's* shells found this steamer on the 6th, a direct hit setting *Somali* on fire so that the conflagration continued during most of two days, and this one-time useful tender became a meaningless steel carcass lying helpless on the mud.

The next four days marked the end of the first Rufiji phase; and though the Simba Urange mouth was subjected to persistent shelling from the sea, yet the main objective settled down into bottling up the enemy so that he could never emerge. These operations formed the opportunity for some fine naval gallantry that culminated on November 10 when Lieut.-Commander J. C. S. Paterson R.N. in one steam picket-boat; with a steam-cutter in charge of Sub-Lieut. J. P. A. Brembridge R.N.; another under Sub-Lieut. J. H. R. Homfray R.N.; two more captained respectively by Sub-Lieut. A. G. Murray R.N. and Lieut.-Commander G. H. Lang R.N.; took part in a dangerous adventure.

At dawn they escorted into Simba Urange the 3,800 tons collier *Newbridge*, which was to be sunk across the river just before high water (7.53 a.m.), and in this cavalcade was included the 42-years-old iron steamer *Duplex*, 874 tons, under Lieut. R. S. Triggs R.N.R. The *Newbridge* herself was in the hands of Commander Raymond Fitzmaurice R.N., *Chatham's* second-in-command.

This mixed squadron received a hot reception from rifles, machine-guns and field pieces at Kiomboni peninsula, but by 6.35—more than an hour ahead of schedule—the duty had been accomplished, with the S.S. *Newbridge* resting on the river bed and only her upper-works showing above water. True, she had been placed in the deepest water; though caught by the tide, she had settled down at nearer 50 degrees than right angles. Also, thoroughly to have been effective, she should have been taken much further up river. Still, there she now lay, fouling a good part of the channel, and the future ebb tides might deposit a new bank of silt at each of her ends.

Commander Fitzmaurice and his party having been taken off by *Chatham's* steam-cutter (Sub-Lieut. Brembridge), a thrilling return journey past the peninsula to the open sea was made possible only by dint of cool bravery, a certain amount of luck, plus the fire from the small steamboats' machine-guns and rifles. The *Duplex*, drawing 13 feet, armed with a couple of 3-pdrs., had been hammering the peninsula's defences whilst entering but an enemy shell struck her bridge, rendering her temporarily out of control so that she drifted in peril near to the German guns ashore.

Lieut. Triggs having been severely wounded in the shoulder, and other casualties sustained, she was compelled to make her way out before *Newbridge* had been put in position; but that the whole operation ended with only 2 killed and 9 wounded must be partly attributed to the bombardment made from seaward by the British cruisers.

CHAPTER 9

Blockade

The Rufiji situation was now one of great uncertainty and suspense. For Captain Looff the future seemed precarious enough, and common sense indicated that but two courses were possible: either he must make a dash and force his ship away into freedom of the seas, or the *Königsberg* would be by persistent attack robbed of all fighting value. The *Newbridge* effort, incomplete and inconclusive as it certainly was, might be the precedent of other attempts to shut the door; nor could the most optimistic German deny that the sinking of just two more blockships in the narrowest bend of the river would bring finality to *Königsberg's* movements.

Knowing the British naval character and its traditions, Captain Looff might well expect before long to see the mast and funnel-tops of some light-draught man-of-war, getting nearer and more threatening. Later, or sooner, but one day or night with the flood tide helping, a vessel armed with 6-inch or at least 4.7-inch guns would pilot her way towards the secret anchorage. Outside, beyond the delta, he looked out on to the British cruisers, which not merely threatened his exit: they barred the admission of his seaborne supplies. Perhaps one or two small craft, such as *dhows* or tugs, might during the hours of darkness steal in over the bar, yet their cargoes would be casual rather than systematic aid. Already by mid-November *Königsberg's* food-stuff for most of 400 men had again become low: "our rations", bemoaned Ritter, "are getting shorter and shorter."

Her commanding officer, compelled to act on the defensive, now sought (if possible) to gain a mooring-place so far inland as his ship could float, but at the "peak" (so to say) of the wishbone-shaped waterway system: that is, off a village named Kikale, where he could be roughly equidistant from the sea, whether by the Suninga or the Kikunja, so that he might be well placed to repulse attack arriving via the southern no less than the northern branch. Twice in the week ending November 23 he essayed to reach Kikale, but twice he had to take refuge in his present hiding place: the shallow twists and turns defeated a vessel of *Königsberg's* depth and length every time.

It was obvious to the British imagination that the enemy could be dealt with only by short, beamy gun-platforms able to float in (metaphorically speaking) little more than an African dew: or else by the use of aeroplanes for dropping bombs. But no suitable vessel—not even the *Duplex*—at that date belonged to the station, and aircraft were still rare possessions as well as decidedly unreliable. But an old, commercial, seaplane was brought from Simon's Bay, South Africa, in the Union-Castle liner S.S. *Kinfauns Castle* (already commissioned as an armed merchant cruiser) and on November 19 Sub-Lieut. H. D. Cutler thus made the first aerial reconnaissance ever tried over East Africa. It extended, however, for only a couple of hours, as he lost his bearings in the clouds. Three days later he went up again, and on returning to his base Cutler had the misfortune to smash his seaplane beyond repair: yet the adventure was well worthwhile. He had located *Königsberg* from the sky, proved that the enemy could be kept under observation, and indeed from this date caused a new order to be issued by Captain Looff: all hands aboard the German cruiser must henceforth turn out half an hour earlier each morning, to resist aerial attack.

Again, was the *Kinfauns Castle* sent south, and on December 3 arrived back with a seaplane fetched from Durban. At 9 a.m. today Cutler took Commander Fitzmaurice aloft with him in this Curtiss bat-boat, and sighted *Königsberg* a second time. The latter had definitely pushed herself further up river and this morning was endeavouring to work through into the Kikunja when she got aground; shortly after which the Germans sighted the aeroplane, received it with volleys of rifle-fire, but failed to hit.

We mentioned on an earlier page the capture of the German Tug *Adjutant*. Now this able craft had since been armed. with a 3-pdr. and a couple of machine-guns. Flying the White Ensign, she was performing useful service as part of the inshore patrol off the Rufiji, her opposite number being Sub-Lieut. C. J. Charlewood's *Helmuth* that we first saw on September 20 signalling *Pegasus* off Zanzibar. Similarly armed to *Adjutant*, the *Helmuth* was fortunate in having a very keen and plucky commanding officer who used her shallowness to best advantage, whilst further out to sea in deep water several bigger vessels (e.g. H.M.S. *Fox*, *Chatham* and the armed merchant cruiser *Kinfauns*

Castle) were always ready to back up the smaller units.

It was on December 10 that Cutler caused the patrols no little perturbation, but in those early days of aviation and that East African atmosphere, every flight became a daring adventure. About 1.30 p.m. he had flown inland over *Königsberg*, then swung round and passed over the Kikunja branch to its mouth: but, when about two miles seaward, something went wrong with his motor, the seaplane made a sudden dive from 1,000 feet, and crashed on to the water. Flood tide and a strong onshore wind were now his masters so that Cutler's situation became grave, for on either side of the Kikunja mouth were enemy guns and rifles which had no difficulty in hitting a target drifting rapidly towards them.

As quick as possible Sub-Lieut. Charlewood in *Helmuth*, and Midshipman Galleyhawk R.N.R: in a motorboat from *Kinfauns Castle*, went to the rescue. It was exciting enough, even for the most junior officers, to enter the approaches within close range; but neither young man flinched from his dangerous duty: yet what had happened to the seaplane already? Was she below water?

Then at last Galleyhawk, up a creek on the mouth's northern shore, sighted it and took his motorboat in. Meanwhile a couple of field guns that side were making themselves a dangerous nuisance until *Helmuth* at 2,800 yards replied and silenced them with her 3-pdr.; but things developed quickly when mounted German troops were seen galloping to cut off Galleyhawk. He had found the seaplane lying well up the shelving sandy beach and was having no end of a job trying to persuade her to float, at what time some Germans only a hundred yards distant were heavily spraying bullets from rifles and quick-firers.

As if this were not awkward enough, the motorboat now got aground, and still nearer drew the galloping horsemen. *Helmuth* steamed as close as her 8-ft. draught would permit towards the beach, though 1,800 yards off became the limit. Galleyhawk and his men lightened their boat by jumping overboard, and floated her; next, getting a line on to the seaplane, he completed his difficult task and hauled her off. With no seconds to spare, he brought motorboat with 'plane out of danger zone, back to *Kinfauns Castle*.

He had robbed the enemy of their prey from under their very eyes—but it had been indeed a near thing. Galleyhawk himself had been grazed by a bullet, his rifle shattered whilst in his hand; the motorboat was found to have five holes, *Helmuth* the same number, whilst sixty bullets pierced the aeroplane. The sad feature was that

Cutler did not return with this gallant coterie: he had already been taken prisoner.

Eight nights later were seen *Königsberg's* searchlights, and their signification could not be appreciated at the time: actually, under cover of darkness and therefore not likely to be interfered with by airmen, she had begun to shift her berth so that by December 20 she at last reached a more secluded, back-of-the-beyond, up-stream, corner opposite a tree full of weaver-birds with their wonderful textile nests.

A strange Christmas this year for Germans and British alike: for the barely floating *Königsberg* among the swamps, as for the watchers outside compelled to maintain a ceaseless vigilance. But peace or war, in submarines or aboard surface ships, German sailors never were known to celebrate Christmas Eve without the usual routine. A service was held that night, a small mangrove tree had been fetched from the swamps and hung with presents that had mostly come from Dar-es-Salaam colonists. Nor did this enforced tropical inactivity prevent mess-tables from being beautifully decorated. After service Captain Looff made a speech to his men and handed each a gift. Toasts were drunk in pine-apple juice, followed by beer: it was this last, together with cigarettes, which to German sailors after long denial of such luxuries gave no little pleasure.

On New Year's Eve beer and cigarettes were again handed out, whilst in the morning a wireless message from H.M.S. *Fox* arrived, (*Chatham* was no longer on the station, she had sailed for Mombasa, there to coal and undergo repairs, after which she left Mombasa on January 2 for Aden): "A Happy New Year. Expect to have the pleasure of seeing you soon. British Cruiser."

Those were the days when naval warfare had not been completely robbed of traditional sea-courtesy, so the reply was flashed: "Many thanks. Same to you. If you want to see us, we are always at home. *Königsberg.*"

But after comedy, so frequently hurries tragedy.

By January 10 the health of Captain Looff's men had begun to break down heavily, thanks to the mosquitoes. There were no fewer than fifty cases of malaria on board today. A week later two men died of typhoid, and next day their bodies were taken down by boat to be buried at Salale. The same sad ceremony had to be performed on the following month; for the German cruiser was having no river picnic. Thus, with sickness in the ship; other cases removed ashore to a Field Hospital within the colony; the probability of further aerial attacks, and some possible plan maturing in the British minds; *Königsberg's* captain had more than his share of anxieties.

But incidents became more numerous.

Mafia Island, facing the Rufiji delta, had been a useful outpost for flashing signals to Captain Looff from the sea, and it was being held by 12 German Europeans plus 40 *askaris*; yet now from Zanzibar the *Kinfauns Castle* brought British troops who landed on the island under her covering fire and that of H.M.S. *Fox*, so that from January 12 Mafia passed under the Union Jack and a British Military Resident became the local authority. Next day from New Zealand arrived H.M.S. *Pyramus*, a light cruiser of only 2,135 tons, but her eight 4-inch guns strengthened the watch against any chance of *Königsberg's* emergence.

At present the latter gave no signs of wishing to move. None the less the domestic fight on behalf of morale, against monotony and physical deterioration, went on bravely. January 27 happened to be the *Kaiser's* birthday, and it began with service in the morning, followed in the afternoon by athletic sports. For the winners in jumping, somersaults, stone-throwing, and other competitions, there were no silver cups; but very simple awards that seemed, up the Rufiji, far more valuable than pure gold. Biscuits had become very scarce, so the champions deemed themselves lucky to receive such rarities; soap, likewise, was worth contending for; cigars, tobacco, and bottles of beer all made life temporary bliss. Still happier were German minds at the set-back which overcame the British patrol on February 6.

The adventurous tug *Adjutant* this early morn was standing in to reconnoitre the Simba Urange mouth in order to locate the enemy guns at the peninsula, when she was hotly received. A shell severed her steam pipe at 6.50 a.m., she was put out of action, on fire aft, and lying aground at the north shore helpless. She could only hoist the white flag and surrender. H.M.S. *Hyacinth* having witnessed the affair, steamed in towards the mouth and from 10,800 yards shelled the concealed batteries on either side, until the ebb compelled her to withdraw or get aground.

Later on, the *Pyramus*, needing less water, approached the peninsula. Flying a flag of truce, she got as near as the shoals allowed, then lowered a steamboat which was met by a German boat off the entrance. A list of *Adjutant's* casualties was asked for and given: they consisted of one able seaman killed and another severely wounded. All the rest, comprising Sub-Lieut. W. Price R.N.R. with nineteen crew, had been taken prisoners. (They were sent to Morogoro, the inland base due west of Dar-es-Salaam. The body of Seaman Piddock was buried by the Germans at Simba Urange.) To the British request for an exchange of captives, a firm refusal was made, and the parley ended.

After the captors had hauled down *Adjutant's* white flag, *Pyramus* from a distance of 4,000 yards fired nine shells into this tug, that now for the second time in life had become German-owned. A conflagration broke forth, and the prize was still burning next dawn. Three days later, whilst yet aground, *Pyramus* assisted by *Pioneer* (which had just arrived from Australia) again shelled the unfortunate vessel, as did H.M.S. *Weymouth* likewise. (The *Pioneer* belonged to the Australian Fleet. She was a sister ship of *Pegasus*, and each of these ships had the same armament and practically the same tonnage as *Pyramus*.)

Now the loss of *Adjutant* was to us a three-fold disadvantage. Not merely did it mean the forfeit of an inshore unit at a time when comparatively few light-draught ships were available; but it provided the Germans with a very useful river-plus-sea vessel, whilst strengthening the Simba Urange defences at the mouth. For she was presently refloated, taken up stream to be repaired, given a German gun, but her 3-pdr. and two Maxims were mounted on shore at that river's entrance. Thus, on April 11 she came into the German Navy commissioned as an auxiliary cruiser.

On the other hand, Britain's marine resources in South Africa could still be tapped, and the whaling industry had developed a small fleet of very seaworthy, stalwart steamers, yet possessing moderate draught. These whalers were in design an improvement on the familiar North Sea trawlers, and by February 11 there arrived from the Cape: *Pickle*, *Echo*, followed that same month by the *Fly*; whilst, *Childers* and *Salamander* appeared later. These five having been armed, and placed under officers of the Royal Naval Reserve, were to carry out excellent service not merely off the Rufiji but eventually up and down the whole coast of German East Africa.

But the immediate and pressing need was for aircraft with their aviators: thus, when *Kinfauns Castle* fetched from Bombay two seaplanes, Flight-Lieut. J. T. Cull R.N., Flight-Lieut. H. E. Watkins R.N., plus a party of eighteen men—the whole outfit having been sent from England—there awaited them on February 20 off the Rufiji a warm welcome. But within a week one seaplane badly crashed, and the other proved itself far from satisfactory. Result? Much cabling to England, and then an answer that three more would arrive off the delta in the armed merchant cruiser *Laconia* by April 23.

Until the end of February this Rufiji campaign had developed into passive, rather than active, strategy ever since the sinking of *Newbridge*. But from March 1 a British Blockade of German East Africa began, which must inevitably become something far more ambitious than the partially successful blocking by an ex-collier. Various *dhows* attempting to run the blockade were chased and captured, patrols were strengthened, and Admiral King-Hall came back to take charge of the new operations, flying his flag sometimes in *Weymouth* but on other days in *Hyacinth*. A most interesting activity, an old-time adventure on modern lines, was about to be attempted.

That which *Königsberg* and the German Army in East Africa most needed at this time could be summed up in the one word *supplies*; and Berlin planned a daring scheme for these to be sent out. For sheer audacity and cleverness this undertaking ranks with some of the riskiest gambles during the whole war, yet also it deserves every respect. Now, consider what chance of success seemed likely to evolve, and ask yourself whether you would have sanctioned such a voyage (had you been in authority), or have entertained real expectation for the enterprise's fulfilment.

A small cargo steamer was to leave Germany, pass up the North Sea, round Scotland and thence down the Atlantic, doubling the Cape of Good Hope, and so up the Indian Ocean where she should make contact with *Königsberg* off the coast. This idea, on the face of it, looked as if it were the creation of the craziest optimist; for such a ship would first have to run the gauntlet of our 10th Cruiser Squadron on the alert between Scotland and Iceland, after which she must penetrate one cruiser-patrol-area after another all the way down south till gaining the East African climax.

The ship selected was the ex-British S.S. *Rubens*, 3,600 tons, which had been arrested in Hamburg, at outbreak of war. Her name having been changed to *Kronborg*, the Germans provided her with faked papers, pretended she was a Dane, selected very carefully both officers and men who looked Danish and could speak Danish: in fact, these were forbidden to utter any other language. The chosen Master was Lieut. Christiansen who gave orders in the Danish tongue, although his naval crew had been wont always to serve in German men-of-war. He was to make believe that *Kronborg* chanced to be just a very ordinary trader.

Stowage of her cargo needed special attention, for most likely she would be stopped and an expert British Boarding Officer would come aboard to look below hatches. So, on the top were wood and 1,600 tons of coal, but deep down below were the real stores such as 1,500 rifles and ammunition for the land troops; machine-guns; shells (in water-tight cases) for *Königsberg's* 4.1-inch guns; tons of dynamite; provisions, medicine, and other items.

The primary motive was to succour *Königsberg*: providing her with everything from fuel to food, so that the cruiser might break out of the river and find her way back to Germany. The military stores for the colony were of secondary consideration. By sending the *Kronborg* ahead to wait at certain rendezvous; by occasionally stopping Allies' steamers just as the *City of Winchester* had been halted; *Königsberg* might never want for coal, and with any luck should gain the Iceland district through which she might have to fight her way.

Luck not infrequently accompanies pluck, and *Kronborg* after leaving the Skaw on February 19, took advantage of the long dark nights, chose the shorter but more dangerous route south of the Shetlands, gave traffic a wide berth, passed well south of the Cape of Good Hope, left Madagascar to starboard, and steamed up still further north. Of course, Captain Looff had been kept informed of her coming, and of the probable arrival date. It was this expectancy which now enthused fresh hope into those aboard *Königsberg* who were despondent, but likewise was it required that his ship might be ready as well to receive *Kronborg* as to go forth and meet her.

Thus, on March 19 he managed to force his ship through the connecting waterway, into the landward end of the Kikunja River and anchored off Kikale village, with the cruiser's head lying roughly in a northerly direction, prepared for steaming out to sea by that branch, rather than by the Suninga along which she had arrived. Early in April *Kronborg's* wireless was heard by *Königsberg*, and the secret which Captain Looff had kept to himself these weeks now spread vaguely through his ship in that mysterious manner which always occurs aboard a man-of-war when some big event is about to happen.

We now come to April 8, and throughout *Königsberg* an unusual activity with disciplined excitement prevailed. The ship's company was being frequently drilled for "Clear for Action", and rumour ran round that they were presently leaving the delta on another raiding expedition. Signalman Ritter wrote in his diary today:

> All are delighted that this odious life is coming to an end at last. Also rumoured that there is a ship outside from Germany,

which is to provide for all our needs.

The yarn was not far wrong, for today we now know that on April 8 *Kronborg* came to anchor off the previously mentioned Aldabra Island. Of course, Mr Mein, the Manager, went alongside by boat, but Christiansen pretended that the ship had come from the Cape Ports bound for Suez with timber; that she had put into Aldabra to effect repairs to machinery, and this would require fourteen days.

★★★★★★★★★★

Before leaving Germany, she had stowed on the upper deck a cargo of wood to make her resemble one of the familiar Baltic timberships. Had she been stopped in Scottish waters, she would have easily passed for what she feigned.

★★★★★★★★★★

Somehow Mr Mein was not quite convinced. Although he himself spoke neither Danish nor German, certainly he thought the ship might well be from Denmark; he noticed even the lifebuoys had "*KO-BENHAVN*" painted on them, and he felt sure that both officers and the crew (who numbered 32) were speaking Danish. Nevertheless, Mr Mein observed that steam was being maintained all the time, which seemed curious if she really intended remaining a fortnight. On the 9th he went off to her again, and asked Christiansen for the ship's Bill of Health, but the Master said he had none, adding that there was no sickness aboard. On the 10th both Christiansen and the chief engineer came ashore, and when requested to produce the *Kronborg's* papers, the former replied that there was no hurry: the steamer would be staying here some time.

That turned out to be another lie, for though she was still at anchor in the lagoon at 8 p.m., she had departed before 6 a.m. on the following day. But why?

We can now fill in the gaps, and the story becomes even still more enthralling. Christiansen weighed anchor on the night of April 10-11 because Captain Looff had: wirelessed to rendezvous him on the 14th in Lat. 6 S, Long. 45 E; that is to say right out at sea some 400 miles northeast from the Rufiji delta, and less than 300 miles north of Aldabra. Yet this meeting never occurred.

For on April 5 news had come from the Admiralty to Admiral King-Hall that *Königsberg* intended breaking out in order to meet a supply ship expected off the coast by April 9, wherefore on the 7th we find the admiral putting to sea in *Hyacinth* hoping to intercept *Kronborg*. The spring tides would have been ready both for *Königsberg's* departure, and for *Kronborg's* arrival in the river, so *Weymouth* had been left off the mouth as the only ship able to catch up Captain Looff's ship if escaping.

On the 9th *Hyacinth* intercepted that wireless from *Königsberg* to the supply ship ordering the latter to Lat. 6 S, Long. 45 E. This rendezvous and the vicinity having been searched without result, *Hyacinth* came back to anchor; being as we have just seen, too early, though on the 11th *Hyacinth* started off again. Now on the 13th all was in readiness aboard *Königsberg*, the drills had ended, *Adjutant* had been repaired and re-armed, (able, if necessary, to put up a good fight against the whalers), and Captain Looff was about to take advantage of the good tides; but, on looking out seawards, he perceived that it would be impossible to take his ship through the steel barrier. His foes had evidently learnt of the intention, and were not going to allow his exit. This is how Signalman Ritter at the time wrote in his diary:—

> *13th Apr.* Today was the day on which we were to have run out. But the English were waiting outside for us, and put a thick line through all our calculations. They lay outside the mouth with three cruisers and two auxiliaries.

★★★★★★★★★★

The diarist is not quite accurate. I find that on April 13 the following ships were guarding the delta approaches: H.M.S. *Weymouth* (cruiser); *Pioneer* (cruiser); *Kinfauns Castle* (armed merchant cruiser); the ex-cable S.S. *Duplex* (armed auxiliary); together with the four armed whalers *Pickle*, *Fly*, *Childers*, *Echo*. Of these, the *Weymouth* with her 25 knots and eight 6-inch guns alone could have been a match for *Königsberg*, but *Pioneer* had a speed of only 20 knots though her eight 4-inch guns would have been effective. The smaller vessels might have done considerable damage to *Königsberg* as the latter steamed cautiously out of the Kikunja mouth, but would probably have then been themselves wiped out: in any case they could not have chased the enemy.

★★★★★★★★★★

This overwhelming strength was too much for us. Everything points to the fact that the English knew our Morse Code, and have caught our exchange of telegrams with the ship. To make sure of this, we sent a wire off a few days later that a steamer would arrive off Lindi at such and such a time, entry free. At exactly the indicated time, an English cruiser lay off Lindi.

Annoying it certainly was for Captain Looff that his long-planned excursion must on the last day be negatived, so he wirelessed *Kronborg* that the blockade was too strict, and that the latter must make for Mansa Bay, which is a good sheltered anchorage in the Tanga vicinity to the north of Zanzibar on the mainland. Thither Admiral King-Hall brought *Hyacinth* with the dawn on April 14, and there in Mansa Bay was the supply ship. The British cruiser opened fire, but Christiansen took his ship further in, and let go both anchors after running her ashore on the sand. Opening her sea-cocks, he and his people escaped in the boats, and *Hyacinth* deluged the burning ship with shells, after which the admiral went back to the Rufiji Blockade.

Unfortunately for us, that did not end matters. When news of *Kronborg's* sinking in shallow water came to Captain Looff, he at once despatched overland two petty officers as divers whom he still had on board, but belonged to that party from the *Planet* which *Zieten* eight months previously was bringing back to Germany. Mansa Bay was this April still in German hands, so nothing prevented divers going down and working in the *Kronborg's* holds. The two petty officers, together with Christiansen's men set to work, salved Mauser rifles, machine-guns, 4.1-inch shells: in fact, almost the whole of her cargo, although the small-arms ammunition suffered badly from the salt water. Christiansen, though wounded, recovered and at a later date came south to go aboard *Königsberg*, where he thrilled everybody with the story of his exciting long voyage.

Well, then, the Rufiji position by the end of April was that Captain Looff's ship still remained off Kikale, lying with bows pointing to the north, just beyond the northwest extremity of Kokotoni Island; for on April 25, two days after *Laconia's* arrival from Durban with the three seaplanes, Flight-Lieut. Cull soared aloft in one of them flew over *Königsberg*, swept low enough to photograph her, noted that she was looking very smart with awnings spread and new paint on her sides. She greeted him with shrapnel, and such good aim, that half a dozen holes were afterwards found in the aircraft; in fact, the engine gradually slowed down and stopped altogether, though luckily not before Cull had brought his machine down to water a little distance from the blockading squadron. Two days later another aerial reconnaissance was made successfully, but the undeniable truth had to be faced: in those early days of aviation, of unreliable engines, and unsatisfactory seaplane construction, aggravated by the hot dry climate, it was too much to hope that *Königsberg* could be destroyed from the sky.

So, after all, the attempt must be made by specially shallow gun-boats able to go right up the Kikunja within easy range. And the only suitable units which the British Navy at this date possessed, were those ex-Brazilian monitors waiting at Malta. It is worth noting that had Captain Looff actually tried to come out from his anchorage, he might have got into trouble immediately. Even if he was unaware of the hydrographic fact, a distinct bar existed almost all the way across the Kikunja only one mile north of Kokotoni Island, this shoal being discovered by British naval officers two months later.

But that would not concern *Severn* and *Mersey*. If they had never seen service among the Flemish Banks, or had not fired a gun since leaving Barrow, their existence would still be greatly justified. Time, in its strange sequence, had created the perfect opportunity for monitors; an exceptional task which could be performed by them but by no other existing type. Difficulties, seen and unseen, lay ahead and the long trail of 5,000 broiling miles would be a preliminary testing to those dangerous adventures that still awaited.

CHAPTER 10

In the Red Sea

Lazaretto Creek on the morning of April 28 presented exceptional activity even for those busy days when British and French warships seemed always to be entering or leaving Malta, going into dry dock, or hauling out.

Aboard *Severn* and *Mersey* hands were securing gear for sea, making the last preparations ere the tugs took charge. Once again, the monitors must proceed crew-less, battened down tight against the heavy seas which would have to be endured, but now that *Humber* was being left behind at least more space would be available in *Trent*. And 280 naval passengers through the tropics would find existence not quite so irksome as 420 must have experienced.

Several minor modifications had been made at Malta. In order to obtain greater ease when towing, both *Severn* and *Mersey* had disconnected from their shafts the propellers, so that the latter could now freely revolve and cease to drag. Bullet-proof shields had been fitted round the tugs' bridges for a purpose that will presently be manifest; but *Blackcock* and *Revenger*, having only, recently got back from Lemnos, were still in dockyard care for a day or two longer. Their place temporarily could be taken by the tug *Southampton*.

To make fast cables and hawsers, get clear of harbour, and settle down on their course needed the whole forenoon, but by 1 p.m. the squadron was out on the blue Mediterranean with perfect conditions of sunny weather and a smooth sea. Ahead went *Sarah Jolliffe* towing *Mersey*; astern of her followed *Southampton* and *T.A. Jolliffe* each with a hawser to *Severn's* bows; whilst, one mile astern, the collier *Kendal Castle* carrying over 6,000 tons of fuel brought up the rear, and *Trent* took up a position abeam of the line.

Looking back on that period, it is not without interest to observe that the date of departure was well chosen. Three days previously had occurred not merely the historic landing on Gallipoli peninsula, but the setting out from Germany of Hersing in U-21 as the first enemy submarine bound for the Mediterranean. If Captain Fullerton's mixed cavalcade had come out of Malta on May 10 instead of April 28, then a quite unusual situation must have followed. It would have been difficult for Hersing to resist attacking seven easy targets steaming through the water at 5½ knots; yet U-21 happened to be so short of oil-fuel that she ultimately reached Cattaro with only half a ton to spare. Whilst it is hard to believe that so able and enterprising an officer as he would have let the rich chance go by, a distinct twist must then have changed the war's progress.

Quite possibly he might have sunk both monitors, though it is a little doubtful whether his torpedoes would not have passed clear of those shallow flat bottoms: not less probably *Trent*'s guns might have engaged U-21 and robbed the spoiler of his designs. For, be it remembered, Hersing's one expectation of ever reaching the Adriatic depended on two items: proceeding along the surface at slow speed, and avoiding much diving. With his loss, we should not have had the sinking of H.M.S. *Triumph* and *Majestic* at the Dardanelles, and our bombardments need not have been withheld from the army's support. Contrariwise, the loss of *Severn* and *Mersey* would have given *Königsberg* a new lease of life. (For the full story of U-21 and how she ran short of fuel see my *Dardanelles Dilemma*.)

But the end of April was so full of uncertainties, that the British Navy could not say definitely whether German submarines had yet entered through Gibraltar Straits; wherefore Captain Fullerton ordered a specially vigilant look-out to be maintained and his ships were to be in complete darkness at night. Navigation lights were to be switched on never, except just in time to avoid collision. This soon led to an amusing incident when at 2 a.m. a steamer westward bound signalled: "Your bow lights want trimming." The navy smiled, and made no reply.

During this lengthy voyage two matters were of daily concern: preserving the utmost secrecy, and keeping every man in good health. The crew might have their own ideas and suspicions, yet not one of them yet knew their destination, and during the next five weeks any shore leave would be denied them. Whilst traffic was being given as wide a berth as possible, nothing could prevent Dutch liners altering course to have a good look-see. At the first port doubtless news of these odd-shaped monitors would be discussed by pilots, seamen, stevedores, and German agents would be there listening.

Cooped up aboard *Trent*, men were kept fit with physical drill, and in the afternoon the ship would be stopped for them to bathe over the side. Awnings were spread, and in the cool of even they would be yarning on the foc'sle or listening to a gramophone, whilst officers played games on the saloon deck. Wireless from the Eiffel Tower each day brought news of the war's progress, and this in turn was signalled across to the lonely crews aboard the tugs.

Each ship was of course a little world of its own, possessing its separate domestic crises and human problems, separated from the rest of civilisation; and under these circumstances every minor incident developed into major import.

May Day showed a steamer of somewhat striking appearance approaching on the starboard bow, and officers began disputing as to which line she belonged: some even swore she was German. "What is your name?" the *Trent* signalled, and back came the spelled reply: R-O-T-E-N-F-E-L-S. Then, "Where are you bound?" was answered by "Hull". The German prize (S.S. *Rotenfels*) was now being taken to England for a new utility.

Next day *Kendal Castle* was sent on ahead to make arrangements for coaling the squadron at Port Said, with strict instructions that no one was to be allowed ashore, and no stranger permitted aboard; neither conversation as to whither the ship was bound, nor any uncensored letters to be sent off. It was on the afternoon of May 3 that the tugs *Blackcock* and *Revenger* joined up at sea, enabling *Southampton* to make her way back into Malta, and, as a final severance of old conditions, with her went Captain Fullerton's dog. The weather would soon pass from warmth to intense heat, and already the ship's doctor was making his inoculations as protective measures.

At Port Said the French men-of-war cheered the arrival of monitors and wondered at their purport, but within seven hours—just time to fill up with coal, water, provisions—tugs were hauling *Severn* and *Mersey* ahead bound through the canal for Suez. We have seen that bullet-proof screens had already been fitted round the tugs' bridges, and whilst waiting before entering the Canal, sand-bags were erected round the port side of *Trent's* bridge as protection for wheel-house, compass, man-at-the-wheel, and pilot. To each monitor was also sent an armed party so long as the ships should be passing through the Canal.

For though the Turkish attack on Egypt, which had begun on

February 3, was so short-lived that eight days later the Canal was reopened for night traffic; yet a certain amount of sniping from its eastern bank might still be expected. Some delay had been caused at Port Said, owing to the scarcity of searchlights, but eventually two had been commandeered for the tugs from merchant ships. At midnight of May 5-6, when half way between Ismailia and Suez, the *Sarah Jolliffe* (towing *Mersey*) was able to give proof that the iron plating had not been a superfluous notion, for the Turkish riflemen made her a target, six shots spattered themselves around the port side-light but spent themselves against the protective shield.

Remains of the February fighting were still visible in an occasional Turkish pontoon, the graves, old boots, empty cartridge-cases, trenches loopholed for rifle-fire: Indian and English troops in numbers, an armoured train and plenty of lookouts, were evidence enough that should the Turks make another effort to get across the Canal, a hot reception was awaiting. "Where are you going?", called out some of the soldiers to the squadron; but the only answer was made in eight words: "Will let you know when we come back."

Men and ships may change, but Nature through the ages retains her principles and laws unaltered. For thousands of years, the Red Sea has been ruffled by the fresh NNW winds that wafted the square-sailed Dynastic ships from Egypt to the Land of Punt for ivories and incense, and still enable Arab *dhows* to trade along the coast. So, too, from May 6 after leaving Suez astern and during the next five days this British squadron of steel vessels was favoured with the same breezes. A nasty, tumbling, sea rose up astern, but it was far better so than had it been ahead.

And now the heat from Africa's deserts began to impress itself, in spite of the fact that everyone had shifted into "whites". Canvas baths were being fashioned both for officers aft and the men for'ard, yet the following wind brought with it no cooling comfort. A sense of monotony crept over monitors' crews, which was not wholly relieved by being able to enjoy one bottle of beer twice a week, on Wednesdays and Saturdays. Ships were steaming at their full speed, yet mosquitoes flew aboard and annoyed everyone. Then, all of a sudden, at five o'clock on Sunday morning (May 9) *Trent's* wireless intercepted one German war vessel summoning another.

This was disconcerting, if not alarming, at such a stage. If an enemy cruiser were waiting about in the Red Sea, she could certainly wipe out most easily each of these eight ships from a chosen range. Had

Königsberg eluded the Rufiji patrols, and escaped northwards? Was she being directed, thanks to secret intelligence, so as to meet the slender British squadron at its weakest, and to leeward of its nearest base, whilst Aden was still hundreds of miles distant?

The responsibility on Captain Fullerton's shoulders at that moment could scarcely be envied, but only one alternative offered: his first duty was to preserve the ships committed to him, which meant running back against the wind towards Suez. He accordingly ordered collier, tugs with monitors, to turn round; meanwhile all boats were to be provisioned, every man to be called and kept awake.

Tugs were to be ready for slipping the monitors, and, should a German cruiser be sighted, *Trent* intended making a signal for the tugs to let monitors go but scatter themselves, keeping well inshore on the Egyptian side and make for Suez. At Port Said they had seen H.M.S. *Proserpine* (sister cruiser to *Pegasus* and *Pyramus*) flying the flag of Admiral R. H. Peirse; whilst in the Bitter Lakes they had passed H.M.S. *Dufferin* of the Royal Indian Marine lying at anchor.

The suspense continued for several hours, but at length after trying to get in touch with these two ships, Captain Fullerton decided to swing back on his original course at 8 a.m. and continue down the Red Sea, though a keen lookout was being made unceasingly. Then, somewhat late in transmission, came the news that off Ireland the *Lusitania* had been torpedoed. But Sunday midnight completed the day's exciting moments dramatically, when a large steamer was descried astern quickly overhauling the tugs.

She had almost got up to the latter when out went all her lights.

Was this, then, the raider? At once *Trent* made towards her at full speed and began Morseing across the dark waters.

"What ship is that?"

"*Trioba*", the other winked back on her lamp.

"Where are you bound?"

"Bombay", came the reply.

"Your movements were very suspicious. Why put your lights out? I might have fired on you."

"Very sorry", apologised the stranger. "My dynamo failed for a moment."

And now she was recognised for a British transport, whereupon *Trent* bade her "Goodnight. *Bon voyage*".

Another hot day dawned and the NNW wind churned the seascape into white-crested tops. Up mounted the thermometer, and

Captain Fullerton was thinking of the firemen sweltering below at the tugs' furnaces.

"When sea is a bit smooth, will send you some ice and fresh meat?" he signalled across to Captain A. P. Weir of *Blackcock*, in charge of the tugs. "At Aden I will try and get two coloured firemen. How are you all getting on, and are you feeling the heat?"

But Captain Weir, the ever-cheerful sailorman and optimistic mariner; a born tugmaster who always could be relied upon, whatever the circumstances; contented himself with: "Ship's company are all well, thank you. Beginning to feel the heat a little. Many thanks for ice and meat, which will be appreciated."

It was not till after another twenty-four hours that conditions allowed engines to be stopped awhile, and a boat could be sent off from *Trent* with the ice and beef. By now the flying fish were skipping across the squadron's bows, and one of *Mersey's* officers caught a 6-ft. shark which Captain Fullerton shot with his revolver, to the immense interest of the youngest seamen.

Still higher rose the thermometer, which soon registered 90° in the shade; lime-juice began to be served out at noon instead of rum, salt water bathing on board became one of life's necessities, but everybody was feeling the heat and some men were feeling it very badly. For the wind had now settled down to light northerly airs, so that though the temperature at night rarely fell below 87°, it even mounted to 100°. The tug-men were indeed enduring a pretty bad time, whilst in *Sarah Jolliffe* one engineer and one fireman were rendered unconscious after the engine-room heat went up to 145°. Aboard the *T. A. Jolliffe* two more firemen were similarly prostrated, and the *Blackcock's* mate became a sufferer.

Now all this personnel in the tugs were hard-case seafarers accustomed to severe conditions, but it must be recollected that such vessels had been built for the cold climate of northern Europe. Against the trials of hot weather—and the notorious Red Sea in particular—tugs possessed no sort of fittings or cooling fans: nothing save the awnings and windsails which Malta Dockyard had provided. Many of these men, too old for acceptance as recruits in the Services ordinarily, were aged somewhere between 45 and 63. Not for them the condition of eight hours on, and sixteen off duty: it was watch-and-watch day after day, week after week, with no sort of contrast and never a chance to get ashore out of their cramped quarters. Nevertheless, they managed to keep that anxious towing so steady that the average daily run down the Red Sea was 157 miles.

Then it became known that the squadron was bound into Aden. The *Kendal Castle* was sent on two days ahead, but only so as to be ready for the others' arrival. The "buzz" persisted that Aden was really the expedition's final destination, and the *Trent's* own crew began volunteering for land service. Yes: they were now being taught rifle drill, but they would suffer some disappointment soon. Even when *Trent*, tugs, and monitors on Friday, May 14, came past the fort of Bab el Mendeb (which H.M.S. *Duke of Edinburgh* on November 9 had laid in ruins) and next day were anchored in Aden harbour, no news could be learnt by the most inquisitive: in fact the squadron's arrival quite surprised the harbour authority in the Examination Vessel.

It was whilst at anchor off the barren rocks of Aden that two deaths from heat stroke indicated how severely human nature had been tried these last ten days. First succumbed Engineer-Lieut. H. H. F. L. C. Beaton R.N.R., 2nd Engineer of the *Trent*, who passed away about 9 a.m., though he had been attending to his duties during the night, and to the coaling that very morn. Several men from the tugs were brought to be under the care of *Trent's* doctor for a day or two; but that same night died Edward Phair, one of *Severn's* stewards. The *Mersey's* butcher collapsed, and was revived only with difficulty, whilst other men normally vigorous could scarce refrain from fainting: altogether the naval surgeons were as busy as anyone. When, however, the squadron started off again on the 17th, tugs had been supplied with Arab firemen, ice, and ice-chests.

So now they were steaming through that area which *Königsberg* had visited during the first days of August, and a Japanese merchant steamer today must have been reminding herself of the fact, for she anxiously inquired of *Trent* if there was an enemy about. Before gaining Cape Guardafui, Captain Fullerton sent *Kendal Castle* into a remote corner of Italian Somaliland named Cloch, where she anchored off a sandy beach just long enough for *Blackcock* and *Sarah Jolliffe* to coal before relieving their sisters who followed suit. A number of native canoes came off with their chief to the collier, demanding as harbour dues a bag of biscuits.

With all its monotony and the merciless heat—for now it was 100° in the shade, and the "worst ever"—always some surprise seemed to come, a fresh happening or new sight. A great nuisance next was the visitation of locusts, which possessed the ships and covered the sea. Then on the horizon steaming up the Gulf of Aden this May 19 was sighted a fast cruiser. She turned out to be no German, but *Königsberg's* particular enemy, *Chatham*. Captain Drury-Lowe's ship had come back to East Africa on April 20 after the *Kronborg* affair, and here once more she was bound up the Red Sea at 18 knots. "Wish you the best of luck and success", she signalled Captain Fullerton. "Left Zanzibar 9 p.m., 16th. Strong SSW winds to Cape Guardafui and strong northerly currents all the way." Within twenty-five minutes of being first sighted, she had passed below the line where sea meets sky.

CHAPTER 11

Tropical Arrival

The first leg of the monitors' long voyage having ended at Port Said; the second stage finished abreast of Cape Guardafui which was rounded at a distance of three miles on May 20; but the third and final lap had its own problems that were to test striving men to their limit.

No longer that fiery Red Sea heat and northerly fair breezes, but cooler weather; the strong SSW winds, and current setting to the northward, exactly as Captain Drury-Lowe had signalled. Instead of greeny-blue water hitherto experienced, the Indian Ocean with its dark brown colour seemed to present a different hemisphere. But progress against the united strength of current and wind down the African coast was grievously hindered, so that instead of averaging 157 the daily run dropped to 77 miles. At first a course was shaped to pass close under the land in hope of avoiding the big seas, but after three days' trial this had to be abandoned; the current inshore being too strong, and at times reaching 5 knots.

It became clear to Captain Fullerton that, under these arresting influences, the tugs would all have finished their coal ere reaching the squadron's destination, so he must devise some new scheme or the war might be finished and done with too quickly for any aid from monitors. Therefore, on the evening of May 22 *Trent* took over the towing of *Mersey* from the two tugs, and the evolution (none too easy on the rough seas) was excellently performed. Those readers, to whom seamanship appeals, may care to visualise the exceptional picture of a liner towing a man-of-war. From either quarter *Trent* veered out 100 fathoms of 5½-inch wire hawser, to which were attached 110 fathoms of 14-inch hemp rope, and then came another 100 fathoms of 5½-inch wire, which were made fast to *Mersey's* anchor cable; two shackles (=25 fathoms =150 feet) of the latter having been slacked out.

Ocean towage, accompanied by high crests and deep wave troughs, is one of the most accomplished marine arts. Not only has the length of rope to be right, but much depends on weight in the right place; for the danger might be that whilst *Trent* was sliding down into one valley, and *Mersey* was coming up towards the intervening crest, a sudden strain would either snap the towing gear, tear out the fittings (such as bollards), or even pull monitor bodily through the crest with ensuing damage to her decks. The ideal conditions are where both ships rise and fall simultaneously, but that is not always possible.

Plunging into the steep, ugly, seas off the East African coast was bound to create sudden tightening of ropes, and this was guarded against not only with the amount of spring afforded by the 14-inch hemp, but also by the monitor's own cable. For the latter, from its sheer weight, made a continual sag in the water, thus exerting an elastic force as another spring. There were some who feared that *Trent* would seriously damage herself in towing 1,260 displacement-tons of steel monitor, but they were wrong. First-class seamanship; 670 yards of warp, wire, and cable; combined to bring about complete success. In fact, the rate of progress was so much improved that Captain Fullerton decided also to employ the *Kendal Castle* for partial assistance in towing *Severn*.

This turned out a little more complicated. On *Severn's* starboard rope was the tug *Blackcock*, she also being connected ahead to the *Sarah Jolliffe*; but the monitor's port rope led to *Kendal Castle's* stern, from whose bows another rope led to the *Revenger's* stern. Thus, three tugs and one collier were hauling *Severn*, whilst the *T. A. Jolliffe* steamed independently on the beam ready for emergencies. The nett result shewed itself when the day's run from noon of May 24 to noon of May 25 became 142 miles.

Gradually the weather calmed, the barren uninteresting coast was receding, and soon they would be abreast of German territory. Assembling his petty officers on Sunday evening, Captain Fullerton now revealed to them the purport of this voyage. He told them that they were bound first for Chaki Chaki Bay, Isle of Pemba, (lying NNE of Zanzibar), where the monitors would fit out, thence make for the Rufiji delta and go in to attack *Königsberg*, but he emphasised that they would first have to deal with the enemy's machine-guns, rifles, and 3-pdrs. on both sides of the river entrance. Having steamed inland, it would be the monitors' duty from a range of 7,000 or 8,000 yards to fire as rapidly as possible with their 6-inch guns, and destroy the German cruiser so as to release British warships needed elsewhere. Up till now, owing to their deep draught, the watching vessels had not been able to get within range of *Königsberg*.

So at last the secret was out, the men knew what to expect, and *Severn's* gunnery lieut. gave them a lecture on the method of firing against enemy-lined river banks. A clear, definite, objective could be looked forward to, everybody was anxious only for the voyage's ending and the beginning of the river trip. Perhaps in little more than a week from now the long trail from Malta and the Medway would be over?

But the unexpected occurred when at 3 a.m. of Tuesday a thick fog settled down over the Indian Ocean, nor did it clear till noon. It was then that Captain Fullerton, having counted his chickens, realised that two were missing: the independent *T.A. Jolliffe*, and the *Revenger* which should have been ahead of the collier. What could have happened to them?

The *Kendal Castle* signalled that the *T.A. Jolliffe* when last seen was three miles away on the port bow; as to *Revenger*, she had been unfortunate, and at 6 a.m. in the fog had got athwart the tow, slipped her hawser, leaving the collier to haul in till they got to the hemp when they were compelled to cut and let the remainder fall to the bottom. For some reason *Revenger* had then steamed off in search of *Trent*.

Now the possibility of such contretemps having been foreseen, *T. A. Jolliffe* had received orders that in case she lost sight of the squadron she might go on to Mombasa or Pemba Island. But *Revenger*? A signalman was sent up *Trent's* masthead to scan the ocean, and, though the thickness was gone, he could see nothing of her. It had been arranged, too, that in case of distress, tugs were to call up *Trent* by firing Very's lights. The afternoon passed, and at sunset *Trent* began using her searchlight against the sky in hope that the laggard might thus locate her mothership's vicinity. Night set in, the collier and two tugs in charge of *Severn* were instructed to continue a steady course and speed, but *Trent* with her long tow was still maintaining a watch for something she badly longed to see. Then, suddenly, just before 8 p.m. two green lights were noticed on the port side though a long way off.

One-and-a-quarter hours later, from the same direction were observed three red lights, which signified "In need of assistance", so *Trent* gradually altered course towards the spot: nor was this nocturnal modification rendered easier with the dead weight of a monitor at the end of lengthy cable and hawsers. Guns and rockets were fired in response to the Very's lights, and about 10 o'clock the loom of a vessel showed up: it was *Revenger*, who reported two men injured, one of them seriously. It turned out that the second mate and cook received their hurts that morning whilst in the act of slipping the tow rope, after which they had to suffer pain whilst the tug went searching for *Trent*, who now took them aboard and tended their wounds.

So almost every day had its excitements, and the following noon, with more than 700 miles still to steam, they were just getting up to the monitor ahead, when *Kendal Castle* signalled the unpleasant news that *Severn* had developed a heavy list to port. One darned thing after another! During the last twenty-four hours an abnormal African current had set the squadron 25 miles to the eastward, so that although an average of 9 knots through the water had been sustained, the actual distance made good amounted to only 72 miles. And now, after all these weeks; the careful nursing of tugs through swelter and stress; *Severn* threatened to succumb.

There could be no question about the heavy list, and it seemed to be increasing. An officer was sent aboard with a party to make investigation. He found two feet of water on the after mess-deck and along the port side, the leak having been caused by the loosening of rivets, so that each time a sea came over the foc'sle it worked through down below. Having regard to the light structure of these river gunboats; remembering all the battering about by North Sea, English Channel, Atlantic, Mediterranean, Red Sea, and Indian Ocean; perhaps it was wonderful enough that they had survived thus far; but no sailor likes to see his ship founder, and especially on the eve of reaching port.

Relays of men were sent off from *Trent* who bailed heartily the rest of that day, and throughout the night until eight o'clock next morning. Then they caulked the holes with lead wire and oakum, making such a good job whilst yet being towed at 5½ knots, that the crisis passed and they went back aboard *Trent* to discuss what they would like to do with *Königsberg*. The most confident of all wished to tow her out of the Rufiji, following victory, and bring her home as a prize to England.

A spell of fine weather assisted the squadron during May 27-28 so that towing became faster, yet neither swell nor current diminished. All the same today's run of 149 miles was the best since leaving Aden, and during the latter afternoon they crossed the equator just east of the 45th meridian, though with little enough ceremony among the officers and none whatever among the crews. On the 29th speed still further improved so that the figure reached 153 miles, and wireless communication with Admiral King-Hall was now established. Already the *T. A. Jolliffe* had joined him.

Yes: rapid advance could not be denied, and it seemed as if nothing might hinder a quick arrival at Chaki Chaki. Alas! Even today things did happen most dolefully. First of all, the *Severn*: she had been shipping a lot of water, which was no new feature, but again she exhibited her former frailty and manifested a decided list. As if this were not sufficiently worrying, next morning the *Mersey* was seen to be very much down by the head: so that in the very period when this long voyage had almost finished, a fresh doubt arose as to the manner in which termination would be made. At any rate the contest against foundering would be continued till the last.

And now the fine weather changed to rainy squalls, with an overcast sky, so that for the next thirty-six hours no sights could be taken; but dead reckoning placed the squadron by noon of the 31st some 47 miles northeast of Pemba Island, of 28 miles off the African mainland. The time had come for modifying the tows in order that *Trent* and *Kendal Castle* might be relieved entirely. This afternoon, then, the great change-over took place, but it was a lengthy business, shifting *Mersey's* hawsers aboard *Sarah Jolliffe* and *Revenger*; after which the *Severn* was taken in tow by *Blackcock* alone. Thus, inevitably were wasted three hours, during which ships drifted some distance to the north with engines stopped.

By the time this procession was again under way, they were abreast of Mombasa some thirteen miles. From that port came out a steam launch carrying the Examination Officer, but Captain Fullerton impressed upon him the necessity of keeping the word "monitor" secret, as of telling the native crew that actually these were no men-of-war. Nevertheless, we shall presently observe how difficult it was to prevent the truth getting about: in fact, the Examination Officer said he had been expecting *Severn* and *Mersey*, as a Norwegian steamer reported passing them at sea.

The "Glorious First of June" began excitingly, though scarcely too gloriously. Since, in her unaided effort, *Blackcock* was not able to tow *Severn* through the current at any better speed than 2 miles over the ground, Captain Fullerton had ordered *Revenger* and *Sarah Jolliffe* to make for Chaki Chaki independently with *Mersey*, whilst *Trent* accompanied *Blackcock*. When dawn broke about 5.30 and eyes looked ahead, they could see Kegomacha Lighthouse on Pemba Island quite clearly about 10 miles off, and the light had not yet been put out; but close thereto lay *Sarah Jolliffe* and *Revenger*, who appeared to be stopped. Further investigation through the telescope confirmed this: both tugs were flying the signal "I am aground".

Away went *Trent* in their direction at full speed, got as neat to them as possible, and anchored. All four motorboats and gigs were next lowered, Captain Fullerton with Lieut.-Commander Wilson accompanied by parties of men at once boarding the *Mersey*. They found *Sarah Jolliffe* hard aground on a coral reef, *Revenger* afloat but with her tow rope foul of the bottom. As to *Mersey*, she was drawing 6 ft. 3 in. at the time, and soundings now showed that that there were not more than 6 ft. 10 in. aft. Seven inches! And the tide ebbing fast from the reef! Terribly bad luck for Wilson to see his ship doomed within a few miles of destination!

Now followed some very smart work. *Kendal Castle* (Captain Richard T. B. Harvey) having been ordered to take over *Severn* from *Blackcock*, Captain Weir immediately slipped ropes in the most seamanlike manner, and then hastened towards the reef. He then excelled himself by a few minutes' brilliant toil, when every second was a lifetime of suspense, and hope had almost vanished. One tug ashore! And his own vessel drawing nearly twice *Mersey's* draught! Yet with caution and remarkable celerity he coaxed *Blackcock* close in towards the monitor, got a hawser fast to the latter's stern, put the tug's engines ahead and lo! the impossible happened. With little enough time and tide to spare, *Mersey* was hauled stern first from her perilous predicament into deep water, and barely saved from breaking her back, as the swell surged and receded. Another few minutes, and it would have been too late, for already the water had dropped a good two inches.

No wonder that both Captain Fullerton and Lieut.-Commander Wilson sent Captain Weir their enthusiastic congratulations.

This latest anxiety having passed, *Blackcock* continued with *Mersey* in tow, and the squadron was free to resume its course, leaving behind *Revenger* to stand by the *Sarah Jolliffe*. Now that same afternoon, as they gradually but slowly passed Pemba Island looking abundantly fertile in its greenery and plenteous palm trees, smoke on the horizon grew into a smudge and the blur cleared into the silhouette of a warship which now began calling up the "*Trent*". It was H.M.S. *Hyacinth*, flying the flag of Vice-Admiral King-Hall inquiring as to the squadron's welfare, and with her steamed *T. A. Jolliffe*. So, the latter was safe, though very short of coal.

For that reason, she and *Blackcock* (also seriously in need of fuel) were ordered into Chaki Chaki where they could fill up from *Hya-*

cinth's bunkers, so again did *Trent* take over *Mersey*. Down came the tropical rain relentlessly, penetrating oilskins of everyone on deck, and sunset, preceded a dirty night: it was as if to render the final hours during a trying voyage difficult beyond dispute. Mothership, monitors, and collier, were punching against the strong current and making good only little better than 3 knots. The sea got worse, threatening to submerge *Severn* and *Mersey* as they crashed through the waves; but even the wireless in its belated news that Lord Fisher and Mr Winston Churchill had resigned their appointments at the Admiralty did its best to depress stout hearts.

Somehow, too, Admiral King-Hall was disappointed and under an unfortunate delusion at that stage: he seemed to suppose that, after 5,000 miles, these monitors had only to anchor, open up hatches, let crews go aboard, and both units would be ready for service within a few hours. Nothing could have been further from reality, although we can well sympathise with a Commander-in-Chief desperately anxious to get *Königsberg's* fate settled. Neither monitor had anchored since setting out from Malta, but always in harbour had either secured to a buoy or lashed up each alongside a tug. True, *Severn* kept one anchor ready for letting go, but it could not have been employed until a party of men were put aboard and given adequate time. *Mersey* likewise could have used a single anchor, yet she must have ridden to 5½-inch wire: for, her chain-locker being full of water right up to the deck, she could not yet use her cable. And in any case, with no steam but everything battened down, there would have been considerable difficulty afterwards in weighing.

It had been reckoned, before quitting Malta, that on arrival off the African coast each monitor would need ten shipwrights and fourteen days' keen labouring ere the vessels were even habitable; for below decks they were just one mass of heavy timber baulks measuring 18-inches square. Temporary breakwaters on the foc'sle must needs be unbuilt, from every hatch and hole a plate would have to be removed; and since both monitors had spent most of the last five weeks chiefly under than on the water, doubtless many of the bolts securing timber had rusted.

Then, too, whilst each man-of-war had plenty of coal and oil-fuel, their main and auxiliary machinery would necessarily require more than a mere glance; their 3-pdr. guns, their ammunition, stores, and much else needing to be put aboard. Two motorboats and a couple of gigs from each monitor would also have to be transferred back into davits from *Trent*; but, besides all these items, various minor matters (such as unplugging ventilators and funnels, refixing rudder-guards at the stern, removing fillings from conning-tower apertures, readjusting binnacles on forebridge) demanded attention.

The admiral decided that monitors, instead of making for Chaki Chaki, should go some 200 miles further south to Barakuni Island which, being adjacent to Mafia Island, would be conveniently close for the Rufiji delta. Thrashing their way against a heavy sea and a head wind, collier and mothership were making monotonous advance, and some apprehension was felt as to whether the much-worn hawsers could last out. On Wednesday, June 2, the reappearance of *Blackcock* and *T. A. Jolliffe* after coaling was hailed with delight: but not less gladdening was a wireless message from *Hyacinth* to say that *Sarah Jolliffe* had floated off the reef at high tide, apparently undamaged. *Revenger* had really been more unfortunate, having snapped two of her propeller-blades off, and lost her tow rope which comprised one 14-inch hemp, one 5½-inch wire, and one shackle of *Mersey's* chain cable; the whole lot now lying below, caught in the coral. (In the Royal Navy a 'shackle' measures 12½ fathoms: in the Merchant Navy the length is 15 fathoms.)

But at length Zanzibar came and went, Mafia loomed up large and not unpleasing with its vegetation, coconut trees, white houses of natives, and the *dhows* left idly heeling over on the beach by the ebb. Before seven o'clock on the evening of June 3 *Trent* had come to anchor, with a monitor secured to either side, the long trek was completed, the steel boxes were still afloat, and now every hatch could be opened to admit fresh air for the morning's toil.

This voyage, apart from any operations performed by monitors off the Belgian or any other coast, will long be regarded as notable in naval annals and illuminative as regards future undertakings. There were not wanting those who had prophesied failure for the scheme, but whilst ocean-going tugs during our generation have thought little of towing such things as floating-docks or oil-tankers across the world, yet the monitors were unusually awkward creatures and just live-bait for any German raider.

History has only a limited value if it does not present conveniently the results which are produced by certain causes, and thereby afford ready-made lessons against the future. Looking back on the past, we can see simultaneously opportunities lost and mistakes made by German and British alike. Instead of having been sent back to do no useful service at Dunkirk in mid-December, the monitors should have been at once ordered to East Africa where they could have arrived by-the end of February and then begun their job, thus saving at least three months.

For, later on in these pages, we shall find that *Königsberg* caused the British Navy to waste 255 days off the Rufiji mouths, and (at varying times) tie down 27 fighting ships, to say nothing of supply-ships and colliers. Leaving out the immense cost of sending war vessels to this area, their wear-and-tear, as well as the payment for aeroplane service; this Blockading Fleet by running expenses alone inflicted on the British Government a charge of £70,000 to cover wages, food, fuel, whereas the German had built *Königsberg* for a mere £270,000— which shows that one solitary cruiser, immobile up a tropical river, can silently fleece her foes for months.

On the other hand, it cannot be denied that the German Admiralty was curiously short-sighted in allowing Captain Looff to remain all this while in the Rufiji. If we are to believe the evidence of a German naval prisoner, S. E. Diaz y Rodriguez, whose information generally was found very accurate; *Königsberg's* officers were at all times anxious to come forth and tackle *Hyacinth*. Had the German cruiser chosen high water to coincide with darkness, I consider it by no means improbable that she could have dashed out of the Rufiji past the whalers and dodged her way northwards: then, by falling upon the monitor cavalcade somewhere between the equator and Mombasa, she would have justified weeks of delay. Another *Pegasus débâcle*! One more blow to British pride!

She possessed ability to run away from the 21-knot *Hyacinth*, avoid range of the latter's 6-inch guns, and then turn south for that previously mentioned voyage homeward to Germany by the Cape of Good Hope. Better a bold gamble like this, surely, than waiting at Kikale to be killed?

But did the Germans know about the monitors?

Of course they knew.

When?

Impossible to say. But *Königsberg's* first officer possessed the information at least five days before June 2.

How?

Through Dar-es-Salaam definitely; but watchers on the coast, spies in Zanzibar, neutral steamers along the Malta-Mafia route, would all have passed on the news.

CHAPTER 12

Preparing For Battle

The long busy prelude to the Great Day began immediately with the morning of June 4; and the work of dismantling heavy timber baulks, which had been so necessary for the voyage out, went ahead at great pace.

Shipwrights and A.B.'s, sent from ships that had been patrolling off the delta, assisted the monitors' crews to get *Severn* and *Mersey* back into a fighting condition after all these passive weeks. So urgent was the matter that the monitors' officers themselves joined in and worked along side the men, even doctors and paymasters toiling with spanners and hammers to demolish the temporary breakwaters. Night and day, Sundays the same, everyone tackled the job with a will but under conditions that might have been pleasanter had they been less abnormal.

For, be it remembered, this matter of refitting was carried out only twenty miles from the enemy and in an open roadstead: almost it seemed to invite the *Königsberg* forth from her lair, and perform a quick desolation, wiping out *Severn* and *Mersey* with the same rapidity that she mortally wounded *Pegasus*. Thus, every hour was suspenseful, eyes were frequently turned towards the direction of Rufiji's mouths, but what might happen between sunset and dawn was always a riddle. Moreover, the heavy tropical rains, the surge and scend of the Indian Ocean, the bursts of hard winds, and the continual bumping of frail gunboat hulls against mother-ship did not help progress. All very well to borrow from the flagship those stout bundles of hazel-wood fenders, but still the crashing and bumping could not be lessened until *Trent* with her two *protégés* shifted nearer the land.

In every maritime country there are critics who reckon naval strength only in terms of ships and guns, but neglect to consider the value of naval bases—to the extent of begrudging so much as a floating dock. What these monitors just now needed was all the facility which a dockyard, with its specialist personnel and shore departments, is able to provide. Quite justly and properly the Admiralty showed their appreciation of the accomplishment in bringing *Severn* and *Mersey* so many thousand miles, but the intermediate period between voyaging and fighting has scarcely received adequate praise.

Additional machine-guns had to be borrowed from the squadron and mounted in the monitors, whose boat-decks were built up now with protective sand-bags; steel plates of half-inch thickness were sent from Zanzibar and laid along decks as simple armour against German plunging fire; more sand-bags were required for such important places as on the fore-bridge, around the after-compass, hand-steering-wheel, after-capstan; whilst further defence would be formed by mattress and hammock screens.

The little ships were to go up a river of uncertain depth, and any sort of fate might await them: there might be floating mines concealed below surface and cunningly laid well inside the river, or perhaps an electrically controlled length of explosives to be fired from the shore merely by pressing a button within an outpost battery. In either case the monitors could be turned into scrap with celerity, long before gaining *Königsberg's* range. Then, too, one lucky shell from Captain Looff's cruiser might burst, after penetrating hull, and during the very first phase, render all these lengthy preparations of no avail.

Still, naval warfare must always be a great gamble and human ingenuity can but guard against likely possibilities. A steel house that was being erected on the forebridge would afford some relief against snipers and splinters, but what about the engineering officers and men sweltering down below? To shut down the engine-room hatch would be unthinkable, so the opening was to be covered with splinternets only. Topmasts were not to be hoisted, and the officer in charge of the gun-control would occupy a sufficiently exposed position at the masthead within the fighting top, whence voice-pipes for transmitting orders were now being connected to the guns below.

Against *Königsberg's* assaults the only real protection consisted in rendering monitors as little conspicuous as possible. From the information obtained by aeroplanes, the German ship was lying in such a position that (1) her starboard broadside of five 4.1-inch guns could be brought to bear, but not one of those on her port side; (2) the monitors, if choosing the Kikunja approach, would be separated from their target by a dense patch of thick jungle with lofty mangroves. Therefore, advantage must be taken of this intervening cover, and the fire be made indirect—over the trees—at a target invisible to the British gunners.

As further precaution, a simple naval camouflage was attempted by painting both monitors various shades of green patterned to suggest mangroves; but lest either Captain Fullerton's or Lieut.-Commander Wilson's ship should quickly founder, it was decided to use 10,000 empty kerosene tins tightly packed below decks. With the peculiar characteristics of the monitors themselves, this comic painting, the shiploads of empty tins that kept arriving from Zanzibar by tugs, *Duplex*, or other vessel; there was ample opportunity for humourists to contribute their jesting comments, and ask "What next?" For some of those half-inch plates had actually been salved from the poor *Pegasus*.

Thus, the toil went on, with plenty of rain, but the monitors still rolled so terribly that it was difficult to climb aboard *Trent* and transfer stores: for all excess supplies were being taken out and placed in the latter vessel. At the end of four days such progress had been made in both monitors that steam became now available in the auxiliary engines, all guns had been mounted, most of the bullet-proof plates put in position, after which the ammunition could be received. Yes: things were already ahead of schedule. Wherefore on Thursday the 10th, Captains and officers from the monitors together with Admiral King-Hall went off in the cruiser *Weymouth*, steamed down to the delta, closing the mouths as near as depths allowed, and had a good look at the locality. They sought to familiarise themselves with the few landmarks; the appearance of Kikunja entrance, its banks dense with brush and trees. Very little could they see round the corner, though sailing across the river was sighted a ship's boat of sorts: man-of-war's cutter, she might be from her appearance. (For explanation see Chapter 15.)

Two days later, as a result of ceaseless energy, '*Severn's* crew were able to forsake their habitation in *Trent*, and, for the first time since leaving the Medway, they went to live aboard their own ship. Thus, notwithstanding many a difficulty, the task which was to have taken fourteen days had been accomplished in eight: a very remarkable achievement. Furthermore, on this same afternoon of June 12 *Severn* slipped hawsers from *Trent* and set out for a short trial under her own main engines which had not been used for more than three months. Everything worked so well that from now onwards it was just a period of adding the final touches, making adjustments, and rehearsing for the terrific adventure that still remained.

Captain Fullerton had given considerable detailed study to the problem, and invited his officers to write fully their suggestions. Many points demanded most careful weighing, as for instance whether it were better to send *Severn* by the Simba Urange, and the *Mersey* up the Kikunja, thereby attacking *Königsberg* from aft and for'ard simultaneously; but finally the decision was made for both monitors to use the Kikunja. In any case it must be a leap into the unknown, for if they were not waylaid by mines or shoals, there might yet be booms or wires across the upper reaches, torpedoes in the creeks ready to be launched as the gunboats came slowly swinging round the turns and twists of the river; whilst the thick growth on either bank would be ideal both for spotting and snipers' stations. Add to this the extreme unhandiness of both units: although twin-screwed, they steered very badly, soon became unmanageable, and their turning circle was 683 yards. Displacing 1,260 tons, a monitor was quite a large vessel for manoeuvring up narrow, uncharted inland waters.

Then the tides had to be just right. A good time to enter would be during Neaps but when already beginning to make towards Springs: some day when High Water occurred moderately near 9 a.m. If monitors made the entrance three hours before High Water, they ought yet to reach their anchoring-and-firing position half an hour after coming into the river and still have time for going still higher, should that be desirable: moreover, by taking with them plenty of flood, they need not sound all the way, and on returning with the ebb there would still be ample water available. It was judged that the stream probably ran at 1½ knots.

The advantage of a 9 o'clock tide would be that the Kikunja could be entered about 5-30 a.m. (daybreak), assuming that the date for attack was to be during the last days of June. And by strict adherence to plan, there was a possibility of rushing past the peninsula into the river with the first streak of dawn: thus, surprising the outer defences of field-guns, machine-guns, rifles. The following table shows the days on which conditions would be more or less suitable:

Date	Time of High Water (Neaps) in Kikunja
Sunday, June 20	8.39 a.m.
Monday, June 21	9.43 a.m.
Tuesday, June 22	10.57 a.m.

But the tides after June 22 would be unsuitable for most of a fortnight until:

Saturday, July 3   7.58 a.m.
Sunday, July 4   8.40 a.m.
Monday, July 5   9.52 a.m.
Tuesday, July 6   10.55 a.m. (just after Neaps)

It is obvious from the above that Sunday June 20, and Saturday July 3 would have been good enough dates, but for one reason or another so grave a matter had to be postponed, principally because of one essential item. Just as other ships this year at the Dardanelles had shown that, without accurate spotting arrangements, the best-laid guns are of little worth; just, too, as the monitors when shelling the Germans in Belgian territory, had been similarly handicapped; so the same difficulty threatened up the Rufiji. Granted that " *Königsberg* was an invisible target, the whole success against her must depend on the monitors knowing where shots were falling. Correct direction? 'Too far to the right? Too far left? Over? Short?

Of course, the problem for Captain Looff would be not less important, but whereas he could choose his own spotting establishments and erect platforms among the trees anywhere down the banks, or on the high ground of Pemba Hill (to the north of Kikunja); the monitors had little selection. It was the air, or nothing. And, so far, the brave flying men had been badly handicapped by machines which on some days were reliable yet on other occasions failed notably; troubled also by the local atmospheric conditions, for each aviator reported on the aerial difficulty of making over this river area. That was one part of the proposition, but another unsettled question was the method of communication between ship and aeroplane.

Nowadays, when wonderful voyages are made across the Atlantic without losing wireless touch, it is necessary to remind ourselves that the Great War burst just a little too soon and overtook the young, struggling, art of aviation: many of us still recollect that in August 1914 serious-minded experts much doubted whether flying would be of the slightest utility during hostilities. Off the East African coast, the experimental trial-and-error stage had not been passed even twelve months later, but the immediate matter in June was how to effect good signalling so that at the critical moment the bird-men could not fail to transmit news down below, destined for the gun-control officers.

So, the latter days of June found the monitors still learning, still seeking a solution by repeated tests, and delayed by unsuitable sky weather. Not till the 21st did Admiral King-Hall begin to search out among his naval officers one who could select on Mafia Island a site that would do for an aerodrome. What length of ground must be provided for landing? Thus, rapidly had modern invention affected an ancient sea service that the commander-in-chief was astern of essential knowledge. Fortunately, however, Lieut.-Commander Wilson of *Mersey* chanced to be one of those few seafarers with practical experience of the air, so he could reply that a Maurice Farman biplane would require 200 yards, and a monoplane 150 yards. Next day a suitable stretch on the island was staked out.

Another twenty-four hours and a machine went up from Mafia to practise her wireless, but the latter proved a failure so far as concerned the monitors, who received no signals. And the same disappointing result occurred on the 24th. It was disheartening for the monitors thus to be hindered after such strenuous days of fitting-out, yet some sort of conversational method must certainly be established ere ships could go up the river. The two commanding officers conferred with Major Robert Gordon of the Royal Flying Corps, and it was decided to employ coloured-light signals as well as an arc lamp in conjunction with wireless. When an aeroplane once more soared for experiments, the arc lamp turned out a failure, but this time both wireless and coloured-lights proved so successful that they were now accepted as the best method for communication.

It was thought by the admiral that *Königsberg* was still in excellent fighting condition, that she had on board coal for at least three days' steaming, but at present was burning wood for maintaining steam on her auxiliary engines. She exhibited no sign of intended departure so far, but whether she happened to be short of ammunition and stores was another affair altogether. That she must be destroyed, and not merely maimed, was essential because her existence kept too many valuable units hovering off the delta which were badly wanted elsewhere, such as in the Aegean, the Mediterranean, patrolling the ocean trade-routes. The moral effect of the German cruiser on her country's colonial troops, the practical value of her ten 4-1-inch guns if used ashore, made it additionally imperative that the British effort must produce more than partial success.

Yet this would be no ordinary naval operation, and anything might happen: the one certain thing was its uncertain result. "Never underrate your enemy". The Germans were keen fighters, and most likely had thought out some original surprises for any vessel who should try invading the Rufiji territory. Formed by a remarkable maze of creeks, most of which communicated with the rivers, though some were shallow, others blind, and many of a depth unknown to the British; this area covered about 35 miles from north to south, but little more than one quarter of that distance reckoning from east to west. As to the swamps, islands, shoals, and depths, scarcely anything further was known than we have already enunciated. No navigational difficulties were expected in the Kikunja entrance, which was the widest of all the mouths, nevertheless, there might be sudden shallows of mud brought down by centuries of November floods meeting the tidal stream.

Whilst it would never do for the monitors to get aground on the ebb, and remain up river during the dark hours as perfect targets for any torpedoing expedition, would not the enemy have devised some scheme for closing fast the door after *Severn* and *Mersey* had once entered Kikunja? True, these monitors hoped to accomplish the bombarding within two or three hours, but that would allow sufficient time for some boom—heavy baulks of timber with spikes and wire hawsers—to be drawn out of tidal creek across the river, thus denying the ships' return passage. Imagine for yourself such an obstruction placed at a sharp bend, suddenly discovered by *Severn* and *Mersey* retreating at full speed down the ebb! Consider these gunboats' unhandiness, their inability to avoid fouling the boom, damaging alike hull and propellers: then the confusion, but easy target at point-blank range for gunners and riflemen lining the banks!

On the other hand, a plan for torpedoing *Königsberg* by using dropping-gear from small craft, such as steam picket-boats, had been examined though rejected. Under all circumstances—even cover of night—it would have been the most desperate of ventures. There were not wanting ardent young officers and men prepared to undertake the risk, but the chances of success were remote: it would have meant approaching to within 500 yards of Captain Looff's hull, preserving complete silence of engines, evading the rays of blinding searchlights, but even then, too much accuracy cannot be guaranteed with dropping-gear. (Nevertheless, it might have succeeded, just as a picket-boat *brilliantly* achieved on the night of April 19 1915 up the Dardanelles, For this exciting incident see my *Dardanelles Dilemma*.)

Supposing, too, the little craft did not get ashore among the shadows on the return trip, and be left dry above the mud, it would have been miraculous had she dashed safely past the German soldiers entrenched at the mouth.

But the reliance on gunnery, on 6-inch shells, and the choice of Neap tides, made it requisite that *Severn* and *Mersey* should not draw one inch more water than Nature's own laws of flotation demanded: in fact, the draught of 6½ feet must be cut down to a maximum of 4 feet. Now could this actually be done, seeing that so much extra weight had recently been added by mounting extra quick-firing guns and bringing aboard so many steel-plates?

The answer is that it was done.

The reader will recollect that in our first chapter we saw each monitor had capacity for 187 tons of coal and 90 tons of oil-fuel. She likewise normally carried 22 tons of boiler water and 16 tons of drinking water, to say nothing of her two 30-ft. motorboats and two 27-ft. gigs. Each ship now possessed two 6-inch guns (one for'ard, and one aft); two 4.7-inch howitzers; four semi-automatic 3-pdrs.; one 3-pdr. on high-angle mounting; four .303 *mitrailleuse* machineguns, and four Maxims. There was also a crew of 150 men plus 10 officers.

A good many tons would have to be removed without taking away personnel, fighting ability, or motive power.

First, *Severn* (like her sister) was cleared of all woodwork, bales of canvas, and everything of a combustible nature. Store-rooms and flats were emptied of spare gear; sofas from the Ward Room, officers' spare clothes and private effects, were sent aboard *Trent*. Only one chair per officer was retained, and on the last night before battle such items as cabin curtains, cupboard-doors, beds, desks, were to be removed, but provisions sufficient merely to last four days must be retained. From the men's mess-decks, tables and stools were to be taken away forty-eight hours preceding action, galley-fires drawn ere leaving for the mouth; all clothing put out of the ship, except one bundle per person of khaki and underwear previously soaked in disinfectant.

There would be no time, or opportunity, to have meals up the Kikunja, so on the final morning each officer and man was to be given four large meat-sandwiches, and baskets of oranges were to be placed in different positions about the ship; whilst plenty of fresh-water bottles and buckets filled with oatmeal-and-water were conveniently to be set ready.

The kerosene tins were stowed as low as possible in messdecks and store-rooms, firmly wedged; no petrol was to be carried other than four tins filled for working the after-capstan, and covered by sand-bags, which throughout the ship numbered no less than 1,500.

Firehoses were to be rigged, all decks kept wet, but in case monitors should have to be abandoned, detailed arrangements had been provided for disabling engines, boilers, hull and guns. Should a monitor get stuck hard aground, it would be the thrilling task for the tug *Blackcock* to go in and haul her off: for which reason the Liverpool civilian crew was now replaced by naval ratings.

It was the absence of a really good, up-to-date, chart which made exact intentions difficult to define beforehand, so the best had to be done with incomplete hydrographic data presented in map form; but the essential project was to hurry up the Kikunja till abreast of the first large island (which seemed to be over 9,000, but less than 10,000, yards from *Königsberg* as the shell flies). Assuming the range was found to be in fact not more than 12,000 yards, monitors would then let go anchor from the bows and swing head to tide. But with this fore-and-aft position each ship could obviously fire not both of her 6-inch guns.

Therefore, in order to enable the for'ard as well as stern armament to bear, it would be necessary to moor ship athwart stream, which could be done in one of two ways: by bending a "spring" on to the bower cable—that is to say leading a wire from stern to anchor-chain and then hauling the ship at right angles (actually done at the Dardanelles by some British battleships, so that in spite of wind and current a full broadside could be fired when bombarding) across river—or simply by letting go a second anchor but from the stern. Possibly the latter would be found the quicker way; so aboard each monitor and over each quarter an anchor, with wire shackled on, was now secured ready to be released quickly.

For the purpose both of weight saving and preventing a conflagration, *Severn* discharged the whole of her oil-fuel into *Kendal Castle*, and all her coal except 60 tons, thereby shortening her draught to the extent of about 9 inches through this one effort alone. Frequent rehearsals of letting go anchors, mooring quickly ahead and astern, then firing across the SW corner of Mafia Island at an old *dhow* invisible to the monitors but with the aeroplanes spotting, produced most encouraging results both as to rapidity and effectiveness. Nor could a sense of humour be altogether ruled out during these busy moments. Since *Severn* was anxious not to send her shells zooming in the direction of Admiral King-Hall's flagship, which was observed getting under way, Captain Fullerton made the following preliminary signal:

Captain of *Severn* to Captain of *Hyacinth*: "Will you please tell me your ultimate destination as I want a clear range for firing?"

This was taken in, read, and answered as follows:

Captain of *Hyacinth* to Captain of *Severn*: "My ultimate destination is Heaven I hope, but at present I am bound for Tirene."

Then came:

Captain of *Severn* to Captain of *Hyacinth*: "Thank you. I hope to meet you there."

The wish was two-fold, for presently monitors shifted to Tirene Bay (Mafia Island) as their future anchorage. Here was deep water with plenty of fine fish, whilst in the background stood the well-built ex-German Residency near the landing beach. Black natives in their long white "nightgowns", the new aerodrome and aeroplane sheds, the former Customs House, the roughly constructed *dhows* and waving palms, were henceforth to become familiar enough sights ere this East African campaign should end. But besides the mother-ship *Trent* and the flagship *Hyacinth*, Tirene Bay gave monitors for companions the cruisers *Weymouth*, *Challenger*, *Pioneer*; the armed merchant cruiser *Laurentic*; the whalers *Salamander*, *Rattler*, *Charon*, *Styx*; together with the collier *Kendal Castle*.

Never before had those sun-drenched waters witnessed such strange and interesting preparations. Nothing indeed was left to chance, and even the entering of Kikunja River was practised "dummy"-wise: a series of buoys being placed off Tirene to represent the width and twist of the mouth. Then along came *Severn* between the buoys, steaming awkwardly as if she were part of a fortress that had broken away from the land for sheer envy of ships that cruise.

The *Laurentic* reached Tirene on June 18 from Aden bringing 2 Henry Farman and 2 Caudron aeroplanes besides personnel, yet Mafia's aerodrome, overgrown with small trees and scrub, having a swamp at one end, was everything but ideal: if the hangar consisted of only a few wooden sections and corrugated iron hastily put together, yet it had to suffice. What mattered anything so long as the aircraft would be ready on the appointed day to keep aloft? And now arrived *Duplex* with a mixed cargo of kerosene tins, vegetables, fruit, fresh drinking water.

This ex-cable ship of the Eastern Telegraph Company was manned chiefly by survivors from *Pegasus*, and mounted some of the latter's light guns. Although *Duplex* could do her 7 knots, and no better, she was already a well-tried warrior of some fame, as the two shell-holes in her funnel proved. Had she not passed through a thrilling time on the day that S.S. *Newbridge* was deposited across the Suninga channel? But also, *Duplex* knew more than a little of the Kikunja entrance, with whose batteries she had exchanged animosity. So, whilst today she was discharging cargo, an opportunity occurred for plenty of good yarns.

Interesting items revealed that on the fatal morn of September 20 when *Pegasus* lay anchored off Zanzibar, she was awaiting the arrival of a store-ship, against whose advent the store-room had been emptied of many provisions which were laid on the upper deck, the intention being to replace these after the new supplies had been packed below. Thus the cruiser was in no perfect state for a fight, and during that evening it had been remarked: "If the *Königsberg* were to come now, she will catch us napping."

When at dawn a whiff of smoke was sighted in the distance, this suggested the store-ship's approach, but *Königsberg's* salvoes soon brought disillusionment and death. Decks were still being cleared of wounded when more salvoes caused further havoc. A sad and regrettable incident. All very well for the *Pegasus* people in *Duplex* to make light of the Rufiji guns by comparison with that memorable occasion, and to encourage monitors' men by saying the Kikunja batteries contained no big 4.1-inch guns: that would remain to be experienced.

So, the final preparations gradually concluded, further realism being added to the rehearsals by gunnery practice at 9,300 yards range and at the very matutinal hour determined for attacking *Königsberg*". So satisfactory was the co-operation between aircraft and gunners that a further test of firing enabled the range to be tried at over 13,000 yards, monitors being again moored head-and-stern, and *Königsberg* represented by a couple of *dhows*. Although the latter were visible only to the aviators, there could be no doubt whatever concerning results. The shooting had been first-class, for one *dhow* was badly damaged and the other so perfectly shelled that she went to the bottom and could not be salved.

CHAPTER 13

Secret Plans

Such then, was the manner in which *Severn* and *Mersey* spent exactly four weeks since their arrival off this coast; but before we accompany them into battle, and witness the climax of all endeavour, it is well to take a glance elsewhere. June had run its course, July had set in, but how had the enemy been faring whilst monitors voyaged between Malta and Mafia? Fortunately, the private, unpublished, documents afford us a clear sequence.

Of the German naval patriotism and anxiety to assist *Königsberg* by personal effort, even at great inconvenience, we have notable testimony. The reader will not have forgotten that we last saw her tender *Zieten* at Mozambique releasing the *City of Winchester's* people. Now after the former's internment some of the German sailors got away and reached Mombasa, this party comprising not merely *Zieten* men but certain of those who originally had been serving in S.M.S. *Planet*, the surveying ship.

How did they manage to elude the British patrols?

The answer is that no blockade can ever be inviolate: at various times, and under special circumstances, daring runners will succeed in getting through. During the first three months of *Königsberg's* captivity we had too few ships watching, and their vigilance was confined almost exclusively to the Rufiji exits, so that they were not able to look out along the lonely seas a hundred or more miles eastwards. Consequently, some small vessel, such as a sailing *dhow*, might work her way northwards from Mozambique, hugging the shore, darting into any of the numerous rivers or creeks when alarmed; then, having got so far north as Cape Delgado, she could altogether avoid the Rufiji approaches by taking a long leg out into the ocean till sighting Aldabra Island. Having fixed her position from that lonely spot, she could head up towards Mombasa giving Zanzibar a wide berth and making the coast again during the dark hours.

Also, obviously, the reverse voyage was not less practicable.

In an earlier chapter we watched the enterprising supply-steamer *Kronborg* (ex-*Rubens*) burning in Mansa Bay on April 14. Shortly afterwards there set sail from Mombasa, a little further to the north, a small fore-and-aft two-masted schooner containing the above-mentioned *Zieten* and *Planet* escapers, who realised that their services could be far better employed under Captain Looff. On April 18 the schooner passed so close to Aldabra as to be seen by Mr Mein, who very much wondered why the stranger did not call at the island. When last visible she was heading to the SSW, but eventually bore away for Lindi where she safely arrived. Thence the adventurers were free to make their way over land, as well as river, till they finally reported aboard *Königsberg* on May 16.

So successful was this round-about journeying that several more small craft later carried courageous mariners to their destination, and in this connection we may cite S. E. Diaz y Rodriguez, of whom we have previously made slight mention but he will come into our story more prominently later. This highly intelligent, remarkably well informed, subject of the *Kaiser* at one time served in the German Navy, and at outbreak of war was Chief Steward in a German mercantile steamship; but after being interned at Mozambique, escaped, hid himself in a *dhow*, got passage so far as Lindi, and from there proceeded to join the *Königsberg*. His ship was S.S. *Khalifa*.

Yes: notwithstanding the inshore patrols of whalers, no one could guarantee that the Rufiji mouths were firmly barred. Thus, one dark night late in April, when tides suited, the 250-tons tug *Adjutant* of many exploits steamed out of the river with a German naval crew, dodged her enemies and, after negotiating the reefs, actually got safely into Dar-es-Salaam: a very plucky performance, though many a man in *Königsberg* bored with inactivity longed to go with her and share any risk.

But it was the growing persistence of British aeroplanes keeping an eye on *Königsberg*, and preventing her complete concealment, that made Captain Looff apprehensive. Although he had taken every advantage of local conditions, lurking behind dense mangroves, this could not make his ship invisible. When on Sunday forenoon of April 25 Lieut. Cull had flown over in a seaplane, the visit was received with the most unpleasant shower of shrapnel, shells bursting so near that the bullets could veritably he heard. The Germans believed their aim had been ineffectual, but the contrary was true; for five holes were discovered in the 'plane, a rifle bullet fired from one of those river outposts at the mouth tore away air-intakes, closed most of the main oil-pipe, and only by the slenderest margin did Cull's machine survive into safety.

Two days later the delta was reconnoitred aerially twice, but a week afterwards, when Flight-Lieut. H. E. Watkins was swifting through the sky, a German shot off Simba Urange mouth hit his rudder and the seaplane crashed seriously among the sharks. Fortunately, Cull had seen the situation, and up in the air he steered, to discover the wreckage with Watkins and his Observer hanging perilously on the floats. Down to the now boisterous sea Cull swooped alongside, picked up the two anxious men, and with them on board taxied over the waves till succoured by a patrol whaler.

But the aircraft sank and could not be salvaged. For the British at such a time it was no small loss when these machines were at once so few and yet so necessary, yet at least the fewer bursts into German privacy now seemed to accentuate the enemy's old monotony of swamp imprisonment. Captain Looff's birthday (May 2) was celebrated by the allowance to each man of one bottle of beer—"a long denied joy", as bitterly remarked Signalman Ritter, though this break soon became forgotten. Certain of his shipmates seemed less unlucky, and their faces on May 11 suggested new hope when at dawn a party of them were mustered on deck for final inspection. Whilst the ship's band played them over the side, and boats catried them ashore, many a longing look followed them till out of sight.

These valedictions between sentimental Teutons were very trying for all. Through many a month and all sorts of trouble; in victory and suspense, high hope and despondency; out upon the Indian Ocean amid freedom of the seas, or as prisoners up this pestilential river; they had always shared together. But now something more than a sudden separation of messmates was taking place: it was for many of them the final earthly goodbye, and though not one could have foretold the curious coincidence, nevertheless exactly two months from that day would end *Königsberg's* career as a fighter.

One portion of this departing procession was bound eventually for Moshi (northwest of Tanga) to assist in military operations, but 2 officers and 80 men were destined for Kigoma and naval warfare on Lake Tanganyika which could now be reached by the recently completed railway from Dar-es-Salaam. (For the exciting naval campaign on Lakes Tanganyika and Victoria Nyanza the reader is referred to Chapter 19 *et seq* of *Königsberg Adventure*.) Ritter wrote sadly:

"We envy them, we who must stay here behind to lead this inactive life for ever; whereas they are going to be allowed to take an active part in the Colony's protection."

So far as Dar-es-Salaam the *Königsberg's* first officer went to accompany the party on their long march, and thereby an interesting fact emerged to be related presently; but when on May 12 it was learnt that a British cruiser shelled the road on which the cavalcade had rested only the previous night, the word treachery leapt to the lips immediately.

As yet the secret of *Severn* and *Mersey* had not reached Captain Looff, but his mind now considered how he could break the patrol encirclement by making the act of blockading too dangerous for the British. His officers and men by no means had lost their pluck or determination to fight till the end: on the other hand, a certain despondency had afflicted them. True, the *Königsberg* was doing her nation good so long as she attracted many useful British men-of-war to the Rufiji vicinity urgently needed elsewhere. Against this, however, had to be reckoned the waste of a fine cruiser and her 4.1-inch guns, the decaying morale of a smart crew. Someday the German Admiralty would doubtless send south another *Kronborg*, and Looff must smash his way out to meet her.

How was that to be done?

Of course, the solution could have been found in a submarine: one U-boat with torpedoes might break up the East African Blockade just as U-21 ruined the bombarding operations off Gallipoli, so that she became known as the "Deliverer of the Dardanelles". (*"Der befreier der Dardanellen,"*) She was about to thrill the world by the ease with which she sent those two battleships *Triumph* and *Majestic* to the bottom; and today we know that, with just a shade more luck, her attacks on *Swiftsure* and *Vengeance* might also have succeeded. What wouldn't Captain Looff have given for a similar submarine just then?

Here off Africa existed not a *distant* blockade (as off north Scotland) but a perfect example of a *close* blockade in force during eight long months—November 11, 1914 till July 11, 1915. The routine generally comprised one fast cruiser of the *Weymouth* type in the offing plus one or two armed whalers inshore watching the Mafia North Channel; whilst a cruiser of the *Hyacinth* or *Pyramus* class, or at least one armed merchant cruiser (ex-liner), watched the Mafia South Channel in the offing, assisted by an inshore whaler. These were normally under way during daylight hours, but at night usually anchored in Tirene Bay, where they could find 10 to 12 fathoms within 100 yards of the golden-sandy beach. At all times a careful watch was maintained, and the first alarm would send units to sea, but during Spring tides an extra-keen vigilance was always kept.

Of course, the Germans were not unaware of this routine, and since no submarine could be granted, the *Königsberg* officers during May were working on another scheme. They planned to destroy the bigger cruisers under cover of night, selected a couple of local dug-outs, lashed them together as torpedo-carriers, rigged the steam launch *Wami* with dropping-gear, and waited for a favourable chance. Now *Wami* was 55 ft. long, with a speed of 7 knots, armed with light guns, Maxims and rifles. For fuel she burned wood, and her customary employment consisted of carrying stores down river from *Königsberg* to the party entrenched at the Rufiji mouths.

On a certain night she chose her tide, stole forth across the intervening ten miles of sea, was not observed, crept towards Tirene Bay . . . but alas! for her, the best-laid plans sometimes go wrong by sheer coincidence: this happened to be one of those rare occasions when the big cruiser had weighed anchor and got under way!

That failure was followed up by the receipt of news which brought no sort of hope, for on June 2 after three weeks' absence arrived back from Dar-es-Salaam the first officer of *Königsberg*, who had accompanied the marching shore-party during the initial stage of their journey. At Dar-es-Salaam he had learnt that "the English now have two monitors (river-boats) here on the German East African coast", of very small draught, and therefore probably intended "for work in the delta".

Today we may regret that, even before *Severn* and *Mersey* had ended their voyage, and in spite of the scrupulous care Captain Fullerton took to preserve secrecy, their approach was made known aboard *Königsberg*: yet the same meticulous caution for concealment was continued till the very last moment, and monitors at anchor were sometimes rendered invisible by placing bigger ships on either side to overshadow them.

A cheering effect on the Germans, however, was made on June 14 by the welcome visit of Lieut.-Commander Christiansen from Mansa Bay. He brought Captain Looff not only thrilling accounts of how the *Kronborg* successfully dodged the north Scotland Blockade, and

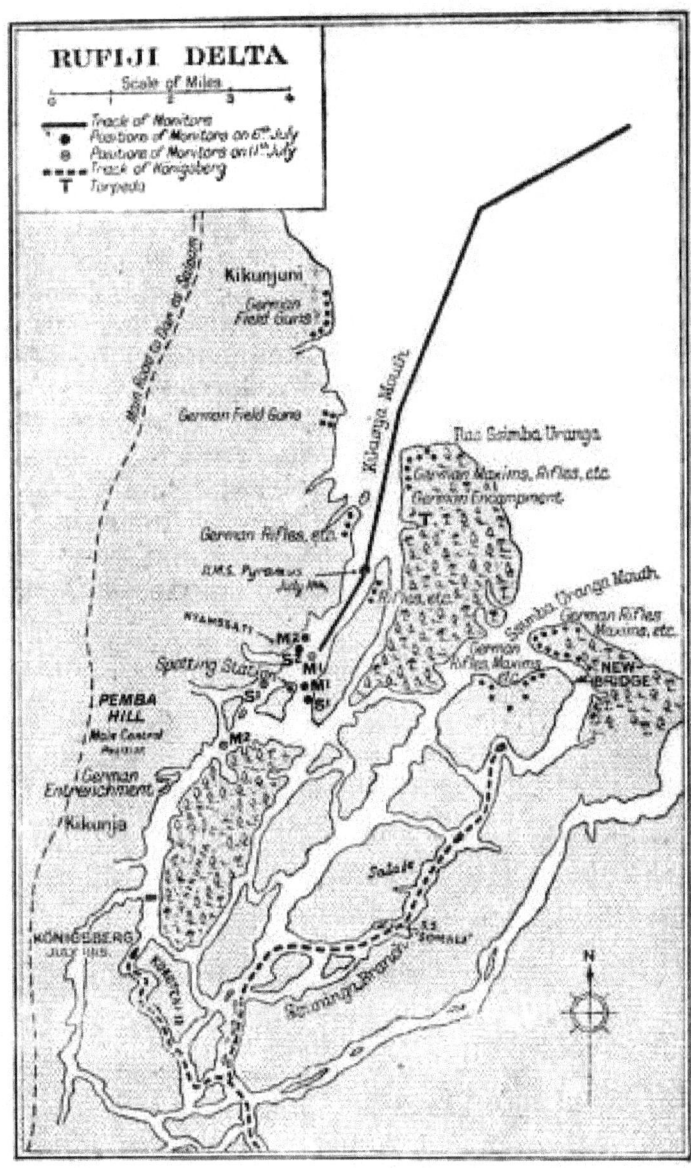

THE ATTACK ON "KÖNIGSBERG"

In accordance with full knowledge this plan now shows the correct position of the S.S. "Somali" and Salale village. The track of "Königsberg" is shown till her final position off Kobotoni Island, to the north of which a black mark represents the bar found across the channel. The track of monitors on July 6 and 11 should be compared with illustration on page 167. The anchored positions of "Severn" and "Mersey" are indicated by S and M.

had just failed to elude Admiral King-Hall; but also, lots of news from Germany and concerning the progress of war in Europe. Quite curiously, following nine days' respite, Christiansen's arrival synchronised with further visitation from British aviators who appeared at 4.45 this afternoon, and about the same hour on the following day. In the meantime, some 2,500 natives, with divers from *Königsberg* and *Möwe*, had been working day and night salving the valuable stores from *Kronborg's* water-filled holds.

****

Möwe was a German naval surveying ship. When Dar-es-Salaam entrance had been blocked by sinking the floating-dock, it had bottled up *Möwe* together with German East Africa liners *Tabora*, *König*, and *Feldmarschall*. *Möwe* (not to be confused with the famous raider of the same name) was little more than a steam yacht of 650 tons and 10 knots speed.

****

It was now learned that she had brought for Königsberg a year's supplies, including a thousand 4.1-inch shells and five million small-arms ammunition. The first of these goods came aboard *Königsberg* on June 21 just in time, and although very rusty they were quickly renovated.

From now onwards a nerve-trying element of suspense dominated the enemy in all seriousness: sooner or later something would be attempted by those two newly arrived monitors, but meanwhile the aerial visits were becoming too determined. Suddenly on June 22 an airman was observed only when right over *Königsberg*, and a brisk fire failed to touch him. Then on July 2 another appeared at about the usual hour (4.30 p.m.), and this time dropped four bombs which did not hit, though they fell into the mangroves barely 200 yards from the ship, signifying that immunity could not be promised the Germans much longer. Of course, the monitors were heard practising their salvoes behind Mafia Island, but the *Königsberg* mariners in their seclusion imagined it was *Weymouth* shelling the shore anterior to making a hostile dash up through the Simba Urange mouth. Thus, when next day (July 3), Christiansen left ship on his way back to Germany as a "Swedish farmer" with a forged passport, his final impression was that of Captain Looff's anxiety; but had the blockade-runner delayed his departure just another three days, he would have carried with him most alarming tidings.

For the long prelude had now been played out, everything was ready and awaiting the grand climax planned to take place on July 6.

In accordance with full knowledge this plan now shows the correct position of the S.S. *Somali*' and Salale village. The track of *Königsberg* is shown till her final position off Kokotoni Island, to the north of which a black mark represents the bar found across the channel. The track of monitors on July 6 and 11 should be compared with illustration in chapter 14. The anchored positions of *Severn* and *Mersey*' are indicated by S and M.

CHAPTER 14

The Great Occasion

The general idea for attacking *Königsberg* was that the monitors should come up Kikunja River and begin shelling when 9,000 to 12,000 yards away from the target, assistance being rendered by aeroplanes whose duties would include: (1) informing *Severn* and *Mersey* as to how these two were firing; (2) dropping bombs on the German cruiser, and any shore guns or entrenchments. Only two Henry Farmans were available, besides the Caudron who could do the bombing, but the most important thing was to afford accurate spotting.

For this momentous occasion Tuesday, July 6, had been selected, High Tide in the river being as we have seen at 10.55 a.m. During Monday the monitors' men were given a rest, but the other ships began to take up positions for supporting the invasion: the *Weymouth* at 6.30 p.m. anchoring off the delta with the intention of closing Kikunja mouth at daylight on Tuesday, so as to engage any guns or entrenchments on the banks; whilst *Hyacinth* was to demonstrate off the Simba Urange entrance, and the armed merchant cruiser *Laconia* (Cunard liner) would appear further south at Masala River's exit. Lest the enemy should be inclined to send troops for reinforcing the Rufiji defences, a feint was to be made off Dar-es-Salaam that early morn by the armed merchant cruiser *Laurentic* (White Star liner), accompanied by three transports from Mombasa and a collier to suggest an imminent landing.

Admiral King-Hall had chosen the three whalers *Echo*, *Childers*, *Fly* and the cruiser *Pyramus* to work under *Weymouth*, but one other whaler—*Pickle*—besides the cruiser *Pioneer*, would assist *Hyacinth*. Before quitting Tirene Bay he made the following signal of encouragement:

The Commander-in-Chief desires to wish the captains, officers, and crews of the monitors every success for tomorrow. He is confident that all ranks will uphold the honour of the British flag for King and Country.

Leaving behind the *Trent* to act as hospital ship off Tirene, *Severn* and *Mersey* weighed anchor after dusk, steamed very slowly towards a position near the Kikunja approach, guided by lights from *Childers* and *Echo*, which could be also relied upon presently as leading marks direct for the river. By 10.30 p.m. both monitors had quietly brought up in their assigned places, and nought else could be done till the morrow; so, Captain Fullerton having impressed on his men the importance of allowing no lights to be seen, he lay down for a few hours with his mattress stretched across *Severn's* dewy deck, whilst the ship's company sought a brief unconsciousness before the arrival of fresh anxieties. Perhaps for some of their mates this would be the last sleep afloat?

According to schedule, monitors would begin shortening in cable at 4.40 a.m., but actually they were under way nearly an hour earlier and steaming through darkness towards the land. It was dead Low Water now, as *Severn* led the way cautiously, followed at a short interval by *Mersey* whose captain had been promoted to Commander only last week. At either side amidships each monitor was towing a motor-boat, which might seem an unusual procedure for men-of-war shortly going into action: but the whole naval operation was unusual, the navigation up an unvisited river unusual, and anything surprising might happen any moment.

Luckily neither gunboat got aground on the outlying shallows, and already the young flood coming in from ocean to raise the river's depths had begun; hulls would soon be across the bar, and the trickiest bit of pilotage be passed. Captain Fullerton was on the bridge; his Gunnery Officer Lieutenant E. S. Brooksmith R.N.; Lieut. Grenfell R.N.V.R.; and the range-taker; were aloft in the fighting-top peering through the blackness that precedes dawn.

As the ships headed to the west of south, the mangrove-covered peninsula should be fine on the port bow, whilst broad on the starboard beam to the northwest must lie the sandy coast stretching northwards, said to be defended by German rifles and guns. Msungu was that district's native name, and today we know it happened to be just one of the fourteen look-out stations which the enemy, with great thoroughness, had arranged for protection of the Rufiji district.

These were all connected by telephone with Pemba Hill, which rose from the shore about six miles up the Kikunja but neatly two miles inland (roughly northwest) from the river, or some four miles north of where *Königsberg* lay. Thus Pemba, besides being something of a local health-resort for Captain Looff's fever-stricken invalids, was also the headquarters and telephone exchange. Through here every movement of any British ship had been always reported these months, and thence the news was passed down another telephone which led to a tent erected on the shore less than 1,000 yards from *Königsberg's* anchorage, each message being finally sent from bank to ship by means of signal-flags.

For protecting the deltas, the fourteen posts were being run by 240 men, of whom many were German colonists turned into temporary soldiers. Each station was a day's journey from the next, the whole of this shore organisation being under the command of an older, more experienced, naval officer than Captain Looff. Seeing that the latter was still on the active list, and that *Königsberg* continued an independent unit; but the Commandant of Defence Force happened to be of junior rank and on the retired list; not unnaturally there existed a certain amount of friction. Complaints were made that the delta defences were too weak, and that because of their isolated positions there could be no mutual succour on a crisis; yet we can well understand Captain Looff's objection to lending them some of *Königsberg's* 4.1-inch guns. Was it not his duty to keep the ship in all respects ready for going out at short notice, fully prepared to fight?

****

Inasmuch as *Königsberg* was lying with head to the north, so that only her starboard guns could bear seawards, the defence *commandant* did his best to beg use of the five unemployed port guns, believing that they could thus prove themselves invaluable at the delta entrances. Whilst we can sympathise with the arguments of the two rivals, yet the situation was delicate and abnormal, Looff possessing the rank of Captain (*Fregatten-Kapitan*), and the *commandant* being a Commander (*Korvetten-Kapitan*).

****

Now in charge of the Msungu area was Lieut.-Commander Paul M. Koohl, one of *Königsberg's* officers, and about 5.20 on the morning of July 6 he was walking with a party of his men along the beach, keeping a routine lookout immediately to the northwest of Kikunja's mouth. Aboard *Severn* the vague loom of the sandy shore had been observed by Greenshields simultaneously with Koohl's glimpse of something that startled the senses and almost froze the imagination. It was only twenty minutes before dawn, the hour when human nature is at its feeblest and the mind least inclined to register exactly: yet that which the German officer saw was no fantasy of imagination.

This is what he wrote in a letter a week later:

> How can I describe our astonishment, when we discerned shadowy looking ships coming rapidly up the middle of the channel? They could not be ships to be sunk: I could see that at once. They were war-ships of a kind, and I saw that we were going to 'get it in the neck'. I at once made a telephone report to the captain of the *Königsberg* and the *commandant* of the M.E.K.D., (the Rufiji Defence Force was known by these initials), and so I was the first one who warned the people on the river of the impending danger.... The monitors advanced gaily up the stream 6,000 to 7,000 yards, as if they were at home.

It is true that during the previous late afternoon the various British cruisers and whalers steaming out from Tirene Bay had been noticed in the offing, though this did not cause the Msungu station

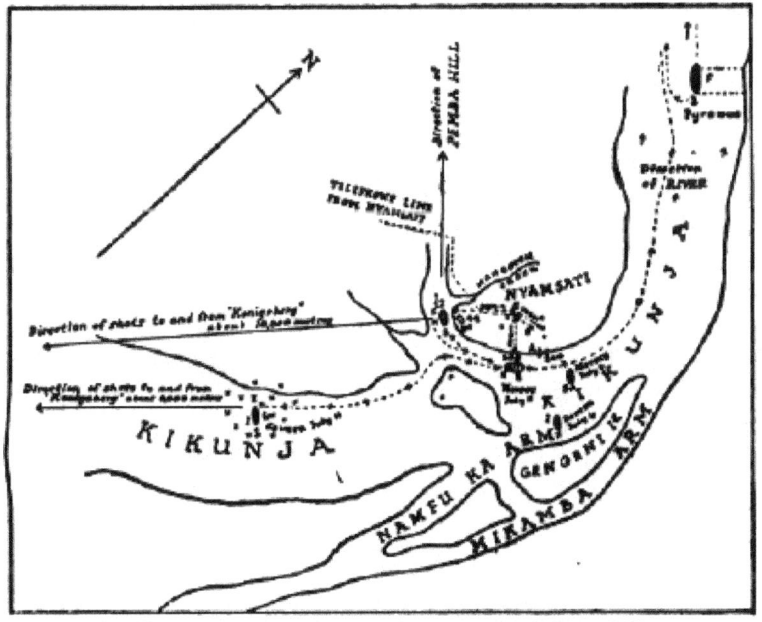

DETAILED PLAN OF THE MONITORS' ANCHORAGES

This shows the various movements of "Severn" and "Mersey" during their bombardments of "Königsberg" on July 6 and 11. The position of H.M.S. "Pyramus" will be noticed nearer the mouth.

great alarm: several similar naval displays had been seen before. Koohl thought he could individualise two of that miscellaneous squadron as cargo ships, but at such a distance he must have mistaken the whalers' outlines.

> We all imagined that their (the British) idea was to sink the two cargo ships in the middle of the deep-water channel, and we all went peacefully to bed.

It was when this matutinal expedition revealed an effort very different from the *Newbridge* affair that the troops, detailed to defend the banks, no longer regarded the "foolish" English so light-heartedly: indeed, one German afterwards admitted that, on seeing the well-armed monitors burst with the dawn into virulent shelling, no member of the Defending Force imagined his own life worth a penny.

At the best of times monitors scarcely inspired beholders with admiration for beauty, and today they looked to German eyes such odd monstrous water-beetles, with guns sticking out everywhere. Another of these Germans wrote to his friend Hans:

> If you have never had any dealings with monitors, you will have reason to congratulate yourself. Dear Hans, they are beastly things, and not to be trifled with.

****

Although the Germans did not see a monitor off East Africa until the morn of July 6, their Intelligence System must have been remarkably thorough, for they possessed the following particulars which were little different from absolute accuracy: displacement 1,400 tons, draught 1.10 metres; guns—one 6-inch, four 4.7-inch, six machine-guns.

****

A German gun from the northwestern shore boomed out from somewhere, showing that if the enemy had been surprised, he had wasted no moments in jumping to his job. *Severn* and *Mersey*, having timed their arrival with perfection, were definitely river-borne by 5.50 and the fast-rising sun made the course so clear ahead that speed could now be accelerated to 7½ knots, whilst the tide became stronger every minute. In running the gauntlet between the two shores, monitors realised this would be the first crisis, so now they were using quick-firers and machine-guns at short range fiercely. Lucky for them that Captain Looff had not landed any of his 4.1-inch: or two British gunboats would suddenly have ended their journey.

Certainly, all confidential books had been left behind, and we have

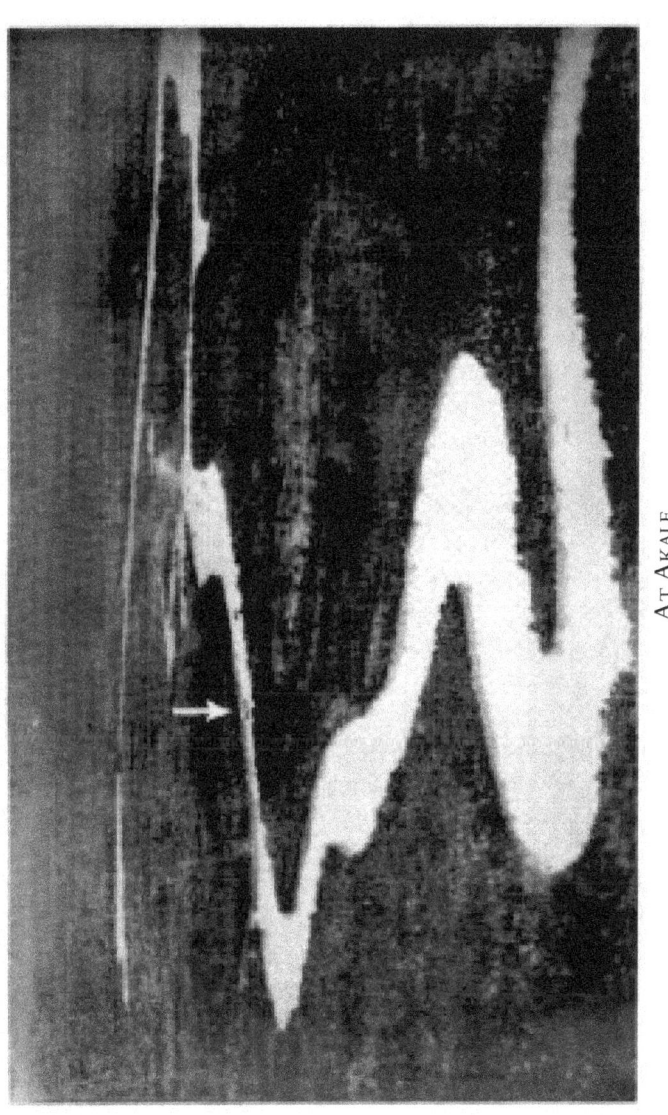

AT AKALE

This aerial photograph shows the sinuous reaches through which "Königsberg" forced herself to the final position up river. She will be noted some distance to the right in background, with white smoke issuing from her wood-fuelled furnaces. Here she was to fight and lose battle. To the left, marked by arrow, will be seen one of her small attendant vessels.

already noted the precautions for abandoning ship; but, even if the sinking of both units might cause some inconvenience against *Königsberg's* future exit, yet the monitors' failure at the end of much voyaging; the losses of personnel by death and capture; must have created a doleful effect on the British public just when things were not progressing too well in Europe.

Some of the enemy's shots spent themselves against the protective steel plating installed, and this undoubtedly saved anyone from being hit; indeed, the men of *Severn* and *Mersey* considered, rightly, that they had entered on their enterprise far more easily than might have been hoped. Hidden by the dense bush and mangroves, snipers could see without being seen, and monitors had no clear target; but one shot from the *Severn's* 4.7 caused a most satisfactory explosion on the port hand shore where two or three Germans were just about to launch a torpedo.

These missiles theoretically were a fine defence at the mouths, though actually disappointing to their owners. The difficulty was that muddy water used to get inside the torpedoes, which needed to be sent back for cleaning and recharging aboard *Königsberg* all too frequently; for, after being submerged in readiness, the mud would render delicate mechanism useless, although a man would stand up to his waist in the river when starting it off along the surface.

Good work that the first ship had blown this danger to bits! It might have been a terrible death-bringer on the monitors' return journey; yet these gunboats succeeded so well that unhindered they proceeded up river and at 6.23 let go anchor on the seaward side of Gengeni Island, the estimated distance from the hidden *Königsberg* being 10,800 yards. Koohl, however, in a private letter gave the line of flight as about 14,000 yards, which is more likely to be correct; for our chart was found most inaccurate, so that for a time our shells fell short.

The accompanying sketch, (references to July 11 will be explained on a later page), hitherto unpublished, was made by this officer and shows with great clarity how the battle-theatre looked through German eyes: it further supplies valuable details not previously explained. On the right we see the Kikunja as it widens out just before reaching the sea; to the SE of one small island, and over towards an island of greater length, was where *Severn* brought up, followed shortly by *Mersey*. The direction in which shots were to be fired over island and tree-tops at the invisible *Königsberg* is likewise indicated.

North of the smaller island is shown a creek running towards Pem-

(Top) Before the Rufiji Duel
Steel plates laid to protect H.M.S. "Severn's" decks.
(Bottom) After the Battle
Hole in H.M.S. "Mersey's" fore 6-inch gun-shield caused by one of "Königsberg's" 4.1-inch shells on July 6, 1915.

ba Hill, but at the eastern side of this inlet (where it empties into the Kikunja) is marked the important Nyamsati observation station containing pier, powder and munitions shed, the local officer's hut, and lookout posts. The direction in which the telephone was laid from Nyamsati will also be recognised. Now *Severn*, after reaching her selected berth, (*Severn's* position was on the channel's eastern side, *i.e.* slightly to the eastward of Gengeni Island's northern end), swung to port, let go stern anchor veering out 70 fathoms of wire, next let go bow anchor, then put engines astern and tautened up on both cables, being thus a fixed gun platform athwart stream. This necessarily took a little time, but at 6.48 (twenty-five minutes after arrival) she opened fire with her 6-inch guns at *Königsberg* which lay behind Kokotoni Island, whilst concealed snipers were endeavouring to pick off British sailors until monitors' machine-gunners kept down such interference.

As to the airmen, their synchronisation was excellent though they had to fly about thirty miles from aerodrome to Nyamsati. At 5.23 Flight-Lieut. H. E. Watkins went up from Mafia carrying six bombs, which were dropped about *Königsberg* in order to distract attention whilst monitors were getting into position; at 5.35 Flight-Commander J. T. Cull with Flight-Sublieutenant F. S. L. Arnold also rose up, overtook the monitors and by 6.17 signalled *Severn* that he was ready to begin spotting.

Admiral King-Hall had transferred his flag from *Hyacinth* to *Weymouth* since the latter drew less water; so, preceded by the whalers *Fly* and *Echo* (who were sweeping for any mines), accompanied also by the whaler *Childers* busy taking soundings, he was just crossing Kikunja bar when *Weymouth* got aground. This happened at 6.30, which is to say with not quite two hours of flood, and it will be remembered tides were Neaps: the incident was therefore scarcely surprising, but water quickly rose and a few minutes later enabled her to reach the river's entrance.

Having anchored, she quickly began at long range deluging Pemba Hill with shells. Though according to Diaz y Rodriguez, there were no hits on that Observation Headquarters, nor were any German guns there mounted: nevertheless, the din of exploding projectiles, the trembling of the earth around this station, and the expectation of being presently blown up, cannot have assisted telephone operators sending their messages through to Captain Looff. *Pyramus*, as shown in the sketch plan was able to get well inside the river, anchor likewise, and "give the entrenchments hell".

Such, then, was the sudden thunderclap which shocked the delta and astounded the enemy whether ashore or afloat; but before following the duel in detail, let us note how the dramatic instantaneity affected *Königsberg*'s crew. It is not difficult to imagine the feelings of her anxious commanding officer, this tropical morn, rudely roused to terrible actuality, nor to share something of his grave anxiety; for, to quote from another document written by one serving under him at the time, *Königsberg* was caught "as if she had been in a mouse trap". Day after day, week after week, she had been keeping steam up for hurried departure, yet that long period had now ended, and escape could not be contemplated. But in what manner did the awful reality touch those of the lower deck?

So frequently it happens throughout the world's naval history that we get from the diary of a sailor or petty officer a plain narrative, which is as clear and precise as altogether satisfying. Before me lies the diary written by Yeoman-of-Signals Greenshields, with the times and record of developments witnessed from *Severn's* fighting top: these hourly pencilled impressions are the very material out of which true history is fashioned, with the corroboration and enlargement from other eyewitnesses. But, most fortunately, his "opposite number" in *Königsberg* did not neglect to relate an honest account of the story as viewed from an opposing angle, and to that journal I now return.

This is how Signalman Ritter wrote concerning the first events of July 6:

> We were sitting, all of us, at the breakfast tables: the middle watch were still lying in their hammocks, when suddenly the cry rang out—"Clear ship for action!" The alarm gongs sounded, and in a second all were at their battle stations. I was signaller of the central in 1st Div. As so often before, we thought that today again it was only a practice: but this time it was real bloody earnest. Hardly were we at our stations, when our guns opened fire on—as I later learned—two airmen who were approaching the *Königsberg*. Shortly afterwards the signal arrived that monitors *Mersey* and *Severn* had run up the mouth.... The monitors went full steam ahead into the mouth, keeping both banks under a sharp machine-gun and rifle fire. They ran up the Kikunja arm, and anchored off Nyamsati. At the entry five guns directed their fire on the monitors. Naturally there was nothing to be seen (from *Königsberg*), as the boats are very flat and the

mangroves formed a screen. We were, therefore, compelled to fall back on indirect fire. As soon as the monitors had secured, they opened fire on the *Königsberg*.

That was at 7 o'clock, and simultaneously the nerves of one officer in Captain Looff's cruiser collapsed pathetically. The advent of hovering aeroplanes, the booming of cannon, the hopeless outlook at the end of so many "mouse-trap" months, may have combined to break down the last vestige of personal restraint. For now, did Lieut. Jaeger, whilst in his cabin, shoot himself with a service rifle. "There is much gossip over the reason for this." But he did not die immediately, and by a strange irony his life kept flickering for just so many hours as the engagement lasted. This officer belonged to the Naval Reserve, having come from Dar-es-Salaam, where he had served aboard one of the German East Africa Company's liners. Not unnaturally, such a tragedy on such a day, and at so critical an hour, made a deep impression throughout the ship; so that we find it repeatedly mentioned in subsequent letters.

Now *Severn* had been firing for just twelve minutes, her first salvo being reported by Cull as 200 yards short and to the left. Then the enemy began with two salvoes for ranging purposes, which fell 500 yards short. But thereafter four, and sometimes all five, starboard guns set to work with such marvellous accuracy as to elicit admiration from the British naval and flying officers. Both monitors were continuously straddled, shells dropping only fifteen yards short or over, and some of them in exact fore-and-aft line but needing slight deflection. Greenshields noted from his vantage-position:

> She was firing four salvoes to our one, and they were whistling over us, falling just short and into the banks, throwing up mud with bushes into the air.

To the aviators it seemed impossible that monitors still floated, and the splashes were so crowded as often to obliterate the gunboats from sight. Somehow the latter's gunnery now became very wild, shells falling on the land and difficult to spot. At 7.40 *Mersey*, who was moored about 400 yards astern (WNW) of *Severn*, (see sketch-plan), had been struck twice, one shell penetrating (illustrated in accompanying photograph), the fore 6-inch gun shield (made of 2-inch hardened steel) on its port side, knocking out the gun itself, killing four men, wounding four others, capsizing flat the rest of the gun's crew, besides setting fire to a couple of cordite charges. Another shot hit *Mersey's* motorboat lying alongside and sank it, but unquestionably this wooden craft saved her mother from foundering, though the steel ship had been holed below waterline.

So now she must fire with her stern 6-inch, move ammunition aft from forward, and Captain Fullerton ordered her to weigh anchor in order that she might shift her position. Thus, do we perceive the benefit of all that previous rehearsing off Mafia Island. Anchors were smartly hoisted, but only just in time: and *Mersey* had hardly quitted her berth than another German salvo pitched in the exact spot previously occupied. Captain Fullerton now became extremely busy during half an hour of vital consequence. At 7.51 *Severn* made her first hit on *Königsberg*, and for a period of twenty minutes Cull's observer reported that British shells were either hitting or just missing. Keen aerial spotting at last had enabled the target to be found.

In those times it was impossible to confirm that the enemy had been struck, though clouds of smoke rose as if from a serious conflagration, and the cruiser's mastheads became visible. Today, however, we know that the supposition was by no means exaggerated. From Ritter we learn that *Severn's* first successful shell penetrated the officers' galley and killed one of the crew; that a second projectile struck the upper deck, bringing death to a couple of sailors, of whom (says Koohl) one had joined from *Zieten*, and the other from *Khalifa*. Very gallantly did this leading seaman from Diaz y Rodriguez's old ship conduct himself: covered with blood, and ignoring his wounds, he insisted on chanting three verses of a patriotic song, then gave a final cheer of independence, collapsed, and so died.

It was a splinter from this same shell which tore the foot off Lieut. Wenig standing alongside Ritter, who promptly carried his officer below to an ambulance station; but a third shot, striking the signal-bridge, wiped out one more seaman.

With no little relief did Captain Fullerton, when he had a spare second, glance round at just after 8 o'clock to find *Mersey* still afloat. She had anchored some 500 yards downstream, off the opposite shore, but about 9 o'clock *Severn* was being so persistently straddled that it was only a matter of minutes ere she too would be hit, wherefore Captain Fullerton likewise moved her across under the western bank; and the wisdom of this decision immediately manifested itself. For barely had the monitor shifted than one of her officers (Lieut. T. W. T. Lewis R.N.R.) perceived only half a mile away on the smaller island which lay in midchannel, a party of four men up a tree that also partially concealed a platform: obviously a spotting station under a petty officer working in conjunction with Nyamsati and Pemba. But some 3-pdr. and 6-inch lyddite shells soon settled that menace.

Whether the loss of these well-placed German watchers did or did not wholly affect the future can be disputed, for aboard *Königsberg* not much trust was placed in petty officers' reports as to the fall of shells: on the contrary great reliance was made on the messages telephoned from the spotting lieutenant on Pemba Hill, where the best glasses were used to note 'shorts' or 'overs'. But I find it definitely admitted by German testimony that Pemba lookouts could no longer observe monitors after the latter had changed position to anchor under the Nyamsati shore: consequently, Captain Looff's officer aboard in-charge of the cruiser's gunnery control could not now learn how his missiles were descending.

Further evidence from both Koohl and Ritter brings out the interesting fact that the somewhat complicated system of sending signals by telephone wire and visual flags was not a success, the distance being so great and the communication so interrupted that loss of time (with corresponding inaccuracy) resulted: in other words, by the moment reports of the shells reached *Königsberg* these messages were out of date. British gunnery disabled the enemy's wireless, but after a while a party rigged up ashore the radio installation which had been captured from the S.S. *City of Winchester*. On the other hand, our opponents were greatly impressed by the persistence of British aviators. Ritter says:

> They were fired on with shrapnel on various occasions, but without success.

One thing is very certain: whereas from 7 till 9.15 a.m. *Königsberg's* gunners had been firing an average of six salvoes every minute, and merely the element of bad luck had prevented the monitors' annihilation; yet from the time when the latter altered anchorage, German firing right till the end was (to quote Captain Fullerton) "distinctly less, and not so accurate".

Severn having moored some 200 yards to the north and east of her sister, resumed the onslaught at 9.50, the range being now increased to what was thought 11,300 yards. Yet the monitors' gunnery no longer was effective, for at 8.40 Cull's aeroplane had gone back to Mafia in order to refuel and the sky was empty. (On alighting at the aerodrome with scarcely any petrol, one bullet-hole was found in the upper plane, which sufficiently indicates a pretty narrow escape.) This made it impossible to correct fall of shot accurately, and thus the contest resolved itself into that of blind men's thrusts.

****

The following record shows how, in that primitive period of aviation, its utility was being used so far as practicable. From 5.25 to 6.47 a.m. Flight-Lieut. Watkins was doing his bombing trip; from 5.40 till 8.40 Flight-Commander Cull with Sub-Lieut. Arnold was spotting, this period being overlapped by Flight-Lieut. Blackburn and Assistant-Paymaster *Badger* also spotting from 7.37 to 10.17. Major Gordon and Sub-Lieut. Arnold were also spotting from 9.30 until 12.5. Then, however, followed that hiatus which continued till after Flight-Lieut. Watkins with Assistant-Paymaster *Badger* took the sky from 11.17 till 1.2 p.m., when they had to return because of engine trouble. Flight-Commander Cull with Sub-Lieut. Arnold were again aloft spotting from 1.15 to 3.50; as were Flight-Lieut. Blackburn and Assistant-Paymaster *Badger* from 2.48 to 3.59. This made a total of more than 15 flying hours including the passage from Mafia to and from the *Königsberg* scene.

****

Presently *Severn* and *Mersey* weighed, but at 1.30 after a bumpy passage Cull's aeroplane once more arrived and resumed her wireless signalling.

Then occurred an alarming incident—the very sort of thing that had been guarded against as likely to bring disaster. *Severn* was making for her original position off Gengeni Island to anchor again, tide was now ebbing, man in the chains sounding, ship getting near the bank; when six feet were suddenly reported, and without further warning the monitor stopped dead. Ashore on a falling tide, and opposite the enemy's lookouts! Those were terribly anxious minutes for her captain, yet with such an unhandy vessel was it surprising that she could not be turned sharp round against stream?

The minutes ticked by, engines were reversed, and with the aid of her stern anchor she fortunately floated off just in time. At 10,800 yards she was again firing over the forest, a second aircraft had begun spotting, yet monitors had to endure inefficient signalling though different in kind from that of the German stations. Two shots this afternoon seemed from the air to reach *Königsberg*, and nowadays we can assert that one definitely was a most useful blow. Ritter says the shell pierced the German hull underneath waterline, tearing a hole in a fore-and-aft bunker of the stokehold, which gradually filled with water, and the water-tight door had to be shored up.

That made a total of four hits: the other three being twice on the upper-deck and once on the signal bridge. During seven hours the cruiser was in a state of conflagration and, whatever might henceforth happen, no impartial person could pretend that Captain Looff's vessel was fit for cruising. The hole might be temporarily patched-up, although never could she venture far, until some dock might receive her. Thus, again do we realise the supreme necessity of warships having within reach the facilities of a well-equipped base. Alas for *Königsberg* that the Dar-es-Salaam floating dock was not for her available!

Nevertheless, Captain Fullerton in the absence of full knowledge, did not feel too optimistic as to results. Both *Severn* and *Mersey* had suffered from wireless confusion, and an incomplete system of spotting. Moreover, during this afternoon, the guns had become very hot and were getting worn. As to the men, they had been at the peak of their endeavour since 3.45 a.m. It was accordingly time to pack up, the ebb was racing down seawards, so exactly at 3.45 p.m. both monitors weighed and made towards the mouth, *Severn* having to leave one anchor behind.

And the river defences?

As the two gunboats with full speed hurried along, they opened a terrific fire against both banks of the entrance in reply to the enemy, whose field guns at Msungu were so well aimed that shells came uncomfortably close, one flopping only fifteen yards beyond *Severn* whilst another actually carried away a 10-ft. sounding boom on *Mersey's* starboard side. But the German gun-layer on this northwestern shore was an expert at his work, and received such high commendation for his efforts against the monitors, that he won promotion to a bigger gun at Tanga, his successor being less gifted.

By 4.30 p.m. the gauntlet had been rushed a second time, and the river left astern, where tugs and the bombarding squadron awaited the adventurers. It was a moving scene as sympathetic crews manned rigging and cheered, till they were hoarse, men weary and nerve-tried. Aboard *Severn*, lent to her for the day, was one who had served in the *Pegasus*, and with joyful satisfaction he now shouted, "We've got some of our own back".

"What is the final result of today's operations?", the admiral wished to know. And Captain Fullerton with justification answered that whilst *Königsberg* had not been totally destroyed, she must have become too damaged to come out again "this war".

We have seen the casualties aboard *Mersey*, and two of the wounded died. Captain Looff, however, had lost four men killed, and thirty-five wounded. That evening he solemnly addressed his ship's company, said a few prayers over the dead, whose bodies with the injured were sent up river in a paddle-steamer to Neu Streten. It would be hard to say which survivors were the more fatigued—British or German—following such an arduous day. When once secured alongside *Trent*, the monitors' crew ate their supper and then turned in to a deep sleep before a moderately busy morrow.

The *Königsberg's* men, who had existed on sausages and biscuits during the fight, were allowed little enough rest. Captain Looff, knowing well the British character, assured himself that the monitors would certainly return, and most likely next morning: the job would not be left unfinished. But the Germans equally would strive till the end. So on the night of July 6, they all worked feverishly getting rid of paint and everything combustible. Secret papers were carried ashore, and even a spare propeller was laid in the earth after a pit had been dug. Next day the men toiled for twelve hours from 7 a.m., for when the flood tide brought with it no renewal of attack, one lot of men were put on to try repairing ship's damage as best they could; others began improving the telephone system from Pemba, carrying the wires direct on board; torpedoes were got ready in case monitors should nose their way round the corner of Kokotoni Island to shorter range; whilst on land, marks were erected as aiming-posts for more accurate gunnery.

And, all this being done, they waited for the next development.

CHAPTER 15

The Result

A biplane, having been sent up on July 7 came back with news that though *Königsberg* had received damage aft, amidships, and elsewhere, she still very much existed; which, of course signified that the monitors had yet to finish their task. It would be requiring a great deal of them to repeat their performance, even under probably more difficult conditions, but unquestionably the enemy had to be wiped off the chart.

Admiral King-Hall decided that this second attack should be made generally on the previous principles, but in order to prevent wireless confusion and let it be quite clear for whom the aeroplane's spotting message was meant, monitors were to fire in turn—one at a time—changing over each fifteen minutes.

Lest the enemy should be warned of their coming, the intended day was kept secret until a few hours before. All the same, when crews saw an iron-cask brought aboard *Severn* to be fixed at the masthead for the gunnery lieutenant's better observation; and the ship went out to calibrate guns with a *dhow* as target; everyone rightly guessed that they would soon be smelling the Rufiji swamps and perspiring in the river heat once more.

On Saturday afternoon all tables, beds, woodwork, were bundled into *Trent* again and the monitors became little else than mobile steel boxes. Captain Fullerton lectured his men on Tuesday's results, told them that the Admiralty's orders demanded that destroyed she must be; so that if the duty could not be performed at the original range, monitors would have to advance closer and closer.

Frankly the crews were not looking forward with much enthusiasm to this almost hand-to-hand tricky warfare. Remarked one of them, "It is not like tackling a ship at sea. One never knows where a gun or torpedo might be placed on the banks." But that attitude was perfectly natural, and shared by the other side. Koohl hated it even more, and his spirit loathed this confined fighting, he complained:

> If it was a question of hurling happy infantry against happy infantry, then one could see who is the better man: but against bombardment from a ship one is so hopeless.

Late on Saturday monitors received orders suddenly for the morrow. There was a universal feeling that this new Kikunja jaunt would be even less of a picnic than previously, and commanding officers had been instructed not to hesitate blowing up their ships if the latter should begin to sink. On Tuesday *Mersey* had been lucky to lose so few men, and *Severn* was miraculously fortunate to have escaped any casualties at all. But would such favours be vouchsafed on Sunday, July 11? And in this mood the ships' companies laid themselves down on deck to snatch a few hours' rest, their hammocks being in place round the guns as protection against those rifle bullets which the shore stations would doubtless spit forth.

It was arranged that in each monitor the navigating lieutenant should be in the conning-tower, gunnery lieutenant in the foretop, one lieutenant in charge of the forward 6-inch gun, and a sub-lieutenant at the after 6-inch; also, that ships should anchor head and stern as before, to enable both guns to bear. The position would then be plotted on the chart, range and magnetic bearing of the enemy next obtained.

Sunday's tide-times were a little awkward, High Water being at 3 a.m. and 3.21 p.m., which meant that the flood would not make into the river till just before 9.30 a.m. so the possibility of using darkness as a cloak was out of the question, and a hot time might be assured for all on gaining the river mouth. The commander-in-chief flew his flag for the time being in *Weymouth* and by means of her radio might maintain touch with the monitors, but if the latter's installation should be shot away, communication would be made by sending up river that fast motorboat *Talawa* which we last saw being put aboard when the expedition left the Medway. For her there might perchance be some exciting moments pacing past the entrenchments.

After a good breakfast all hands were ready, and shoved off from *Trent* at 7.30 a.m., the tug *Blackcock* picking up *Severn*, and *Revenger* towing *Mersey*. Soon after 10.30 hawsers were slipped, and a course laid for Kikunja mouth which was being approached an hour later. Oh yes! That expert German behind the field gun on the northwest shore had not yet gone to Tanga: he and his mates were pronouncedly vigorous as ever, three successive salvoes falling respectively only 20 yards short, 40 yards over, and 30 yards short of *Severn*, though they got *Mersey* on the starboard quarter, wounding a couple of men. Both monitors however barked back so fiercely as to overawe the enemy into silence, whilst machine-guns soon put to flight snipers. Lest this statement may seem excessive, we may quote Koohl's reaction, since his station was on the northwest side.

He wrote only two days later:

> It is a wonder, that today, after the two bombardments, I am still alive. The first on 6th July was very sharp and damaging, but child's play compared with the second on 11th July, one Sunday. ...I can only tell you now that the 11th July was an experience of hell, and the dispiriting effect is so great as to make one ill to think of it, trying with two or three men and rifles to stand up against such a bombardment, knowing one can do nothing.

As they advanced, the monitors were surprised to see a ship's boat being rowed across river from east to west, but, when the oncoming British warriors suddenly showed up, something like panic seized these oarsmen. One look was enough, they pulled for salvation to the nearest bit of bank, hastened on their way by *Severn's* shells, then leapt ashore and disappeared from destruction among the bushes. Not till long after was this mysterious matter explained.

At first glance she might have been a man-of-war's cutter sent down river on some hostile mission such as mine-laying, or running an obstruction across. Today we can say that she was a British-built boat, originally belonging to the S.S. *Newbridge* whose role as a blockship was noted in an earlier chapter. The Germans had removed this lifeboat from the collier's davits, expended a lot of trouble fitting her with mast and sails, after which she performed most useful service bringing stores to the troops at this river's mouth. Today she was loaded full of such provisions, when her crew so narrowly cheated death.

It was part of today's plan that in order to give *Severn* a free opportunity, unmolested, for attacking *Königsberg*, Commander Wilson should so manoeuvre *Mersey* as to invite Captain Looff's attention. Wherefore, having arrived off Nyamsati, (see previously mentioned sketch-plan), the two monitors separated; *Severn* carrying on up the starboard channel another 1,000 yards and there mooring, whilst *Mersey* let go in much the same position as last time. But *Königsberg* declined so to be tempted, and at 12.12 started getting the range with two guns, five minutes later firing 4-gun salvoes once every sixty seconds, straddling Captain Fullerton's ship as the first anchor was being let go. This became one of the most critical, though brief, periods of the whole adventure, indeed (viewed from *Severn*'s foretop) it looked like a race between the latter's gun-layers and receiving the first German shells; but here came the advantage of much rehearsing and cooperative smartness.

By 12.25 *Severn* had finished mooring bow and stern, three minutes later her spotting aeroplane (with Cull and Arnold) arrived, and at 12.32 this monitor opened fire, guns having been laid in the record time of seven minutes, which was five minutes quicker than had been done in practice. Anxiously she awaited the result, but the aeroplane wirelessed:"Did not see fall of shot." A great duel of wits now ensued, a fast fight for life and victory between rivals separated from mutual sight by the intervening mangroves of Kikunja. *Severn* now lowered range but was still firing over, and then immediately *Königsberg* sent shells which fell just short. Which of the two would reach the target first?

You can imagine the suspense, the eagerness of swift workers, the slamming of breech-blocks, the short sharp orders the breath-taking excitement during such an amazing contest. Far from all but a handful of spectators, not even witnessed by the Admiral, this was one of the finest shows in maritime history, and the drill more rapid than naval tournament could ever provide. Any football crowd would have waxed hysterical over this competition, yet not one head ashore dared show itself.

"Down 400!"

The British seamen fired again, but the aviator signalled: "Sixth salvo 100 yards over and a little to the right." At this moment, however, the enemy got in a perfect salvo, one shell missing *Severn's* quarter-deck by three yards, scattering steel fragments aboard yet without damaging one person. Another marvel of luck! Could it last?

Then something remarkable happened, something that brought incredible joy.

The seventh British salvo had been too far left, but the eighth at 12.39 was an unmistakable hit. "HT" the aeroplane kept reporting persistently, so that during the next ten minutes seven more hits were made. The climax had been well passed, the battle had turned determinedly in favour of the British, but the enemy projectiles still fell short and over. That was the position at 12.48, and no praise could too generously be offered the aviators for their accurate and exposed work: without such aid, monitors' endeavours could barely have attained success. Yet, at 12.49 the flying men were in difficulties and had become themselves a target. "We are hit. Send a boat".

No mistaking that message, though how unfortunate anything should go wrong just at this stage! Either rifle fire or more probably the bursting of German shrapnel, had slowed down the engine which now stopped dead. Cull had been a naval officer ere he took to flying, and he was ever cool in peril, gallant in a crisis. He glided in the direction of *Mersey*, and on the descent his observer (Arnold) with equal imperturbation wirelessed no less than three valuable spotting corrections which enabled our guns to be brought slightly left, thus hammering the enemy right amidships instead of forward. "You are hitting beautifully forward. Train a little left."

So, the three salvoes, which followed, settled *Königsberg's* fate for all time. At 1.16 terrible explosion occurred aboard her, with dense smoke, and then other eruptions of a similar nature. From the *Severn* it seemed like unto an earthquake, flames shot up, the smoke took on the shape of a mushroom-cloud rising twice the height of the tall trees, or not less than 200 feet. Meanwhile, just missing the mangroves as he had also avoided falling in the enemy's direction, Cull brought his machine slowly with no little skill to the water, where it promptly insisted on capsizing.

Such a possibility had long since been thought out, and the *Mersey's* people made a smart rescue evolution. Within two minutes her motorboat was off, and half an hour had barely elapsed before she had rushed to the scene, picked up both officers, brought them back on board without giving the crocodiles one chance. Presently the boat returned and blew up the wreckage with gun-cotton.

At half-past one Captain Looff's ship having been silenced, *Mersey* was ordered to weigh and move closer, for the instructions were that *Königsberg* should be destroyed. Just as Commander Wilson got about 7,000 yards off the latter a second aeroplane arrived, so the monitor began firing at once, loosing off 28 salvoes (securing a hit the first shot) until 2.40. Now in this movement up river a very interesting bit of information was obtained, for *Mersey* crept along through the narrow channel close under the northern shore finding 14 feet, which presently deepened to 36 feet when clear of the bank formed off Pemba Creek. But just before reaching the assigned (7,000 yards)

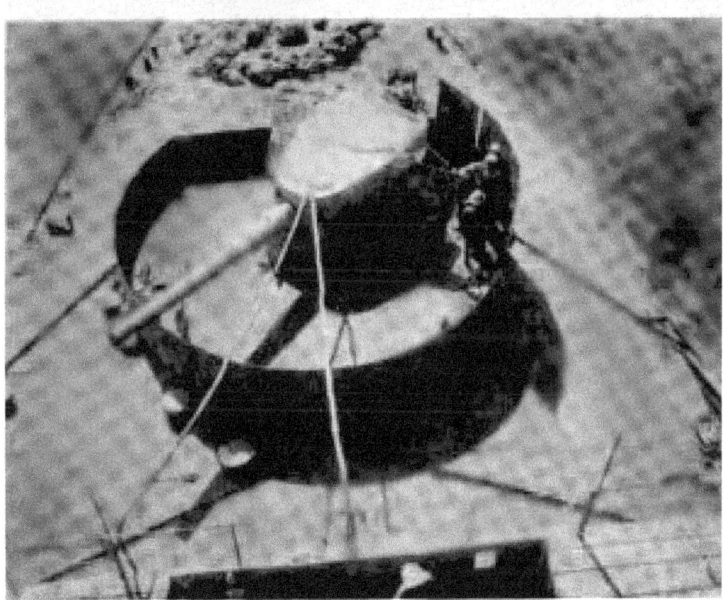

(Top) Fighting Top in H.M.S. "Severn"
During the engagement of July 11, 1915.
(Bottom) H.M.S. "Severn's" Fore 6-inch Gun
In action July 11, 1915. Note sandbags protecting capstan.

position, the water was seen to shoal, soundings of only 8 feet were discovered, so she put her helm over and anchored.

Eight feet! The tide within an hour of High Water! And Springs! Surely Captain Looff, needing 17½ feet, could never have brought his ship out by the Kikunja after all?

Whilst *Mersey* was on the move, Captain Fullerton went to the topmast-head of *Severn* and saw the impressive picture of *Königsberg* fiercely burning throughout her length, the hollow steel after-mast smoking like a factory chimney (due to wind fanning the conflagration from below), the foremast leaning over; but volumes of smoke hid from sight the gap which had been caused when her middle funnel disappeared. That assuredly looked like the end, the fulfilment of orders, the completion of their mission: so now *Severn's* commanding officer could wireless his admiral outside that the target was destroyed; nor was there much use in steaming further up river, risking such likely traps as mines or underwater obstructions.

At 2.30 came the commander-in-chief's reply, ordering both monitors to retire. Ten minutes later *Severn* weighed just as the tide was easing and, whilst she waited for *Mersey* to follow, amused herself knocking down with 6-inch shells some of the poles that bore those telephone wites. Then, proceeding at half speed against the last strength of flood, the triumphant monitors had to look out lest German attentions should at the ultimate stage negative today's success.

All the way down, the two gunboats blazed away at everything which might be hiding an opponent, flattening the vegetation of each bank, receiving for answer a few shots from creeks or through the trees, but no serious opposition until abreast the expert gunner at the entrance's northwest shore. Was he ready for the final bit of hate? Would he even now send along a lucky shot to crash through decks?

Severn steamed through the defile untouched, and somehow those field guns seemed to direct their missiles not quite so uncomfortably close this time. Perhaps this was because H.M.S. *Pyramus*, profiting by the state of High Water, had come inside and fairly deluged both shores, yet the unfortunate *Mersey* once again received a blow on her quarter-deck though without more damage.

It was now 3.55, ships were out of the river, and firing ceased with a few parting shells that fell short of the invaders; then with the young ebb making and engines full speed ahead, fatigued men could relax, wipe the sweat off their brows, and congratulate themselves on a good day's work. If a few hours ago they had been dutiful and determined, rather than afire with unmodified enthusiasm, this afternoon had roused their emotions to fresh heights. "The luckiest ships afloat", was how the crews now spoke of their habitation, and they knew that presently when the great news began to be cabled round the world, *Severn* and *Mersey* people would be the envy of thousands.

But *Weymouth* came forth flying more than her ensign and admiral's flag: she had just hoisted a few bits of bunting which meant a very great deal to every officer and man.

"Well done monitors," the signal read, and now the flagship steamed round the victors in welcome, white-clad sailors rending the drowsy air with wild cheers, and the *Severn* arraying herself with every White Ensign in the ship. It was one of those moments which belong only to conquerors and would be remembered long after the war; to be pondered over by men and officers alike when the navy might cease to have further demands on them, and greying figures by the fireside would tell out these episodes for the younger generation.

So here came the tugs to pass their tow ropes, and before 8 p.m. the monitors were secured alongside *Trent*. Then supper, and wearied bodies turned in to relish that unrivalled, all-satisfying sleep which makes toil so worthwhile. But among all the happy messages which began to arrive for the monitors none was more appreciated than that from "The captain, officers and ship's company of H.M.S. *Humber*. . . proud to have been associated with them during the first nine months of the war."

So far have we seen one side of the picture, and this memorable July 11 becomes yet more interesting as we piece together the broken bits of historical mosaic. *Severn*, no less than *Mersey*, had been perilously near to disaster. The effect of German salvoes bursting under water, in close proximity (sometimes only 10 feet distant) had so badly shaken the former that when presently she was put on Zanzibar spit for examination several holes allowed big spurts of sea to leak through. Again, and again have we stressed the frailty of these hulls, and we can never cease to marvel that they withstood so much battering by open seas as well as exploding shells: yet the greatest risk of all will shortly be related. Let us, then, begin imagining ourselves aboard *Königsberg* at a time when the Kikunja watchers by the coast, noted outside the assembling of British men-of-war.

Four suspenseful days had come and gone, but now a message was telephoned up to Captain Looff from the delta that most likely a second attack was about to be made. Hands in the cruiser were therefore sent to their mid-day meal an hour earlier. Ritter says that today, after anchoring under the mangroves "the monitors shot with bewildering rapidity and accuracy. Salvo after salvo crashed into the ship forward. . . . . As in the last fight, I was in X Division forward", and a couple of stokers fell wounded. "One I carried down to the dressing-station in II Division, near the refrigerator: the other dragged himself off alone to the steering-room. Soon after this I was wounded myself and, having been attended to, went to the Deck Officers' mess—as the steering-room was full—to get bandaged." Suddenly the cry rang out, "All hands abandon ship."

Thus, within fifteen minutes of *Severn* having moored, *Königsberg's* crew began to realise that a German victory was impossible. Another letter says that during this first half hour *Königsberg* was hit twenty-four times. From Diaz y Rodriguez we can, however, quite understand why the enemy gunnery was so excellent at first, yet kept on just missing. It appears that an observation officer had hidden his body in a tub buried in the mud less than 30 yards from *Severn*. Only his head kept showing, but with telephone to his mouth he lost no time sending Looff valuable information whilst Captain Fullerton was in the process of mooring. Thus did *Königsberg* quickly get almost on to the target: but the spotting failed to improve because one of *Severn's* initial salvoes severed the wire, and communication promptly ended.

Ritter, whose statement as to "Abandon ship" is confirmed in the previously mentioned letter, goes on to describe this disembarkation in some detail, but the most impressive facts are: (1) that less than half an hour was needed to conquer *Königsberg*, and (2) the abandonment was accompanied by panic: it would be indeed difficult, with such evidence before us, to assert that perfect discipline was maintained till the end. Rather does it become certain that the cumulative effect of all these months, and the last five days' anxiety, had been to break down morale.

> I got up on deck as soon as possible, and, as there was no boat, together with Petty Officer Jacobs sprang overboard and swam ashore. While I was attempting to scale the steep bank, a shell exploded so near to me that it filled my ears with mud.

He then goes on to complain bitterly of one officer who:

> . . . behaved abominably, as he pushed any of the crew, who stood in his way, into the water. . . . I saw many, however, who only worried about their own safety, and paid no heed to the

wounded. After we had abandoned ship, the First Officer and Leading Seaman Huber went down into the torpedo room, put detonators under three torpedoes and, as soon as they themselves had left the ship, blew up the *Königsberg*.

Ritter definitely avers that when this took place there were still some people in the ship, including a number of wounded who had not received the abandonment order; but they got away about two hours later. Captain Looff was wounded in the stomach. He, together with Ritter and other casualties, was taken further up river by paddle-steamer to the field hospital at Neu Streten, but two months later was recovered.

And the unsuspected peril to *Severn*?

Well, the reader may not have forgotten the steam launch *Wami* with her torpedo-dropping gear, or that maze of interconnecting channels joining the various delta branches. When Captain Looff on July 11 learned of the monitors' approach, he decided to carry out a daring plan by sending *Wami* a little way southeast (*i.e.* astern of *Königsberg*), and then by turning to port she was to use a channel parallel with the Kikunja till past Kokotoni Island. By again turning sharply to port she could emerge at Gengeni Island suddenly, and torpedo the monitors unawares. It was a clever idea, and might have succeeded, but the launch managed to get aground about 12.30. Not to be thwarted, *Königsberg* then despatched a steam pinnace similarly armed, and she worked her way through, reached the spot assigned, only to discover the Nyamsati vicinity empty. The monitors had departed fifteen minutes ago.

Although *Severn's* losses today again had been nil, and *Mersey* had only three wounded, *Königsberg* suffered ten times that number by death, but all her 125 wounded did finally recover. The hurried finale was doubtless caused partly by Looff's injuries, but, after breech-blocks of the guns had been hurriedly thrown overboard, most of the crew were marched fourteen miles southwest to Kilindi, where they formed a camp; from there, however, some returned the same evening to their old ship and began salving. So also those divers, who had been sent weeks previously to work on the *Kronborg*, were ordered back from Mansa Bay for the duty of getting out *Königsberg's* remaining shells, and the breech-blocks were also recovered.

Not one of her 4.1-inch guns had been seriously damaged: they had all ceased firing only because the gun-crews had been slain. These ten valuable weapons were now brought ashore, put into waggons, five of them being thus hauled by 200 natives to each waggon as far as Dar-es-Salaam, but two more were sent on to Tanga, whilst one reached Lake Victoria Nyanza, and two went to Lake Tanganyika. As to the *Königsberg's* survivors, they were within two days turned into soldiers; given reduced pay, a rifle, side-arms, and became known as the "*Königsberg* Detachment" of the Defence Force. Under the cruiser's First Officer, Lieut.-Commander Koch, they set out on July 30 and four days later reached Dar-es-Salaam.

Of the excellent service, which these naval guns subsequently rendered in different parts of East Africa with the German against the British Army, this book is not concerned; but more than one British military officer has told me of his own personal experience, and in particular one relates how his 4-inch weapon in the neighbourhood of Lindi was almost daily having a duel with a *Königsberg* 4.1-inch until the enemy's ammunition gave out.

Criticisms have been made that, after all, the *Königsberg* never was destroyed; and in its most literal sense this is quite true. On August 5 Flight-Commander Cull again flew over it, to find she was lying mortally maimed with a list of 15° to starboard so that the water on this side was over the battery, and her quarter-deck after being completely submerged every High Water had become red with rust. Her middle funnel lay athwart the hull, topmasts were gone, but the worst damage was hid from the sky; for when Captain Looff had ordered the torpedo to be fired, this broke the ship in half.

Thus, in addition to the damage of July 5, the hull had been ruined for all time, and you can imagine the engines' condition after a couple of tides and deposits of mud. In so far as steel survived, she was not destroyed but she was most certainly conquered if words have any meaning at all. Admittedly the enemy showed no little enterprise in salving guns, and British soldiers have since commented on the fact that this was permitted by Admiral King-Hall.

On the other hand, a similar professional jealousy between the two services existed amongst our enemies. It was General's chief staff officer who thought very little of what the German Navy performed in East Africa, (von Lettow-Vorbeck was Commander-in-Chief of the German land forces in East Africa at the time), and he had no sympathy with Looff's policy of allowing *Königsberg* to withdraw up the Rufiji. "Its speed and armament ... would have caused more damage" to the British and have been of more help to the German Army "than were its crew and armament acting with their land forces."

But the monitors needed structural attention after their experiences, and news came from Zanzibar that a sixth man belonging to *Mersey* had died in hospital from wounds. Extra shipwrights went aboard to help in restoring both gunboats to their former condition; getting rid of the sandbags, iron-plates, kerosene tins, and so on, filling up with stores from *Trent*. Then, leaving behind only a couple of small units to keep watch over the delta, *Severn* with *Mersey* towed by the tugs went off northwards for Zanzibar, where *Pegasus* still showed at Low Water portions of her sad wreckage.

Severn's foremost bulkhead, having been knocked out of position by her own 6-inch gun-fire, needed the help of dockyard men who came aboard whilst the crew busied themselves with paint and brushes over the side, making her look smart and grey once more instead of an imitation mangrove scene. There were plenty of defects to be remedied, for monitors could not be released from the coast just yet a while; but the joy of at last being allowed shore leave, of picnicking and playing games away from sight of the ship and miles from the hated Rufiji district, was most invigorating. When however, divers went down to examine *Severn's* bottom, they discovered a large dent on the starboard side below water forward (where enemy shell had exploded so closely that it felt like a hit), and it was noticed that several rivets were missing, thereby causing leaks.

So, the flat-bottomed monitor one day was taken over to a convenient level spit, allowed to dry out; and this afforded an overdue opportunity for scraping a hull already made foul by tropical waters. Many other dents—under the stern and round the quarter where another shell had burst—now revealed themselves and had to receive attention. All this meant inevitable delay, but just when the Zanzibar scene had begun to spell monotony, a healthy breeze of excitement blew through the ship. *Severn* was off to sea in the morning on another "stunt", though *Mersey* would remain behind.

What sort of experience would it be, this time?

DASH INTO TANGA, AUGUST 19, 1915
(Top) German S.S. "Markgraf". Photograph taken from H.M.S. "Pickle" at 7.37 a.m. The German battery ashore was almost in line with "Markgraf's" port quarter.
(Bottom) German S.S. "Markgraf" burning furiously after eight minutes' rapid independent shelling by H.M.S. "Severn".

CHAPTER 16

Dash Into Tanga

The Blockade caused by *Königsberg* had lasted 255 expensive days from October 30 to July 11, tying down 27 ships and causing the consumption of 38,000 tons of coal; which can remind naval students that just one light cruiser worth originally £270,008 could cost her enemies £275 a day in watching. Two years later, long after Captain Fullerton, Commander Wilson, Flight-Commander Cull, and Flight-Lieut. Arnold had each been awarded the D.S.O., the matter of *Königsberg's* defeat came up before Sir Samuel Evans, President of the Prize Court; and this was the first time in history that prize bounty was claimed by aeroplanes, the sum of £1,920 being divided not only between officers and ships' companies belonging to the two monitors but also among the aircraft.

It was for the Admiralty a great relief that some of the more valuable vessels could be spared now that Captain Looff's ship had been knocked out, but this by no means ended operations off the coast. The Germans were resourceful, their army out here would need succour from outside—any day perhaps a second *Kronborg* might try rushing munitions ashore—and it was essential that the British Navy should retain command of the sea; even if by reason of the local geography, unhealthiness of the swampy coastal belt, and the difficulty of combined naval-military manoeuvres, actual invasion might be impossible.

On the other hand, there were special and particular activities which small men-of-war could directly perform, and one interesting result had been obtained whilst the monitors refitted at Zanzibar. The reader will remember that in an earlier chapter we saw that as a result of H.M.S. *Chatham* having on October 19, 1914 sent her steamboat inside Lindi and some distance along the Lukuledi Creek, Commander Fitzmaurice had been able to go aboard the German S.S. *Präsident* there to discover documents proving that *Königsberg* was up the Rufiji.

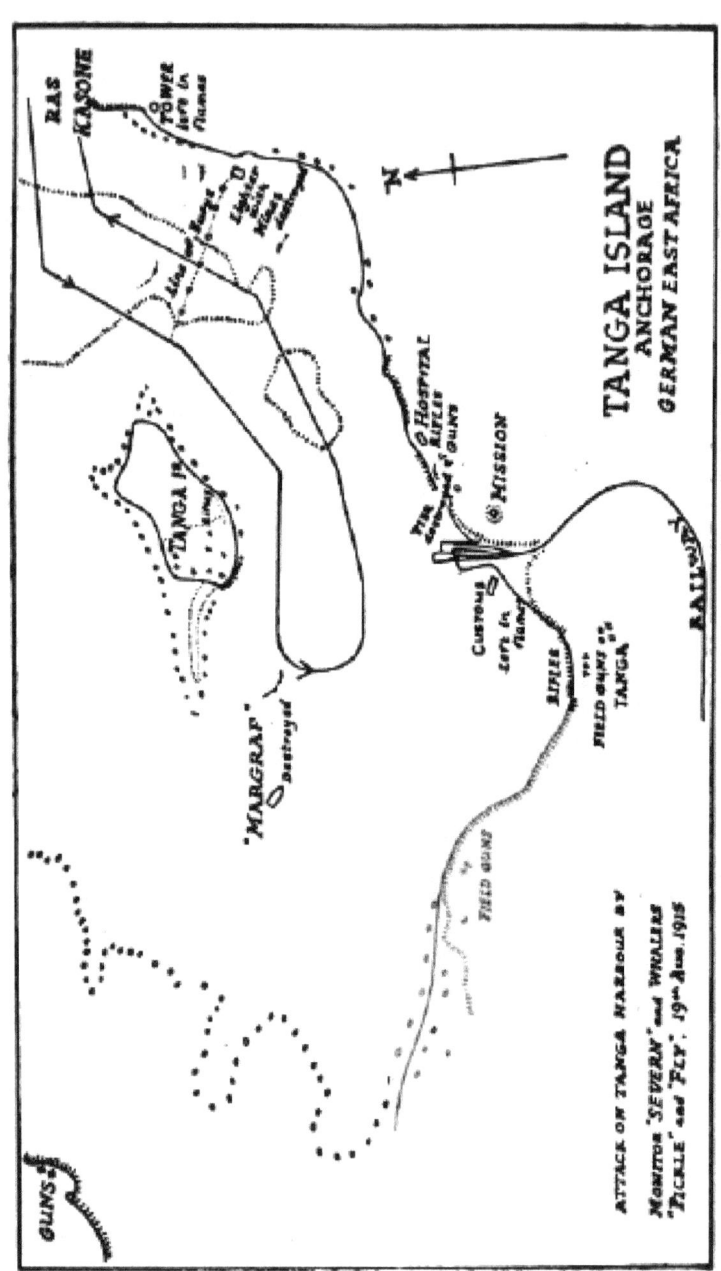

Now nine months later it became known that the former had no intention of suffering the latter's fate, but was about to make her escape. First of all, she would need to fill up with fuel (having sent her coal to Captain Looff), so on July 26 by taking advantage of spring tides she was moved right up Lukuledi Creek, anchors were let go ahead, and wires attached to either bank whence she proceeded to pack her bunkers with wood fuel.

On July 29, however, an effort was made to forestall this escape over the Ocean, and a small squadron of the whalers reached Lindi under Commander the Hon. R. O. B. Bridgeman. Leading a boarding party, he went up the creek, found *Präsident's* engines in first-class. condition and at 2 p.m. he set to work. Having applied some 16½-lb. charges of gun-cotton at vital spots, he blew off her propeller, ruined the machinery as well as wireless, and burst holes in her sides. That settled her fate, to the intense annoyance of the Teutonic populace who saw their ripened plans spoilt only at the last. Nor did East African Germans hesitate to criticise their *commandant* at Lindi for having suffered this to be achieved. News travelled fairly quickly even in those days, a narration of this incident reaching the entrenched watchers at Simba Uranga within a fortnight later; and I have before me copy of a letter from that part of the delta written on August 18 to a friend at Lindi, it says:

> You people in Lindi have during the time had British visitors, for the engines of the *Präsident* are said to have been blown up. All the work you did was apparently of no avail.

But more thrilling by far was to be an affair that now concerned *Severn*, and the scene would be nearly 80 miles north of Zanzibar, in Tanga which the Germans had made a port of some consequence; whence also a railway started up country for fetching such commodities as rubber, gum, and copal, to be put aboard their D.O.A.L. (German East Africa Line) steamers. Here, too, at Tanga some three months after opening of war, there had been an unfortunate ending to a military expedition sent across the sea from India. Although one British, one Ghurka, and one Sikh regiment had done well, yet the inferior troops of Bombay (never previously on active service) had landed immediately after being dispirited by three weeks of sea-sickness, and they failed lamentably in the field.

Now at outbreak of hostilities the single-funnelled S.S. *Markgraf* (see illustration), of the above line remained at Tanga, and H.M.S.

Chatham, voyaging from the Red Sea to Zanzibar, had beheld her still there. In view of what *Präsident* had recently planned, and for the purpose also of ascertaining whether a second supply-ship (generally expected sooner or later) had found shelter during the last fortnight within this northern port, the time had come for a reconnaissance in force to be sent against her. Should she be there found, she must be cut out, and at the same time *Markgraf* must also be destroyed.

From the plan it will be noticed that the harbour lies between Tanga Island on the north and the mainland at the south. Viewed from seawards, the latter presented a peaceful enough small town with green slopes, trees, bungalows, balconied well-built houses, pier, hospital, mission, railway station. With its trim square, band-stand, Bismarck monument, streets, it looked out on to anchored craft, and a lighthouse marked the entrance.

The attack had been selected to take place at daylight of Thursday August 19 because surprise would synchronise with convenient tides. The scheme was that the whalers *Pickle* (Lieut. H. C. Davis R.N.R.) and *Fly* (Lieut. D. H. H. Whitburn R.N.R.), having shipped parties armed, and shod with gymnastic shoes, were to dash in under cover of *Severn's* guns, then go alongside the two German liners, for which purpose each whaler was to carry three scaling ladders. Our old friends, the tugs *Revenger* and *Sarah Jolliffe* would be available for towing the liners out. Three other armed whalers—*Salamander, Rattler*, and *Charon*—were to be used to sweep up any minefield that might be found, and the three-funnel cruiser *Challenger* (5,915 tons) was flagship for the time being. The latter, however, drew 21 feet and her position would be outside Tanga harbour.

On the previous evening the light-footed boarding parties from *Challenger* came over to *Severn* for temporary habitation, and after an early breakfast they were taken off at 5.30 on Thursday morning by *Pickle* and *Fly*. In the former whaler also went Flag-Commander the Hon. R. O. B. Bridgeman, who was to have charge of this adventurous scaling endeavour. No better human choice could have been made than of this very gallant gentleman for a risky undertaking. His family motto—"*Nec temere nec timide*"—always seemed to inspire his studied bravery and sane courage. One of his brother officers wrote to me:—

"We had an immense respect for him out there. Although he was small physically, and might almost have been taken for a Midshipman, I fancy he was generally regarded as the ablest man in the squadron, and a perfect gentleman." Captain Fullerton regarded him as "one of the most single-minded, unselfish, fearless and gallant officers that ever breathed. On him fell practically the whole burden of the operational side of the East African Campaign from the sea point-of-view."

Picture, then, this morning at seven o'clock *Severn* leading the way towards the entrance of Tanga Harbour, with *Pickle* and *Fly* following; but H.M.S. *Challenger*, the tugs, and minesweepers, had stopped behind to await developments. Off Ras Kasone (the headland which had to be rounded at the mouth) *Pickle* and *Fly* went ahead at full speed, passing *Severn* and keeping to the channel's port side. Three minutes later, having got well inside, Commander Bridgeman signalled the monitor: "There is a hawser stretched across the harbour". And, sure enough, *Severn* found it about ten feet below surface but supported every ten yards by buoys. All three vessels had no difficulty in getting across the wire, but its existence aroused certain suggestions, especially as its southeastern end was secured to a lighter.

This was about 50 ft. square with a crane mounted, and mooted in a small bight; but when Yeoman-of-Signals Greenshields called attention to what resembled metal drums stacked in a dozen rows on its deck, Captain Fullerton fired at them with his 3-pdrs in passing. Each row contained ten or twelve objects with horns, which made them look still more like mines, yet in spite of eight shots nothing happened.

The harbour and town were wonderfully still this tropical morn, with not a sign of life anywhere, until at half-past seven *Pickle*, who was then 250 yards ahead, received the first attention when abreast the local hospital, a heavy fire being opened on her and on *Fly* a minute later from four different directions. And extremely accurate it was, the range being only from 450 to 1,500 yards, so that both whalers were continually straddled. *Pickle* and *Fly* as well as *Severn* replied, and the Germans hoisted the Red Cross flag over the hospital almost simultaneously.

From east and west, southwest, and southeast this hot concentration seriously menaced the ships. But where was the alleged supply-ship?

Certainly, she had not yet arrived. There was not a boat or a ship of any sort except one biggish steamer lying in shoal water southwest of Tanga Island, badly aground aft, and her bows heading to the southeast. A fine vessel with a single funnel, and her name on the bows. The lettering spelled *MARKGRAF*.

With great dash away sped the two whalers towards the latter's port side, and the accompanying illustration is of remarkable interest. It was photographed at 7.37 a.m. from aboard *Pickle* when the latter was within a few yards of her objective, and shows the *Markgraf* anchored with two cables at the bows high out of the water.

Assuredly the Germans had made up their mind that she should never be taken captive out of harbour, and they had made most ably selected the shore gun-positions against any such attempt. Over to the northwest, excellently concealed, was a formidable fellow, which may have been one of *Königsberg's* 4.1, and so placed that it could rake any vessel trying to board *Markgraf* from either side. Even when about 300 yards short of the liner, Commander Bridgeman observed this barrage beginning, and the enemy had got the range to a yard.

What to do?

In any case the order to bring the liner out was impracticable, so she must be treated with explosives to prevent the Germans ever hauling her afloat. Through the terrible curtain of shells *Pickle* bravely moved, grappled and secured alongside at the high bows as if the tactics of ancient Greek and Roman Navies had never in long centuries been discarded, and boarding was as modern as in Elizabethan times. Tanga, in fact, witnessed one of the very few episodes of marine warfare when steel hull went alongside steel hull and crew tried to leap aboard.

But the enemy's guns were sending an intolerable opposition, it was too hot for the whalers to remain alongside, and only a question of moments before they would both be sunk, so Commander Bridgeman ordered *Fly* out of the danger zone. The necessary delay in applying explosive aboard *Markgraf* would have entailed certain disaster to his men, wherefore *Pickle* delayed only long enough to fire a few 3-pdr. shots at close range along the waterline, and then retired too.

All this period *Severn* had kept under way, heavily engaging the batteries and thereby considerably helping the whalers, but now she sent the latter out of harbour and at 7.45 dealt with *Markgraf* alone. Opening with both 6-in, 4.7-in. and 3-pdrs., she raked the liner with capped shell during eight minutes "rapid independent", which after penetrating and bursting inside the hull produced the conflagration shown in the next photograph. Then a few lyddite against the bows tore great holes in the side, and settled *Markgraf's* future finally. (*Markgraf* was showing 10 feet at the bows.)

The monitor, being practically stationary, had become the target for every German battery; but except for puffs of smoke occasionally visible from behind the hills northwest of the island and eastward of the pier, there was nothing for her to aim at. *Severn* was thus hit three times, one shell coming through the 4-inch protective steel plate on the forebridge just missing the Yeoman-of-Signals (standing with his eye to the telescope), then exploding on the boat-deck wounding a recently joined Midshipman and two sailors. A second entered a cabin aft and wrecked it, the curious coincidence being that this compartment belonged to the same unfortunate Midshipman; fumes almost suffocating several men at the stern. The third projectile flew into the ship's galley like a wild rocket, scattering lockers and cooking utensils, but hurting no one.

As the monitor turned to come out, she brought her guns to bear against three cranes at the pierhead, knocking out two and setting on fire a large store-shed near the Customs House. Still on her way to the exit, she steamed abreast of the lighter, which had attracted her attention on entering. This time she was able to get in a few rounds and see quick results. First the dump began to burn, next for three minutes this grew into a fierce blaze, then the whole lighter—mines and all—went up in a violent explosion, distributing hundreds of pieces through a smoke-cloud; and when the smoke cleared, there was nothing left to see.

We have noted the efficiency of Germany's East African Intelligence system, but the corresponding British department deserved praise for having provided the right date and exactly anticipated a certain shipping movement. Those mines had been lying across the entrance in line with the wire ready for blowing into fragments any vessel who might attempt to pass; but they had been lifted and placed on the lighter so lately as August 18. This further information, however, did not reach the British Navy for another eleven months. The lighter's destruction was a serious matter, since the Germans had no more mines to lay down, and were of the latest pattern: it may be that they had been brought out from Europe in *Kronborg's* hold.

But, apart from this minefield being out of commission, the enemy at Tanga were thoroughly prepared; their gunnery rapid if unlucky, shells often bursting against the whalers' sides; but though *Pickle* was hit twice, neither she nor *Fly* suffered one casualty. *Severn*'s people had found the Rufiji scarcely a place for a *siesta*, but Tanga was far worse: "a hotter corner to be in than when we went up against the *Königsberg*", was how one of her men described it. And German organisation at Tanga today was so perfect ashore, that from start to finish not one

European or native was visible.

So, after a visit which lasted 27 minutes, the trio passed Ras Kasone headland again giving a final hammering to the round signal-tower over which flew the German flag. The last mental picture was of its cracked walls, and a fire consuming the contents. Soon after 8 a.m. *Severn* joined up with the squadron outside and, transferred the injured midshipman to *Challenger* who at 15 knots rushed off to place him in Zanzibar hospital. A nasty wound behind the calf of his right leg containing splinters of shell would be best tended ashore. But, late that evening, by the time *Severn* arrived, news came that the operation had been successful.

DASH INTO TANGA, AUGUST 19, 1915
(Top) H.M.S. "Severn" with whalers "Pickle" and "Fly" making for Tanga entrance after the engagement.
(Bottom) H.M. whaler "Rattler".

CHAPTER 17

The River Hazard

Back once more at Zanzibar, *Severn* had her holes patched up and minor repairs effected: even on the way thither she had broken down, and had to be taken in tow by one of the tugs. But she was always a lucky ship, and one dreads to imagine what would have been her fate if engine trouble had developed inside Tanga harbour. Somehow throughout her adventurous career she "shuffled"—to quote an apt word which her men often used of this ship—in and out of danger with comparatively few battle scars, yet her list of achievements during the first year of commission already was enough to make a crack battleship in the Grand Fleet envious. Fixed above the quarter-deck, carved in the shape of a ribbon, those who came aboard might now read and note:—

Belgian Coast 1914-1915.
Rufiji River July 6-11, 1915.
Tanga August 19, 1915.

And more records would have to be added ere long.

She was sent this month to patrol off the Rufiji, the monotony being broken to some extent after anchor had been let go in Tirene Bay and fishing parties could go off in a boat. There was no lack of this sport, and good catches were frequent, yet the suspense of war hung over everyone, and by night each gun had its crew watching for sudden events: though *Königsberg* might never emerge, who could say what surprise might not be maturing within the delta?

If the dark hours were often very cold, the days out here were generally pleasant with a refreshing breeze and none of the stifling odours of Zanzibar's harbour. Moreover, the daily menu could be varied not only by fresh fish but by turtle, as well as birds and duck on one of the islands. But as the *Severn* cruised in and out among the tricky reefs where deep water would quickly shoal; and as she stopped to search this or that outlying islet; there could be no question that eager eyes on the mainland were following her every move and reporting to German Intelligence Headquarters.

An elaborate system of white flags and bonfires along the coast had formed the basis of signalling and reporting news right from the beginning of these African hostilities; and whilst this paragraph is being written I am touching a piece of fabric which the German officer in charge of Komo Island employed when communicating with First Lieutenant von Geldein in charge of the next station at Kissiyu. A bit of material, such as used for making tents, had evidently sufficed for the purpose, and the flagstaff on which it had been hoisted was still standing when *Severn's* liberty-men roamed the island that September. (On Komo Island this month *Severn's* sailors discovered a number of notice-boards nailed to trees, and bearing instructions to the natives that they were to make across for the mainland should the English arrive.) *Dhows* and catamarans bearing natives employed by the enemy as spies now and again were intercepted by *Severn*, who would during her investigation enter numerous creeks and small bights containing as little as seven feet of water.

The difficulty of the continent's coast-line was that the offing consisted of awkward shallow patches and rugged reefs—thereby making nocturnal navigation extremely irksome—whilst the shore itself ended abruptly at the sea with almost impenetrable dense bush and lofty trees. It was, in short, exactly what a German described as "an ideal country for defence, but impossible for offence." Those nightly bushfires, with their bright glow against the sky, could be observed for miles yet two significant features were the equal spacing, and the sudden manner with which these symbols were obliterated; thus, proving intentional control.

What precisely was the enemy inside the delta contemplating? 'That question had to be settled? And were the Rufiji defences at the entrance still manned? Granted that *Königsberg* could not issue forth, did that still apply to the *Somali*? And the *Adjutant*? For as yet we did not know definitely that the former had been left burnt out and beached; or that the latter had slipped round into Dar-es-Salaam. What had become of Captain Looff's men, and whether his guns were still aboard or now mounted at the mouths, still was hidden from British knowledge.

So, a reconnaissance was planned for the morning of September 14. On the previous day *Severn* and *Echo* anchored after sunset seven miles to the NNE of Simba Urange, which was the entrance up which *Königsberg* had steamed, and now the monitor's personnel shifted into khaki, preliminary to going into action yet again and up this hateful delta for the third time. Among Captain Fullerton's sailors these strenuous excursions had become such established undertakings that outwardly the men joked and asked each other: "Any more for the river trip? Just about to start—and no waiting!" Yet inwardly every man realised well enough that they were about to penetrate one more tight corner, and be given a violent reception at close quarters.

For the older hands, who had been brought up in the tradition of long-range sea-fighting, this repeated close duelling was a ceaseless wonder and essential annoyance, but they were all of them veteran warriors by now. As to Lieut. C. J. Charlewood R.N.R., commanding the whaler *Echo*, this officer in spite of his youth had received his initiation twelve months ago when in charge of the tug *Helmuth* at Zanzibar and he signalled *Pegasus* concerning *Königsberg's* approach.

Picture, then, the two ships weighing anchor on Tuesday, September 14 at 4.a.m. and making straight for Simba Urange, (the reader is invited to consult the charts of this entrance placed later in the book referring to the dates of May 5, and September 20, of 1916), *Severn* leading the way at 6 knots. It was still dark, but fifty minutes later the mouth was just discernible, and at 5.10 the monitor passing in between the two points as the day dawned. Not a sign of opposition, not a murmur from either bank. No longer any entrenched Germans? Or could they be asleep?

A thousand yards astern followed the whaler, and for her from the Kiomboni (eastern) shore there awaited the loud banging of that 3-pdr. gun which once belonged to *Adjutant*. Thrice the shells shot forth, they curved right over *Echo* and pitched on the other side from an invisible battery, but Charlewood's gunners could see the flashes among the bushes and trees, so replied with 3-pdr. and Maxims till the enemy ceased fire. The Germans still guarded the Rufiji gate after all, and Captain Fullerton wirelessed *Echo* to retire: it was then that the hot time began.

Charlewood turned his ship round, and now the full brilliant light of an African morn offered no protection. He was making for the sea, and, as he once more approached the narrow defile, was fighting his course through at 8 knots, being only 700 yards from the eastern battery but 500 yards from the western. The enemy had him mercilessly

(Top) German Supply Ship "Kronborg" on fire in Mansa Bay, April 1915, after being shelled by H.M.S. "Hyacinth".

(Bottom) German S.S. "Markgraf" at Tanga, lying on her side after having been burnt out.

as between two claws, and pressed him with all their vitality. From the Kiomboni peninsula they scored three hits, severing the starboard cable and thus causing the loss of an anchor which was hanging cock-a-bill; but the single gun on the western bank, being at shorter (and almost point-blank) range did the greater damage. Nine successive shells imposed a terrible toll for this trespassing into German territory.

Two burst in the engine-room, cracking the high-pressure cylinder, whence a heavy cloud of steam issued, another passed through the stokehold and exploded in the opposite bunker, a fourth erupted on deck and amputated all the steam pipes, three blew up on the bridge; whilst the rest did various structural injuries to boiler-casing and steering-gear. An impressive moment of pandemonium! There was *Echo* in a mantle of steam which filled the wheel-house and roared so loudly that orders could not be heard, the foc'sle door knocked off its hinges and eventually found a dozen yards away; winches ruined, small arms (stacked on deck) twisted and distorted out of shape, and one gun disabled.

Nevertheless, something like a miracle happened during these minutes.

Notwithstanding the cracked cylinder, the whaler maintained her speed and—still more wonderful—not a mortality occurred, the only casualties being one seaman with slight wounds and Lieut. Charlewood with a slight injury to his left shoulder. If ever a ship was lucky, let her name be remembered as the *Echo*. And there could be no sort of doubt as to *Adjutant's* British shells being used, for fragments were picked up and found to be stamped "V.S.M" (Vickers Sons & Maxim).

Meanwhile *Severn* was having an interesting time. As she proceeded into the first reach, she must immediately sight the sunken blockship *Newbridge*; whose masts, funnel, and upperworks were still standing conspicuously. The monitor was steering to leave this steamer to starboard, when it was noticed that from her mainmast a wire stretched across river to a high ladder fixed on the (northeast) port bank opposite. The Germans had been quite ingenious, for the ladder was so high that it commanded above the trees a clear view seaward, and the height of *Newbridge's* mast was being employed for supporting the telephone wire to the Suninga shore, whence it passed through Salale inland up to *Königsberg's* final position, thereby having kept Captain Looff in direct communication with Simba Urange defences.

This wire now caught against the monitor's forestay right in front of the bridge, and broke in two but ran clear without fouling person or thing. The river at this bend was very narrow, with several creeks running into the swamps, and from now onwards *Severn* could congratulate herself as the first British man-of-war to have intruded. Less than fifteen minutes after passing *Newbridge*, the lonely channel, where it widened, yielded a surprise; for here was revealed a boat pulling up river with the tide. One round from *Severn's* fore 6-inch sufficed, and the rowers dropping their oars fell down so hurriedly that they appeared to be killed, but presently the khaki figure of a European stood erect holding hands above his head and then four black natives followed his example. On this occasion there was no getting away, the monitor proceeded alongside the boat, and made all five prisoners.

This turned out to be a most interesting event, as we shall see later. The white man was Petty Officer S. E. Diaz y Rodriguez, whose name we have mentioned more than once. Born of Spanish descent at Altona-on-the-Elbe on July 21, 1881, he had afterwards gone to sea in the German Navy, completed his service, but at the beginning of hostilities was Chief Steward in the 8,000-tons S.S.S. *Khalifa*, This German vessel having been interned at Mozambique, he escaped with three others in a *dhow* and after eleven days landed at Lindi but, fulfilling his duty to report, he reached the Rufiji early in November. He was then ordered to join the "watchers" (as they were called) at the Simba Urange mouth, keeping a good lookout at the point and helping to man the guns. Married, with a wife and two children in Hamburg, he happened to be the only one among the watchers who was not a bachelor.

Rodriguez had bad luck this Tuesday. No British ship had come into any part of the delta for two months, and this morning he had started from the entrance on the flood bound for Salale village where he was to buy provisions for his mates, when the squat sight of *Severn* was beheld astern steadily overtaking the boat. Having been put aboard, he was searched and held captive in the monitor's chart-house on the forebridge, whilst the black men were sent down below. Nor was this the only shock of the trip.

Severn had resumed her speed, negotiated a sharp and narrow turn (where the shoals on both sides were probably the cause of the 360-ft. *Königsberg* having got aground), and now straight ahead stretched a long reach, Salale being barely 2½ miles away on the starboard hand. Only fifteen minutes had elapsed since receiving the five prisoners, whose boat was being towed astern, but of a sudden just after 6 o'clock a large steam launch became visible. She had just shoved off from the

(Top) H.M.S. "Severn" after her fight with "Könisberg". Note underwater leaks and damage to monitor's hull from enemy's bursting shells.
(Bottom) German prisoner, Petty Officer S. E. Diaz y Rodriguez, aboard H.M.S. "Severn".

village carrying quite a number of Germans, bound evidently for one of the outposts, when she too suffered a fright.

This, as we can assert, was none other than the *Wami* which on July 11 should have torpedoed *Severn*, so the former may have had a guilty conscience on seeing the monitor approaching. At any rate *Wami* never stopped, but at full speed sought to get away from this unexpected embarrassment. Knowing every twist and turn of the tricky Rufiji channels, her skipper could hope for safety by taking refuge among the luxuriant growth, but he was in an awkward position. Captain Fullerton's vessel loosed off two rounds at her from the fore 6-inch gun, both shots falling short; yet the German was in such a hurry, as to be visible only a few seconds and then she went "all out" for a creek which lay nearly opposite, instantly disappearing behind the mangroves.

Opposite this creek *Severn* therefore stopped engines and lowered an armed motorboat, in which went Lieut. E. S. Brooksmith R.N., and Lieut. C. H. Grenfell R.N.V.R. who could speak German. At full speed they tore down the creek, searched for about half an hour to the extent of three miles, and just as Captain Fullerton was getting anxious for their safety, they came back to the ship unsuccessful. *Wami* had eluded them because of her local knowledge and evidently had crossed over into the River Kiomboni, which runs parallel with the previously mentioned Kikunja, Simba Urange, and Suninga.

This minor incident is illustrative of the natural defences which the delta provided, and ambushes which could so easily be laid against invaders, so that we can well appreciate the trouble which might have been continued had *Königsberg's* homeless crew been split into so many parties aboard mosquito-craft. Dodging round corners, firing their guns, then doing hide-and-seek tactics, they could have made the rivers intolerable for even a shallow monitor. And we cannot fail to agree with the Defence Corps that the wrecked cruiser's 4.1-inch weapons might have shut the entrances tight against all except such ships as another *Kronborg* running supplies into Central Africa.

Whilst waiting for the return of his two Lieutenants, Captain Fullerton had bombarded Salale, destroying a number of corrugated-iron sheds and a brick house which was the residence for the Commandant of the Defence Force. All the village boats likewise were blown up, and it was the blast from *Severn*'s after 6-inch which during this procedure caused Rodriguez' boat to sink. Time passed, the latter's former colleagues at Kiomboni Point one day discovered this craft

At the Simba Urange Mouth

(Top) British 3-pounder gun in German hands at entrance to Simba Urange.

(Middle) Grave of Seaman Piddock, R.N., of H..M.S. "Adjutant". He was killed at the Simba Urange mouth when that tug and the above gun were captured. Germans buried his body and erected the wooden cross.

(Bottom) German soldiers entrenched at mouth of Simba Urange.

among the mangroves, and they rightly inferred from examination that it had been smashed up by the blast of cordite; but as to Rodriguez's fate, and whether he was still alive, they knew not till after the war ended.

Diaz (as he had been known to his friends) could speak good English, and he was what is understood as "a very decent fellow", loyal to his own nation, but well-behaved as a prisoner-of-war; honourable, popular among British officers and men. That he was well-treated from the start merited corresponding appreciation, but—apart from certain regrettable features of U-boat warfare—the great brotherhood of the sea survived international enmity; and "*Sailors always look after sailors*". So, *Severn's* new guest early established for himself a good relationship.

But what he could not understand was that *Severn* did not now continue up river, past *Königsberg*, down the Kikunja, and thence (if she wished) by a side branch back to Simba Urange. Nothing, however, of interest further up was visible from the monitor's masthead, so having hoisted up her motorboat she made for the mouth whence she had come, and the thrill of living began when abreast of *Newbridge*. It was 7.45 a.m. as the first rifle shot smote the plating around *Severn's* forebridge, and two minutes later she had been hit seven or eight times by 3-pdr. shells on that structure and funnel; several cabins and the upperworks being riddled. Yeoman-of-Signals Greenshields says:

> I was on the forebridge all alone, and the prisoner in the chart house, when a shell came through the house low down and burst round the wheel and compass. I was wounded by it, my legs, fingers, and face literally peppered by small fragments, and my helmet blown nearly to pieces. (I am keeping it for luck.)

For Rodriguez it was an unusual experience that a German aboard a British man-of-war should have to endure British shells fired by German friends, but this trying period did not end until a few minutes past eight when *Severn* had got 3,000 yards beyond the entrance and picked up *Echo*, after which they both proceeded to their anchorage at Tirene Bay. Even today it is hard to understand why nobody was killed, and only one man in *Severn* received wounds. The prisoner confirmed that *Adjutant's* shells were being fired, but the most remarkable thing was that the damage amounted to 100 *per cent* more than larger projectiles had caused in Tanga harbour. All men not required on deck had been sent under cover ere reaching the Narrows, otherwise a long list of casualties might have been expected. As to *Echo*, the Chief Engine Room Artificer had doggedly managed to effect temporary repairs and maintain steam so that slowly, though under her own power, she carried on till the end: there had been only the smallest margin between freedom and captivity, which proves that the *Adjutant* incident might have been exactly repeated.

At Mafia the black prisoners were sent ashore, but the German was kept aboard for the present, and had this reconnaissance done nothing else it would still have been worthwhile by reason of the information obtained. From the natives it was learnt that the *commandant* and four Europeans lived at Salale, that guns and Maxims at the mouth were always kept manned by a dozen white soldiers under an officer (naval lieutenant), their habitation being in tents under the palms. (Ten of these entrenched, with rifles, will be seen photographed on another page.)

Rodriguez, in spite of his reticent caution, became a veritable quarry of information, which may be summed up briefly. At first, he seemed, not unnaturally, dejected for he had been suffering a good deal from malaria. No fresh water was obtainable at the watch-stations, and when given a glassful in *Severn* he remarked that this was the first he had tasted for eleven months, having previously contented himself with the boiled brackish river water mixed in tea or coffee. He and his fellows had suffered a great deal from mosquitoes, fever, dysentery, and they had to be extremely careful of cuts, since the tetanus germ abounded in the mud, and even the water for washing had to be boiled; yet, if all were tired of their fate, they had by no means lost heart.

The watchers were well paid, allowed £5 a month each for provisions, and there was plenty of wild pig in the delta, Supplies of food were more than ample, the soil being so fertile that anything would grow—including grapes (from which they made their own wine) and European fruits. Moreover they obtained their mails together with German, British, and American newspapers of late dates; *Königsberg's* wireless communication with Dar-es-Salaam had given them more recent news until her defeat, and from that town provisions used to reach the Rufiji by road in five or six days.

Many opportunities for conversation were afforded this extremely intelligent and well-informed prisoner, for he was allowed to have his meals with the officers in the Wardroom and not sent to his cabin until sunset when a sentry guarded him from outside. Certainly, he possessed a good knowledge of what was happening along the coast, and every movement of a British ship had been reported. Not without interest was it learned how *Königsberg* had managed to find her course through this maze of waterways; for, just before the war, a new Rufiji chart had been completed though never published. Equally notable was the statement concerning the British torpedo which they possessed, and this might have been one of two.

On November 7 during a boat attack at this same entrance, the port outrigger of H.M.S. *Goliath's* picket-boat was hit, so that a live torpedo was accidentally released against the bank. So also, on November 10 when *Newbridge* was being sunk, a picket-boat fired at her hull a torpedo to make the sinking doubly certain, but the wayward missile dived under the ship, struck the mud, and was not seen again by the blockship party.

That which the Simba Urange outpost recovered was probably the former, but in any case, it availed them nothing. So, too, with other explosives. Doubtless the reader will have long since wondered why the Germans never mined these river entrances at the Narrows, but according to Rodriguez an observation-mine was laid in the Kikunja, that it drifted away by the tide and exploded astern of *Severn*; also, that a row of observation-mines was placed across Simba Urange—and still remained there—because the contacts all went wrong and it had not been thought worthwhile to take them up. In spite of experiments, they had not yet succeeded in making an efficient mine.

It is also to be remembered that *Kronborg* carried from Germany plenty of dynamite, and that when H.MS. *Challenger* visited Mansa Bay on July 21, 1915, two extemporised mines were brought to the surface. But neither Rodriguez nor any other German could comprehend why on April 14 H.M.S. *Hyacinth*, after shelling *Kronborg*, steamed away and allowed unhindered the salving of guns or ammunition. This would have mattered less if *Königsberg's* 41-inch guns had all been destroyed on July 11, whilst Captain Looff was running short of shell. That during the ensuing months of campaign there should have been both the original ordnance, and the fresh shells ex-*Kronborg*, has been the subject for criticism.

Admiral King-Hall, who has since died, stated that:

> It was impossible to do anything towards preventing the enemy from salving the arms as soon as the fire was extinguished, for, short of an occupying force of troops to hold the surrounding

district, it was out of the question for a man-of-war to remain in an enemy's harbour day and night for weeks.

Then, a little later, the Germans naturally mined the Mansa approaches, and so the salvage went on unhindered.

Rodriguez told his hosts:

> The *Königsberg* is a total wreck now. Everything has been taken out of her, and if you go up you will find nothing but iron. Her upper deck is awash at high water.

Which agreed exactly with what Flight-Commander Cull had reported. She was even now sinking deeper into the mud, nor could she ever be raised. Gutted by fire, there remained a useless rusting shell.

After nine days aboard *Severn*, during which he had another touch of malaria but was always well treated, being given books and papers to read, allowed to exercise on the quarter-deck in return for his parole, Rodriguez was sent off in a steamer to Bombay. "You are a lucky ship", he told some of *Severn's* people, "in not having got lost up the Rufiji". Then, having expressed thanks to his hosts, he did not omit to hope all officers and men might at the end of hostilities arrive safe home.

The accompanying photograph, taken by a German, shows *Adjutant's* 3-pdr. mounted at Simba Urange mouth, and it is easy enough to understand how impossible the ships found their task of trying to find gun-port or weapon among the overhanging growth. Fortunately I have before me a letter written by the very loader of this gun, and in referring to the tussle of September 14 with *Severn* he admits that:

"Such a scrap is not easily described.... It is good sport when one is in the thick of it, and it was with real relish I loaded the shrapnel ... it is marvellous that there have been no killed or wounded in our crowd."

Yet the mere sight of *Severn* or her sister used to create such an unpleasant morbid condition that it became known as "monitor fever".

This, then, was the fourth hot corner in which Captain Fullerton's vessel saw action since arriving in African waters. Her shot-holes were patched up by men working day and night, but the injured steam-pipes must be sent to Zanzibar. Soon she was patrolling again among the numerous islands, and investigating the mouths further to the southward, going close into the Masala entrance where a lookout platform with a matting roof had been erected.

Mersey had broken down, and *Severn's* refit was long overdue, but the patrolling had to be maintained in the latter assisted by whalers: scarcely a very big force to ensure that no strange vessel should enter the delta, and that none of the several small craft, still within, should dash out. True, H.M.S. *Hyacinth*, which had been away from the station for some weeks having a refit at Cape Town, now returned and became flagship once more instead of *Challenger*, but she had many duties up and down the coast. In short, whilst no blockade was ever absolute and positive, it must also be recollected that ships need to be coaled at intervals, machinery given minor overhauls; and human men herded together in hot steel hulls must be allowed to stretch their legs ashore occasionally.

That is to say you cannot drive a squadron at full ability all the time, and there must be some nights when tired nerves and bodies can rest peacefully behind an island undisturbed by the throb of machinery. On Sunday afternoon, September 26, *Severn* had come in from her patrol and let go anchor off Nyuni Island, giving leave to those who cared to go fishing. The weather was warm but dull, and inclined to rain.

News had just been received that the king was pleased to award not merely the D.S.O. to officers already mentioned but the names of ten petty officers and men of the monitors were to be selected for the Distinguished Service Medal. Great happiness aboard *Severn*! Night fell, gun-watches were set, and the ship remained at anchor till next morning at 6 o'clock.

But during those dark, overcast, hours and along a smooth sea, *Wami* crept out of the Rufiji, past the land and into Dar-es-Salaam unseen and unsuspected by her enemies. For such a small, low-lying, craft it needed only a little enterprise; the working of tide and moon times, settled weather and just ordinary luck. Her existence in the delta, running provisions and men down to the mouths, had become too threatened with danger since twelve days ago, and any way she could perform far more useful work in another area. Badly needed on Lake Tanganyika, the engineers of the Central Railway at Dar-es-Salaam would take her to pieces, put her on trucks, and send her to Kigoma to be launched into the fresh water. Ten months after quitting the Rufiji, she ended her service—not without some more narrow escapes—and today she lies sunk beneath the lake's surface.

Such are the strange chances of ships and men.

CHAPTER 18

Yambe Island

Months of monotonous patrolling, varied by an occasional reconnaissance further north in the neighbourhood of such places as Mansa Bay; unbearably hot days followed often by extremely cold nights; with little chance of looking forward to some useful "scrap"; were the destined experience that awaited *Severn's* personnel. Nothing seemed to happen, or likely to occur, of human interest, so that the vaguest rumour connecting present with future, or even the smallest domestic event, took on a value quite different from its real worth. One day, for example, when the ship's cat was gambolling with the dog and the former fell overboard, so that engines had to be stopped for quick rescue, the incident afforded quite a new and welcome subject for gossip.

The loss of *Königsberg* had, in truth, taken away some of the zest from living and robbed adventurous souls of their objective. The departure of those tugs *Blackcock* and *T. A. Jolliffe* back to England, after long association, seemed the final severance of olden times, and in December Admiral King-Hall sailed south for Simonstown, about to be relieved by Rear-Admiral E. F. Charlton.

Moreover, it was past high time for *Severn's* refit. Her engines cried out for thorough overhaul, she had been on the go for the last seven months and not been docked since February, but all this was the penalty for having become indispensable. Last Christmas Day had been spent in drab Dunkirk and an environment of vile gales, but at least there was then some semblance of festive cheer aboard. But, this African Christmas, *Severn* found herself looking in down the coast of Kilwa Kivinje to see what the enemy was up to. It was a beautiful day, she stood as close as possible to the shore, where three German flags were flying in the breeze, and just as twelve months ago a British cruiser outside the Rufiji had exchanged signals with Captain Looff, so now Captain Fullerton hoisted bunting to wish the German *com-*

mandant of Kilwa the usual greetings.

But, in spite of the brilliant sun overhead, there must have been a glum and gloomy feeling ashore; for answer came there none. Divine service was held aboard in the forenoon, yet of the traditional naval Christmas, with its "fun" party and decorated mess-tables, no suggestion manifested itself. A meal of biscuits and tinned meats, after all, is not the most exciting fare to produce personal happiness. Four days previously the cruiser *Pioneer*, with a view to Christmas dinner, had stopped abreast of an apparently uninhabited bit of shore, sent off a boat's crew to land on the spit, where they might discover cattle and fowls; but barely had the boat approached within a hundred yards of the beach than it was surprised by volleys of rifle-fire, riddling the woodwork, wounding two men in the knee and hip respectively. Not till *Pioneer* began bombarding could the cutter extricate herself, and no further mishap developed; the place being situated a little south of Kilwa, and forming part of the African continent at low water, but with the tide up it was an island.

When least expected, some significant happening would now and then liven seafaring existence, as two days before the eventful Old Year was about to depart. *Severn* had just passed the Rufiji mouths and altered course round Komo Island, when she sighted a dugout containing one native. The latter, having been picked up well away to sea, related a thrilling tale of how he and another African had escaped from German captivity up the delta. He had broken the chain that hung round his neck, but his companion had been killed, and now the former was trying to reach Mafia Island. Naturally in this frame of mind the escaper happened to say willingly all he knew about our enemy, and the information he provided was of no little value.

That same old trouble, which had been so often suffered by *Severn* north of the equator, repeated itself when she was sent up towards the coast where German and British territory met south of Mombasa. Her flat bottom banged so heavily to the ocean swell that again the buckling of her fore messdeck, straining of structure, and leaks through rivet-holes, threatened: yet if she had not been designed, or built, for monsoon weather, her draught once more was enabling her to get into channels and pry about where bigger ships dared not approach. In any case the sight of Rufiji's mouths had become so distasteful, that it was a whiff of relief to gaze upon other scenery.

But at length a new liveliness was foreshadowed in February 1916; important military operations were beginning in the north, so that warships' marines landed to play their part also. Delayed by the weather, *Mersey* at last joined her sister and the two monitors made for Kilindini, where enormous activity ashore was the preliminary of great developments. Transports were arriving with troops, guns, motor-vehicles, stores; trains were quickly filled, and sent off upcountry with much cheering and flag-waving; but on February 19 there disembarked from an ex-German liner General J. C. Smuts to take command of all the British Forces in the field, and he too went off by the five o'clock train that same afternoon.

Now the first of *Severn's* participation in this phase occurred six days later, when patrolling between Tanga Island and Wasin Island. A small fort and lookout station had been located in the bush about 500

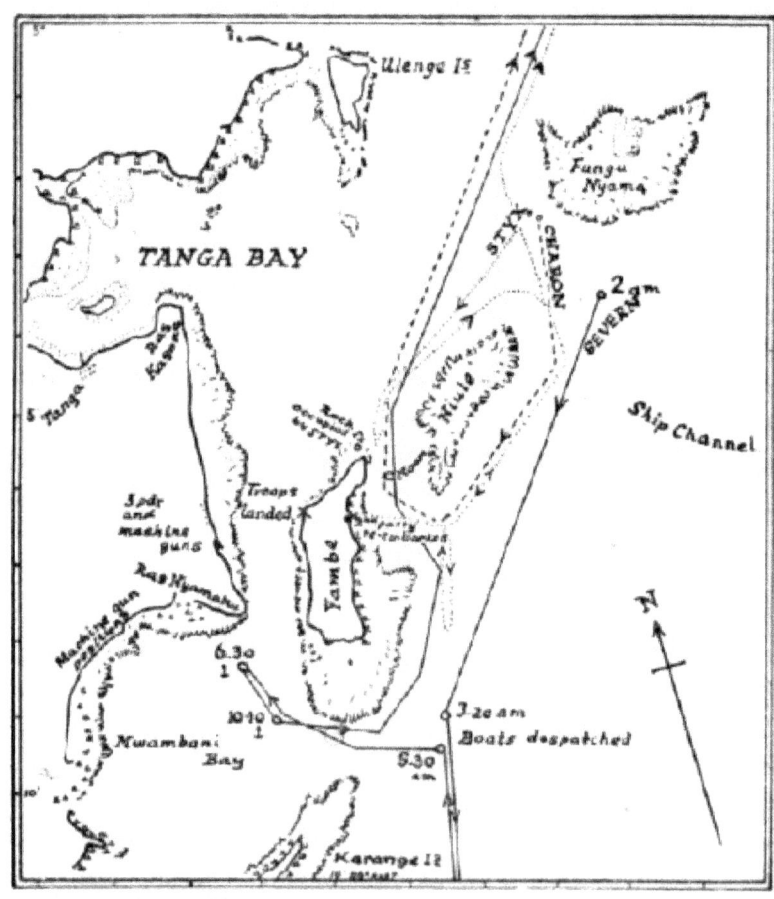

Track Chart of H.M.S. "Severn", "Charon", "Styx", during Yambe attack.

yards south of Ras Kilifi, which is at the entrance to Moa Bay. Using her 4.7-inch lyddite, she hit the fort five times, blowing it to bits, wrecking the huts, and causing an explosion at the back, that may have been an ammunition store. The garrison ran away, and an important telephone station ceased to function.

On the 28th *Severn* chanced to be at Gaze, and whilst Captain Fullerton was visiting the British camp, he met a Captain Dickson, who before the war had been District Commissioner at Shimono, but now was serving as Intelligence Officer. The latter came on board, bringing a black native caught in the military camp acting as a spy for the Germans, having been sent from Vanga by the enemy to collect all the Gaze information. This capture proved most useful, and the spy turned out for the enemy a boomerang. Getting under way next morning, *Severn* anchored head and stern off Vanga, Captain Dickson went into the fighting-top and from the spy's extracted information was able to give the exact position of the German camp. Invisible though it lay, this officer (who knew almost every coconut tree in the locality) provided perfect direction for the guns.

Although the range opened at 8,400 yards, the monitor's 6-in. and 4.7-in were believed to have achieved excellent results, which were confirmed by his own scouts a week later; huts being all smashed up, trenches ploughed, pools of dried blood showing in several places, and every evidence of a most hurried retreat along the road. In fact, here had been afforded yet a third occasion when this ship's gunnery signally defeated a distant, but totally concealed, enemy. It was additionally satisfactory, since Admiral Charlton had during the previous day come aboard to present the five Distinguished Service Medals to men who earned decoration for the *Königsberg* action.

The British naval strategy had thus settled down to getting rid of the enemy's means for receiving intelligence from the vast coastal organisation, its linked up outlying islands, its watchers perched on platforms posted up trees, its telephone and telegraph system, and so on. From now, likewise, all fishermen and their native boats were to be arrested, the general purpose being gradually to render the German command both blind and deaf in regard to news from the sea. Seeing that reefs and shoals up in the north were numerous as in the south, the risks to heavy ships could not be tolerated by allowing them to poke their way through indifferently charted waters; so, on *Severn* and whalers the inshore work had to be borne. (*Mersey* was about to be towed by *Trent* for a refit at Durban.)

The British learned that an outpost and observation station existed on Yambe Island to the south of Tanga Bay, wherefore it was resolved to try capturing the same, and here we have one of those simple yet adventurous stories which read more like the juvenile fiction that once delighted our imagination.

The idea included the employment of *Severn*, the two whalers *Charon* and *Styx*, armed boats, together with black troops of the Zanzibar African Rifles under their white officer Lieut. Deacon. These natives expressed beforehand their delight to have a chance of meeting the enemy, and loudly promised to give them a good defeat. Further interest was created by belief that one of *Königsberg's* 4.1-inch guns had been mounted on the opposite mainland.

Now from the accompanying chart Tanga Bay with Ras Kasone (mentioned in an earlier chapter) will be noted to the northwest, and thence the mainland stretches southwards till opposite Yambe Island. Northeast of the latter lies Fungu Nyama, but in navigating around this area great care had to be taken because of the extensive reefs. Leaving Zanzibar at daylight of Saturday, March 18, *Severn* took with her a native who knew the Yambe region well, and that evening the monitor anchored south of Fungu Nyama, whalers bringing up west of that shoal.

Having turned in early, everyone was astir long before dawn and at 2 a.m. *Severn* got under way proceeding down the eastern side of Niule shoal, but when to the southeast of Yambe's reefs she halted at 3.20 a.m. and sent all boats away containing Lieut. Deacon, Colour-Sergeant P. E. Smith R.M.L.I., with 80 rank and file African Rifles. The two motor-craft and two gigs were under Lieut. E. S. Brooksmith R.N. and Lieut. Leoline W. T. Lewis R.N.R., both of *Severn*; who, after steering for the south end of Yambe and having given the coral reefs a good berth, turned up northward between mainland and island.

The latter measures about 2½ miles long and ¾ of a mile at its widest, but this was pretty well all the knowledge in British possession, so that with them the party brought a black guide. Captain Fullerton had insisted that fire was not to be opened on any of the enemy unless definitely seen to be hostile or the Germans themselves should attack. A captured live German would be the best prize to be brought off, a captured wounded German the next best, but a dead German would yield the least information. Therefore, the orders were to capture a white man, if possible, but in any case, to go about the job with absolute silence and invisibility.

It was a still but moonlit night when at 4.30 a.m. the boats made a landing at Yambe's northwest corner where marked on the accompanying chart, troops disembarking immediately and extending across the island. As they began to sweep northwards, daylight was breaking and they found few paths, but thick bush everywhere thwarting them. On the northeast side a very old camp, which had been deserted apparently for some weeks, was discovered, yet therefrom they found a well-cut track towards the northwest, and here was located another camp so clean and fresh that it must have been deserted only the previous night.

For in both the European and native quarters the ashes in the fireplaces were still quite warm. An examination of the former—constructed from coconut palm leaves—revealed such things as an armchair, native-made bedstead, a table fashioned out of some packing case, a roughly made desk whereon was printed in pencil: "TELEGRAPHEN POSTE YAMBE". Outside lay 250 empty beer bottles, the smell from which indicated that they had contained palm wine. Whilst any telegraph or telephone instruments had already been removed, a scrap of paper containing Morse signals sufficiently suggested that at least someone familiar with the code had been living here.

Moreover, on the edge of the camp stood a huge-stem *baobab* tree, containing three fixed platforms and ladder in the usual manner adopted by the Germans for observation from the branches. The general impression was that the island was certainly used during daytime, but at night the watchers might normally be withdrawn to the mainland.

There is always a fascination in islands, especially those set against a tropical background; but still more so when over them hangs a suggestion of mystery. Yambe caused a sense of expectation, where anything might happen, a mine go up, or an ambush be discovered too late. Perhaps the owner of that armchair was only hiding in the bush, and ready with his men to spring on the visitors at the ripe moment?

But the hours sped by, the sun's rays had become powerful, and at 8 a.m. not a soul had been revealed, so the time seemed to have been wasted. Lieutenants Brooksmith and Deacon discussed the matter and concluded that it would be useless to go any further, therefore the troops must be reassembled on the beach and re-embarked. Some had been delayed by the thick bush, but the greater part moved down to the foreshore, where the tide had considerably ebbed, which meant that the bare-footed *askaris* treading their way over the sharp coral could move only at slow pace.

However, 8.30 a.m. saw one motorboat and one gig filled with the first lot amounting to sixty: these two craft now shoved off and began making towards Ras Nyamaku in Mwambani Bay, where *Severn* had anchored two hours previously after cruising about to the southward during darkness. Now, as she remained covering the channel between mainland and Yambe, watching the first two boats approaching her, a new development without warning changed the whole picture.

For, just as the second section were about to wade out towards the other motorboat with its gig, there came a bang; followed by the sharp *rat-a-tat, rat-a-tat,* from the mainland. Heavy fire of a 3-pdr., machine-guns, and rifles, was concentrating on the landing-place and shells could be descried smiting the beach. The first shot landed overhead, but the blacks leapt to their feet and scattered into the bush, which turned out to have saved them against instant death, since the next two projectiles fell exactly where these men had been sitting, the range being 1½ miles.

Eight more shells followed, but were directed at the waiting boats, and they would certainly have been destroyed had not the coxswain (Leading Seaman F. Date) very properly got under way and cleared out at full speed towards *Severn* also. Keeping his men out of sight, he bade the gig's crew kneel down and with their rifles return the fire. Cleverly the enemy kept out of sight, so that the monitor could not use her guns, but after waiting some time she weighed and anchored where a better view of Yambe's southern end could be obtained.

Captain Fullerton's anxiety for the missing score of men increased as the half-hours passed, and no sign of them was reported. According to the prearranged scheme, troops if fired on and prevented from re-embarkation were to work across the northern part of the island in a southeasterly direction. Meanwhile the whaler *Styx* at 4 a.m. had weighed from her anchorage west of Fungu Nyama shoal, towing her gig already manned and armed. She steamed to the northeastern side of Yambe and when a mile away slipped this boat which rowed into the beach; but when the whaler returned there at 8 a.m., alas! the gig's crew had observed none of the missing soldiers.

Charon likewise started from the Fungu Nyama anchorage and went round to Yambe's eastern side, Captain Fullerton having wirelessed orders for a sharp lookout to be kept. The minutes ticked by, the coast was being scanned in expectation of a rift among the growth revealing the lost wanderers, but hope had become thin.

Then another change occurred.

At 11 o'clock the missing men burst into *Charon's* observation, without waste of minutes got into the gig, and climbed aboard the whaler. Deacon's detached party for two and a half hours had been forcing their way through thick bush that seemed impenetrable, so that they were compelled to hack nearly every yard of progress till they dashed forth in view of the sea. So, the incident ended without casualties, and by noon the few hours' excitement had passed into the list of minor events.

Yet these hours had by no means been wasted. *Severn* herself had made some valuable observations of machine-gun positions and rifle pits near Ras Nyamaku; the *baobab* tree platform could be useful for locating German guns in the likely event of having to visit Tanga harbour before long; and, because this position looked right into Tanga town, it would serve as spotting station for naval guns.

CHAPTER 19

Narrow Waters

The attack on Tanga came almost immediately, though it was particular rather than general, the plan being to destroy its railway station and concentrate against the position where at least one of *Königsberg's* guns was said to have been placed: that is, a couple of miles south of Tanga Pier, by a clump of mango trees. Some of the German cruiser's former crew had been sent thither before the middle of March from Dar-es-Salaam where, incidentally, the dread scourge of typhoid broke out a couple of months previously.

Things were not looking too well with the enemy just now, and the loss of Captain Looff's ship was symbolical of the fate which was slowly stealing over German East Africa, though many of the colonists refused to acknowledge the truth.

> Yes: you may defeat us out here, afloat and ashore, take our islands and bombard our towns, sink our liners or destroy our buildings. But why should we worry? We shall get them all back and you'll have to pay dearly for the damage done; because the war will be decided in Europe, and in Europe we shall win with our armies as well as our submarines.

So, whilst *Adjutant* and *Wami* were being prepared for railway transport at Dar-es-Salaam, in order to take the place of two units already sunk on Lake Tanganyika, the British Army on land began its advance by breaking through, and the British Navy off the coast was rendering the harbours gradually useless. The attack against Tanga was fixed for Wednesday, March 22, and the first operation was to sever outward communications.

Reference to the chart will show Ulenge Island at the northern approach of Tanga Bay, but at low water it was possible to walk from the mainland. Now, apart from the old lighthouse and some buildings, there stood a modern lighthouse which acted as a valuable lookout, being connected with Tanga by telephone. At the deadly hour of 2.30 a.m., this Wednesday, *Severn* sent off one motorboat in charge of Lieut. L. W. T. Lewis R.N.R., the cable was promptly cut and 100 yards of the telephone wire brought aboard. It was a night when the moon should have illuminated, but for most of the period some clouds obscured activities. Not a sign of German opposition anywhere: the enemy must have deserted this outpost. Or were they in ambush?

It was just breaking daylight at 5.30 when *Severn* arrived, opening fire with all her guns on houses and the old lighthouse, so that within five minutes little remained. A party of marines together with some 26 of the black troops, who had been employed at Yambe, landed under the same excellent Colour-Sergeant P. E. Smith, swept their way through the island but found no one; hoisted the White Ensign at the new lighthouse flagstaff, and demolished what remained of other buildings. Evidently the Germans, as at Yambe, were not risking capture by night but using this lookout by day only for, notwithstanding that a few hours previously one white man and several natives in khaki had been noticed, these must have gone back to the mainland by nightfall. That was a great disappointment to the invaders who were longing for an expected struggle, nor was any assault on the modern lighthouse permitted.

The orders comprised holding this for spotting and observation purposes, the landing being a preliminary activity to the day's principal duty. Everything, then, had worked without a hitch, the black troops no longer went bare-footed but had been provided with shoes and boots lent by *Severn's* officers, thus rendering disembarkation much quicker. But now followed the heavy onslaught at 6-19 a.m. when that old-fashioned battleship *Vengeance* (which monitors remembered months ago in the English Channel and during the August demonstration off Ostend) with her powerful 12-inch guns, assisted by the cruiser *Hyacinth's* 6-inch, began a terrific outburst.

The former devoted her attention to Tanga railway station and track, whilst her sister was concerned with the defences. This went on for nearly four hours, and one who witnessed the 12-inch shells hitting their targets, blowing up rollingstock as well, says it was like a series of earthquakes, debris leaping into the air and devastation laid all round. At 12.15 it recommenced for half an hour, and from 2.17 until 3 p.m. the same mighty thundering continued. Altogether about 150 big shells dropped each within a hundred yards of each other, so that the enemy would never be able to use the port for assisting his army until many a month elapsed.

Our intense bombardment had taken place under circumstances of fierce heat, for Tanga lies only 5 degrees south of the equator. With no awnings spread, sailors in khaki 'shorts' felt the sun's rays considerably, and the guns required every interval for cooling; but, though Tanga today was not captured and such an intention was still beyond the present strategy, ship's crews very much longed to know exactly how the "show" looked from the enemy's point of view. What they could not comprehend was that not a shell, nor so much as a rifle shot, reached the vessels.

I have before me, however, a German account written on that same day, and it leaves no sort of doubt as to results. Remarking on the effectiveness of *Vengeance's* shells, the writer goes on to mention by detail the damage done to Herr Müller's shop, someone else's hotel, the Villa Carolina, and so on. He admits that the railway station was wiped out, likewise that local artillery "replied with 200 rounds without success", yet we must concede the Germans' praise for one small enterprise. The British efforts having been completed, ships withdrew and the White Ensign on Ulenge was intentionally hauled down. Next morning at 3.30, whilst yet it was dark, *Severn* made a feint on Tanga in order to make the enemy release one bit of knowledge, which they had kept to themselves and we dearly wished to confirm.

Where precisely was that 4.1-in. *Königsberg* gun? Surely the exact position would be ascertainable if it flashed by night?

So, the monitor steamed past Ras Kasone to stir up the ex-Rufiji weapon. Sending up rockets and coloured lights against the sky failed to attract, and she even fired into the air her 4.7-in. howitzer: in fact, everything that by sound might suggest an imminent landing was loosed off. Yet the Germans neither showed a light, nor barked off a shell; by no sort of dodge would they indicate where their greatly treasured piece had been mounted. On the other hand, whilst Admiral Charlton had given strict instructions that the modern lighthouse on Ulenge was not to be harmed, the Germans doubtless realised how useful a spotting station this would again become. Therefore, during the night of March 23-24, they sent a party from the mainland in order that they themselves might destroy it, the work being accomplished so secretly that next morning *Charon*—the only whaler on patrol—was considerably surprised when she gazed at ruins only.

But on the 23rd, also, H.M.S. *Hyacinth* fresh from the Tanga exploit arrived with *Vengeance* off Dar-es-Salaam to make further sure that German steamers should not escape. Within lay the 8,000-tons D.O.A. liner *Tabora*, besides the *König* and *Feldmarschall*. The first of these three had pretended to be a hospital ship, yet her wireless aerial was noticed by H.M.S. *Chatham* so far back as October 1914 still in position, and such strong suspicions of her genuineness were entertained that shortly afterwards (November) an investigation party, which included Surgeon E. C. Holtom R.N., was sent aboard.

Certainly, she exhibited on her side the Red Cross, and Holtom found both a Dr. Weiss as well as a Sister in nursing uniform, but that about summed up any evidence of truth. Yes, a "patient" had been improvised at the last minute, and there he lay in bed; but when the British surgeon threw back the sheets it was to disclose an interesting phenomenon. The "sick man" had been such a hurried actor as still to be wearing trousers!

Presently there followed a gross act of German treachery, the investigating party were fired at and, to make a short story, Holtom with eleven others became prisoners. Therefore, on this March 23 the *Hyacinth*, having made sure that *Tabora* no longer could be claimed as hospital ship, began with *Vengeance* to shell her. Nine shots inside settled the liner's fate, she heeled over, sank on her beam ends, and was afterwards put up for auction, being sold for 60,000 *rupees*.

All sorts of happenings were now to take place and a quickening of tempo had begun. General Smuts' forces on land were doing well, and there was great joy in *Severn* when news came that troops had captured one of *Königsberg's* big guns. At the beginning of April, the monitor was sent south again to her former patrol area, using Tirene Bay as before, but now for the first time she learnt concerning one of the strangest coincidences belonging to maritime history. The reader will doubtless be aware that during the first three months of war British commercial ships in the Orient had suffered considerably at the hands of S.M.S. *Emden*, this German cruiser under the brilliant and goodlooking Captain von Müller being one of the sharpest thorns whichever the British Navy had to grapple.

Then on November 9, 1914, in the vicinity of Cocos Islands (Indian Ocean), H.M.S. *Sydney* came upon her and after a short action destroyed *Emden* utterly, taking Captain Müller prisoner, the actual position being Lat. 12.5½ S, Long. 96.53½ E. Pass over many months, and many thousands of miles till we come to Boydu Island near Mafia Island, where the vagaries of wind and current deposited one of

Emden's lifebuoys as a curious reminder of the past. Boydu Island, 1½ miles from Mafia, lies in Lat. 7:56 S, Long. 39.31 E.

★★★★★★★★★

Boydu at this date had been deserted by natives, but occasionally *Severn* called here and gave leave to her men for a run ashore. The lifebuoy had been picked up on February 19, 1916, but not till another three months did the monitor learn from the Resident here the exact details.

★★★★★★★★★

The rainy season had now set in with its discomfort, but any sight of the delta scenery gave happiness to none, though there were pleasant visits on those outlying islands to fetch turtle eggs, coconuts, lemons, fowls, and sometimes even cattle or goats, for the larder. On April 11 a party of liberty-men were just about to land for exercise when sudden orders cancelled leave, boats were hoisted in, anchor weighed, awnings furled, and off to sea *Severn* sped. Further south than ever was she bound this time, and on the way her crew were getting ready the splinter nets, covering with hawsers the steam-pipes, in fact generally preparing for action. News by wireless had disclosed that the whaler *Echo* was probably lost by this time, or at any rate in a pretty bad way.

Unfortunately, the Indian Ocean chanced to be having one of its boisterous moods, wind and head sea with a strong current combining to slow down *Severn's* progress and finally to make it no longer practicable. She wirelessed Admiral Charlton, then reluctantly turned back. Now all this was concerned with a very thrilling affair, and illustrates the changes which without warning were wont to occur.

Another supply steamer had reached the East African coast from Germany!

Exactly when or where our Intelligence system did not know, though more than the vaguest information reached them at the end of March. Her name we may mention as the *Marie* and like *Kronborg* she had taken advantage of the long northern nights to rush past Scotland, before coming down the Atlantic. *Marie* had been escorted up the North Sea by U-70. The German troops had profited immensely by *Kronborg's* supplies, but again there was need of stores especially such items as clothing, rifle ammunition, hand-grenades, and any fairly big guns.

That she had not come into one of the harbours north of Zanzibar seemed pretty certain, but less assurance could be made of some southern port. That was why on March 31 the battleship *Vengeance* arrived off Kilwa Kisiwani during the afternoon, and sent in a picket-boat under Commander Bridgeman. It was high water, navigation through the surf-washed reefs a risky business, and a heavy ocean sea was breaking menacingly. But Bridgeman would have been the last person to funk a fence and, though he returned after a narrow escape from disaster, he effected nothing except to reconnoitre the locality.

Next day, however, he took in the two whalers *Childers* and *Echo*, whilst the battleship lay outside the reefs and again supported him with her guns. The whalers also shelled positions observed by Bridgeman the previous evening, but received no reply; so, they entered the river, went up for thirteen miles, ascertained that it contained no enemy shipping, and at 10.15 a.m. began retiring. Nor had they got more than three miles downstream than shots from Mpara Hill fell uncomfortably close. Things were getting fairly warm until both whalers replied and the German firing quietened, but now most unfortunately *Echo* got aground.

There she stuck, and could not be moved on the falling tide. This looked like the end, for the enemy had a perfect target and was believed to possess two guns. Of course, *Childers* did not remain idle, yet the suspense of waiting till the flood might float *Echo* off at 2 p.m. was most trying: it seemed inexplicable that keen German gunners had not availed themselves of a glorious chance, yet eventually both ships emerged from the river safely, setting alight the Customs buildings as they came out seaward.

Six months passed ere the reason for this narrow evasion could be learned, and it shows yet again how little two rival enemies at the moment can appreciate each other's difficulties. *Vengeance* on the evening of March 31 had turned her guns on a position known as Yellow Cliff where the Germans possessed two cannon, but since the battleship's range was 11,000 yards we can well understand that the British found it impossible to say what damage they inflicted. Actually the 12-inch shells knocked one of the two cliff guns out of use, killing three of the four white men plus one native porter. This caused the enemy to shift the other weapon to Mpara Hill, where excellent marksmanship seemed about to conquer, had not *Childers* with her little 3-pdr. put up such an accurate and fierce answer that the Germans found it impossible to stand the hail around them and moved away.

The nett result of this visit was of negative value. Since, however, the *Marie* lay not within Kilwa Kisiwani, she might have entered Lindi, or Sudi Bay, or even Mikindani. Finally on April 11 H.M.S.

Hyacinth with the two whalers arrived off the indentation at Mgau Mwania, and the cruiser anchored outside so that she could look right up harbour. *Childers, Echo*, and a steam cutter, all under Commander Bridgeman now hurried in, but the Germans had made what might have been thought irresistible preparations.

A little distance inside, on the west bank, stood Sudi and here not one but two of *Königsberg's* 4.1-in. guns pointed straight down the inlet as if they were mounted at the top of a street, whilst on each shore were machine-guns besides rifles. Thus, in theory no lightly protected vessel could possibly attempt such a defile and survive: yet Bridgeman in his gallant manner not merely got through this narrow trap, defying shells and bullets. He turned slightly and continued into the next reach where, sure enough, lay the store-steamer *Marie*.

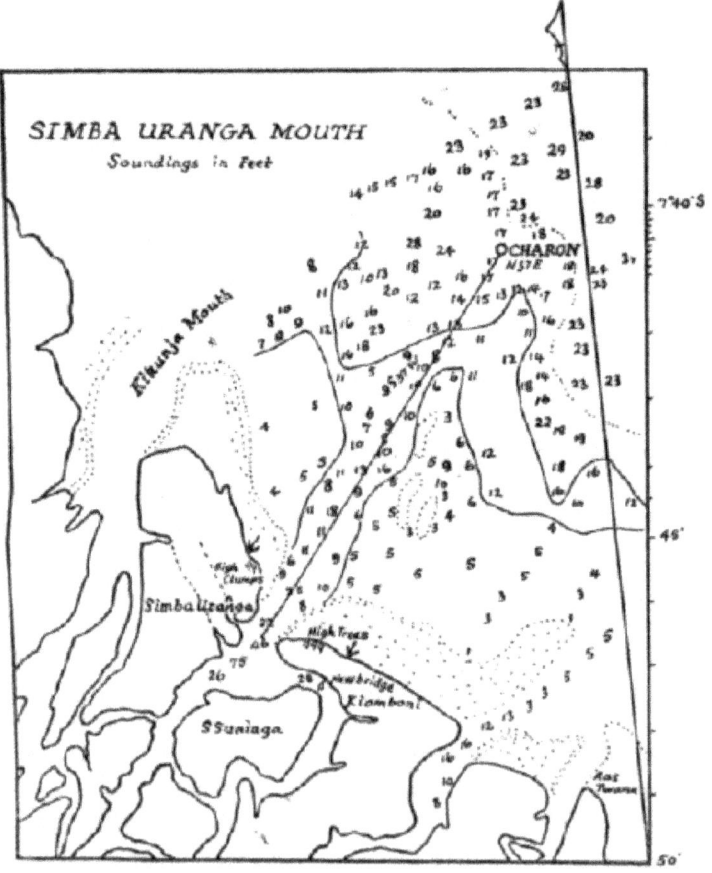

Chart to illustrate the attack on May 5, 1916, by H.M.S. "Severn", "Styx" and "Charon".

Alas! The British were come too late, for the blockade-runner had emptied her holds during the last three weeks and any seaman's eye could note that only absence of cargo would give her the present water-line. Bridgeman was determined to render her of no further use, yet all this German attention from the shore made every moment one long peril. *Childers* by her wireless was trying to direct *Hyacinth's* guns on to *Marie*, the whalers themselves performing the dual role of spotting and shelling. What with having to do this, keep under way in the stream, and dodge the enemy's fire, the task could scarce have been more difficult. *Marie* had been damaged by this intrusion, but if the visit should be prolonged any longer all three craft would be full of dead men.

So, Bridgeman brought his trio out, and past the strong defences again. More vigorous than ever was German anger this time, and the retreating flotilla looked as if they were on a suicide trip. That any human being could issue forth alive belonged to the miraculous, yet whalers and steam cutter with the loss of not more than 5 killed, and about the same number wounded, managed to gain the open sea.

Such bravery, and so many hazards, deserved greater ultimate success; for the adventure was of no more service than that of kicking a hole in the stable-door after the horse has bolted. Or, dropping all metaphor, the *Marie* could well be spared now that she had put ashore on the pier 4 field howitzers, 2 mountain guns, hand-grenades, several thousands of 4.1-in. shells for the remaining nine *Königsberg's* artillery; clothing, in large quantities, every kind of store that the German Army needed—together with a number of Iron Crosses for that same cruiser's company.

That *Marie* should have been even more successful than *Kronborg*; that she should have brought 60,000,000 rounds of ammunition all the way from Germany through two blockades, landing guns complete with officers and crews; is to us a matter for regret, though something of which the enemy might well be proud. But the gamble had to be made, for the reason that we had already maintained such a persistent patrol and denied the enemy use of his principal ports.

Nothing, however, could be more striking and conclusive than the personal statement of General von Lettow-Vorbeck. Some time since I received a letter from a British major who served through this campaign with the King's African Rifles, he wrote:

I have been living for some years in Germany, and by good

fortune about four months ago I met von Lettow-Vorbeck and had a very interesting talk with him. He told me that the blockade runner which got to Sudi was a veritable godsend, as they were getting to the end of their ammunition.

According to Ritter, the *Marie* had unloaded her cargo entirely by night and it was "under cover of darkness" that she slipped out from Sudi on April 13—that is, two days after the Bridgeman affair—"and began the return journey to Germany. The next time the English returned, they sent up their captive balloon, and concluded, as the ship was no longer there, that she had been sunk by a shell."

But if munitions now had begun to be hauled over land northward till reaching the Central Railway, which ran from Lake Tanganyika to Dar-es-Salaam, so that a steady supply came into the latter before being immediately despatched to the front; there was one great privation which the Germans had begun to feel keenly in that hot climate.

Beginning from April 1, the brewery at Dar-es-Salaam had ceased to produce any more beer, owing to the lack of maize!

Chapter 20

Glorious Adventure

Tiny hints sometimes foretell striking episodes, and the crew of *Severn* one Saturday evening towards the end of April guessed rightly that some new adventure was being planned. The ship was at anchor off Mafia, the rain had cleared, and now two native dugouts came alongside, both of them with their black occupants being hoisted aboard.

Was this another spy expedition?

Next morning the monitor got under way, patrolled off the delta, and at dark anchored abreast of Simba Urange. The natives were supposed to know this branch well and, having first been taken up on to the bridge, they were told by Captain Fullerton through an interpreter what was expected of them: to land by Simba Urange mouth, search round, and find out if the German outpost with watchers and guns were still there.

It was a pitch-black night when one dugout with three men cheerfully set forth, being towed by motorboat close towards the shore, a second dugout with another trio remaining on board. A careful watch, with men at the guns, kept minds on the alert in *Severn*, for at such close proximity the enemy might spring any sort of surprise. Three hours passed, it seemed an ideal occasion for stealth, and now the small craft came back: the sea had been too rough for them to get ashore.

On the following night a similar effort took place, and after four hours the men returned. As evidence that they had landed they brought with them some foliage, yet though they had looked along the beach no white man or anything of interest was observed. Had the Germans, then, evacuated the place and left the mouth undefended at last? To make sure, a third expedition went off at 7 o'clock on the night of Wednesday April 26, and at 1 a.m. the dugout was hauled on deck, a lot of green stuff, coconut shells and sand, being offered as proofs that the spies obeyed orders. This time the three scouts had certainly seen something else. Their job being finished, they were sent back to Tirene.

The rainy season was coming to an end, in a few days the tides would be at Springs, and meanwhile there was plenty to do. Sailors were being exercised at General Action Stations, sandbags refilled for protection round the ship, awnings taken down, and all fittings in the way of guns removed. Yes: something was maturing rapidly. For, on May 4, sixty black troops under Major W. B. Brook (Military Commandant and Resident of Mafia) embarked in *Severn*, and tomorrow before sunrise a new effort against the delta was to be attempted. The aim would be to land at Simba Urange; capture guns, gun-positions with their guards, on both sides of that entrance; high water being a few minutes before 6 a.m. The final preparations having been made and the last sandbags put round capstans, a practice landing took place on Niororo Island. That Thursday night *Severn*, with the two whalers *Charon* and *Styx*, as well as a steam pinnace from the battleship *Vengeance*, were waiting off the Simba Urange shore.

With the chart of Simba Urange mouth before us, we can perceive the intentions quite clearly. First of all, Lieut. L. W. T. Lewis R.N.R. was to leave *Severn* early on May 5 in one of her motorboats, during the fourth hour of the flooding tide, dash in between the points of beach, swing round to port past the Kiomboni peninsula and so reach the *Newbridge* wreck. Leaping aboard the latter, he was to cut that telephone wire which led from the mouth to Salale headquarters and thus sever connection with the outpost. This would prevent any succour approaching the latter.

Furthermore, he was ordered to mount a Maxim gun in *Newbridge's* bows, thereby commanding a big stretch of water should the watchers attempt retreat. The monitor's second motorboat was to land Major Brook with 35 of his troops 1¼ miles east of the point at Kiomboni, whilst *Vengeance's* pinnace was to take 25 more of these black soldiers plus 4 marines (all under Chief Gunner James Hamilton) and disembark them 1 mile north of this point: that is to say on the opposite bank.

Severn should be some 2,000 yards from the mouth just as dawn was breaking, and so draw the enemy's fire; but if the attack held out hopes of success, then both whalers were to steam at utmost speed as far as Salale, there to capture any boats which might be about. Captain Fullerton fully realised the riskiness of this venture, impressed upon officers the necessity of making no noise before gaining the above village, lest those Germans at the mouth should be warned and get away by boat into the creeks. The whalers, of course, could keep in touch with the monitor by their wireless; and, to prevent *Severn's* gunners firing on the wrong people, our troops when in sight of the ships were to hold rifle vertically in the right hand above the head.

Charon anchored on Thursday night 7 miles N37E from the mouth, showing white and red lights as a guide for *Severn* and *Styx* to bring up. Darkness still covered the face of land and sea when silent, unlit, activity commenced. It was very fine, with little wind or sea, and no moon; but a strong easterly set of tide slightly upset the landfall. Thus, Lieut. Lewis, with some Marines and a machine-gun crew, after leaving *Severn* at 3.30 a.m. instead of arriving exactly at the mouth, found himself half a mile to the eastward. This was soon rectified, he rushed in with a strong flood at 4.30, and forty minutes later was aboard *Newbridge* with gun mounted.

The Western party in the steam pinnace and towed gig was navigated by Sub-Lieut. F. G. J. Manning R.N.R. who, on nearing the shore prudently altered course slightly to starboard, so that he found an excellent sandy beach on the Simba Urange peninsula, where Mr James Hamilton disembarked his 4 marines and 25. black soldiers who soon had to contend with dense mangrove trees. It was very heavy going through swamp for the first hundred yards, and they encountered no human being, but next they came across several huts, which proved empty, though one had been inhabited by Europeans some time ago. Still advancing towards the south, they discovered, 400 yards from the land's end, a strong fort surrounded by barbed wire and trenches having emplacements for 4 guns pointing seawards; whilst in the rear of these were deep, roofed pits as "funk-holes" against ships' shellfire. It was significant that no guns remained: they had been sent elsewhere.

But a gruesome thing now met the eye. Natives, when captured, had always spoken in fear of German tyranny and cruelty, from which they were only too thankful for escape. Here then was a grim reminder of harsh discipline a little further south-westward. Standing in a small village were two uprights with an iron bar across—ugly gallows for stringing up disobedient blacks—and this now had to be rendered useless. The nett result of such exploration, and sighting another gun-emplacement, confirmed the impression that some time had elapsed since the enemy's evacuation. At 7 o'clock Mr Hamilton was able to signal *Severn* that he had captured the position.

We now come to the Eastern party which shoved off from *Severn* in her other motorboat and gig just after 3.30, Sub-Lieut. H. C. Gaffney R.N.R. being the navigator. The personnel besides the 35 Africans comprised Major Brook, *Severn's* surgeon, and Petty Officer D. Greenshields, Yeoman-of-Signals. Owing to the set of tide, and Mr Gaffney not being well acquainted with the coast, these two boats made the land 1½ miles too far eastward at 4.30. The tide was due to start ebbing in about another seventy minutes, so that, the water being very high, the gig penetrated a hundred yards before anybody could get ashore. Proceeding a couple of miles through this dense jungle, they struck a path along which cattle had evidently passed the day previous.

It was a strange, savage, terrain of coconut and mango trees, overgrown by abundant bush, and over this the party began to advance in extended formation, officers and men very much on the *qui vive*, expectant of surprises, keeping a sharp lookout against sudden ambush and machine-guns hidden among trees. Here is how Petty Officer Greenshields describes this exceptional morning:

> My party under Major Brook made a safe landing and got into a swamp, but was able to negotiate it. Our troops were thrown out and we made for the point: it was very heavy going, and daylight just breaking. After getting out of the swampy ground we struck a kind of grass field and then a path. Footmarks were clearly to be seen on the wet, sandy, soil. We followed the path, having a line thrown out both to right and left of us, and came across posts put up at intervals. At first, we thought they were to mark the range, but, when we saw necks of bottles on tree-trunks and posts, we came to the conclusion they were insulators for telephone wire, which we found as we went on.
>
> After skirmishing over a lot of ground and thick bush, and mote swamps, we came in sight of a lot of huts and roughly-made houses. The troops on our right had pushed on ahead of us and were up to the huts, and captured three natives. They were brought in front of Major Brook and questioned. It was found from their information that the place was evacuated some months ago, but that there was one white man left behind with telephone communicating with white men at Kikunja mouth on the mainland. One of the natives taken was this white man's servant, and he took us to his house. We fully expected to capture him, but when we got close more natives were seen, one trying to get away, but he was caught. We found out that the

THE SIMBA URANGE RAID, MAY
(Top) Showing difficult quicksands at mouth. Major being helped out by four *askaris*.
(Bottom) Lieut. Lewis returning in motorboat alongside H.M.S. "Severn" with his prisoners and the two captured German dinghies.

white man had left hurriedly, and this native took us to where he said he had gone.

We took all the natives, women as well, with us and followed a path for some time, cutting telephone wires as we went along. We had the white man's chest and personal effects with us, having to cross another swamp—bare mud over the boot-tops—and had a look round but could find no trace of the German; so decided to get into communication with Mr Lewis on board *Newbridge*, whose masts were visible above the trees. As we approached towards the ship, we heard three or four single shots fired, which appeared by the sound to be a louder report than from any of our men's rifles. We stopped, listened, the firing had ceased and we went on again.

Now the name of this sole watching German was Allert, who witnessed Lieut. Lewis enter and ordered the natives to hide in the bushes. Allert's house not only was seen to be empty, but his telephone receiver had gone too. Escaping towards that portion of the peninsula where the telephone wire jumped from shore to *Newbridge*, he sought to avoid capture by escaping in one of the two dinghies which were kept at a landing-place alongside the bank. But he was too late.

Lewis had spotted both these boats and seized them. Moreover, he had severed the telephone wire stretching from that shore to *Newbridge*'s mainmast. He found the steamer absolutely gutted of her external fittings, and the Germans had even removed from abreast her forehatch six steel plates from either side—probably now fitted as protection in *Adjutant* and *Wami*. But at low water her upper deck still remained 9 feet above sea level, and this was as well; for at 6.45 some sniper from the bank began firing and the bullets spent themselves against her sides, but more would have followed had not Lewis replied with his machine-gun. A few rounds sufficed, and the sniper desisted. These, then, were the shots which Major Brook's party had heard, yet the former's quest became all the keener because the firing might be of the enemy.

Allert was in a most awkward fix, his retreat to the peninsula's seaward end cut off, and his means of crossing the river withdrawn. Taking with him one native and two rifles between them, he had hidden among the thick bush only a few paces from the riverside, and begun to vent his anger on the Lewis party; but this information at present was denied to Major Brook's people who; after lighting upon those

(Top) One of "Könisberg's" 4.1-in. guns. This was mounted on a platform, used at Tanga, and hauled on rails by natives. (Bottom) One of "Könisberg's" funnels knocked down during engagement with monitors.

trenches where rifle and Maxim fire on several occasions always spat forth against British craft whensoever advance so far up stream had been made; now still hurried like hounds on a good scent. But where was the fox concealing himself?

If this German was almost caught, he intended to make a good effort to save his life, and with him was the advantage of knowing by long sojourn every inch of the ground. Whilst his situation admittedly must be desperate, he still possessed a rifle and with luck might lie motionless among the prodigal growth till the crisis passed.

Then a most dramatic thing occurred. Throughout the African continent, from east to west and north to south, even along the fighting front, no more exciting incident at this second could have been enacted.

Greenshields relates:

> I had got ahead of the party, and with one native soldier, who had got further ahead of his section, went round a bush to make for a ladder which carried the telephone wire to *Newbridge's* masts, when I nearly stepped upon a white man lying prone on his stomach with his rifle at the present. He fired point blank at me, and I was taken by surprise. My pistol was in the holster and before I could get it out—and me falling down behind a bush as well, and calling out "Here he is!"—he managed to shift his position into the bushes.
>
> Breathless moment! Allert only two yards away... pressing his trigger... and the shot rang out into silence... but missed!

The fugitive took speedy advantage of great luck, for the vigilant man behind the Maxim gun aboard *Newbridge* on hearing this rifle imagined the sniper was again aiming at Lieut. Lewis' party, so answered with a spray of lead into the very bushes wherein Greenshields and his comrades had barely retired. Lying down, the latter sought to evade this spatter, but it continued in such a downpour that Greenshields as signalman had to go into the open along the bank and request the gun to cease. It was firing from only 50 yards away.

Now this natural misunderstanding enabled Allert to disappear once more, creeping his way through the bushes, but the hounds were still working around. Sending half his party to dismantle the telephone wire, Major Brook set the others to probe the thick growth. At last, they got on the German's track, followed it for a considerable distance, hung about for most of an hour, but Allert managed to get clean away into concealment. Such was his haste that in the bushes his pursuers came across the two obsolete rifles, together with the missing telephone receiver. Greenshields, too, picked up the empty cartridge as a personal souvenir of his own most narrow elusion from death. Not that the memory ever forfeits recollection of such an episode. "I could see him taking aim along the barrel. I could have touched him."

What happened to the isolated Allert, left with nothing but his life; and how rescue ever came his way; we can but surmise. From *Newbridge* arrived a boat to fetch the native prisoners including a woman, the ladder of the telephone post (which would be useful at Mafia), Allert's box of belongings; the other women being used as porters. So now the party started to wend their way back, picking up the telephone-wreckers, and noticing the *Charon* with *Styx* pass upriver; but at Salale these ships saw nothing, so came down again. Ferreting out gun positions, crossing a bridge made of tree branches and palm leaves that spanned a gully, the united party under Major Brook traversed a large open space of clay-like mud surrounded by swamps and bush, intersected at low tide by deep water-courses, till they gained a cutting in the jungle cleared for more telephone posts.

The defence works on the sea-front had been made extremely well, gun emplacements perfectly concealed from the water and roofed in with growing creepers; deep trenches preceded by a wide ditch so filled with dry twigs that no one could approach without being heard. In order to drain the emplacements, some of *Newbridge's* 2-inch pipes had been tun into them. Everything had been most cleverly thought out, the shelters all neat and well-built: even the several huts and mud houses being so placed with a belt of young mangroves running along the beach as to render invisibility complete.

When *Severn* at 6.45 heard the rattle of *Newbridge's* machine-gun, she proceeded inside the river, anchored, and established signalling communication with Major Brook. Later Captain Fullerton with two officers came ashore and was not less impressed by the nature of this peninsula than had been Mafia's Resident. Thoughts went back to the various attempts in rushing this gauntlet, and it seemed remarkable that any ship should have survived. As to having seized and occupied the peninsula what time German guns and men remained, this idea now presented itself as thoroughly impossible. Such a scheme would have demanded not merely perfect surprise and a large force, but a trustworthy guide.

The nature of this region defied all imagination for its military difficulty. The greatest part consisted of swamps, and the shore side was all quicksands into which men sunk to their knees; the paths so well protected by rifle-pits at the end of every straight stretch, that one man could have held up a large force. (The accompanying illustration is from a photograph taken on that memorable May 5, and shows Major Brook being helped out of these tricky sands by some of the black soldiers). Single file would have been essential, since either side of the path was all soft stuff.

Altogether the visit was more than worthwhile. Firstly, it definitely settled that the last guns had been sent away about two months ago south to Kilwa Kivinje, the transportation being made partly by boat and thence by road. (It was Kilwa which *Severn* had bombarded so recently as May 2, destroying at 3,800 yards part of the Government House.) Secondly, from the peninsula native prisoners was it confirmed that *Adjutant* and *Wami* had reached Dar-es-Salaam. In fact, the delta was now deserted with nothing to defend, and no further use of the peninsula as an observation station would ever be risked.

At 11.30 a.m. troops were re-embarked, the nine women and one old man with a boy who had been carrying gear down to the water now were given their freedom, but no small interest was aroused on board *Severn* when Lieut. Lewis' motorboat arrived alongside with seven prisoners and two boats. One of the latter afterwards was taken in hand by the ship's carpenter, who made her look quite smart. But great was the feeling of joy that at length, after all these trying months, the Rufiji delta could now be regarded without any more apprehension, and to some extent vigilance might be relaxed when off here by night. This morning visit of so few hours sufficed to create a certain sympathy for the life which German watchers by the shore had necessarily to endure. The stench of foul mud, and the virulence of mosquitoes, were the final impression which the British took away with them.

Still, apart from the exciting adventure forming a powerful antidote to baneful monotony afloat, the trip ashore had been of considerable interest, and by no means the least entertaining items were the contents of Allert's box. A large number of photographs taken of his colleagues, the trenches, gun emplacements, and so on, have thus been happily preserved. Major Brook caused these to be reproduced, gave a set to the *Severn* and from these I have selected more than one illustration. It would have been a pity had the fortune of war left behind no picture to remind posterity concerning a delta that won a very special chapter in naval history.

CHAPTER 21

Advance Begins

By the middle of June *Mersey* was back from her refit at Durban, where also her crew had been rested. It had been hoped that now it might be *Severn's* turn for docking and her thorough overhaul be taken in hand: but this was the eve of prolonged naval operations, and just now her presence along the coast seemed more necessary than ever.

Material, however, can outlast personnel; and machinery may endure more than human nature with its sensitiveness. Captain Fullerton's ship's company had been cooped up so many months with such rare opportunities for leave; their nerves tried by such a number of thrilling events; that one wonders how sailors kept so fit. The time, however, had arrived when men must get away from the monitor, and have a few days of plain rest ere beginning another adventure series.

So, *Severn* steamed up to Zanzibar, where was a sanatorium on an island. Hither in three watches the crew took turns to come for a few days' complete change. Football matches, a concert, helped to bring a little contrast among the nerve-weary, and on Monday July 3 this vessel was on her way north to the Tanga area. Here she found Ulenge Island in British occupation, with the Union Jack flying over it and several other men-of-war at anchor. Clearly something was about to begin.

Actually, from now we witness the effect of naval pressure assisting the army in the decline and fall of Germany's power throughout East Africa. Let us remind ourselves that, apart from the adventure interest in these separate episodes, there is the underlying attraction of studying what can be achieved by a mixed collection of ships possessing no sort of homogeneity. The Grand Fleet in European waters was negativing the High Sea Fleet, U-boats were waging warfare against Allies' commerce, only a handful of ocean-raiders broke out on to the shipping routes; light cruisers such as *Emden, Dresden,* and *Königsberg*

215

no longer existed outside Germany, so that a full-dress sea-battle away from the British Isles was out of the question.

Off East Africa there was not one first-class battleship, not one modern cruiser, but old-fashioned units such as *Vengeance*, *Challenger*, *Talbot*; the three gunboats *Severn*, *Mersey*, *Thistle*; and those improvised warships which had been built for the industry of whaling. The squadron looked as if it was but the expression of an afterthought, and not one logical plan: a collection of bits and pieces rather than a unified whole; an assortment of odd craft gathered together from all parts of the world. And that, indeed, was about true. For the bigger ones had come from Europe, others from New Zealand, the whalers from South Africa, and now the 710-tons *Thistle* (with her two 4-inch guns) had come all the way from China.

But they sufficed for the special coastal purpose that was required, and at a most difficult period when not enough armed units could fulfil all the demands for the Narrow Seas, the trade-routes, the Mediterranean, Adriatic, and Aegean. More than ever the army ashore was the spear-head, and the navy along Africa's east coast the shaft of that weapon: but now we are to watch how the latter could be employed during the final thrusts.

The German colony was doomed because command of the sea was not theirs. All very well for Dar-es-Salaam to be *en fête* and decorate itself with lamps when news of the Jutland Battle sparked through to the capital, but that did not materially alter the local outlook. Supplies were getting short, most of the port's guns with crews had been sent away to the front, and though all the town turned out to see them off from the railway station, those cheers and chantings of folksongs were scarcely full of optimism.

Not less heavily did the threat of impending doom hang over Tanga, whose civil population had been evacuated by June 4. The several bombardments going on every few days against Dar-es-Salaam, Kilwa, Pangani, with more to follow, indicated clearly enough to which contending side belonged the initiative. On July 5 *Severn* was still at anchor off the entrance to Tanga harbour, cleared for action, ship's company in khaki, waiting to help the soldiers who had landed at Kwale in Mansa Bay, but now were marching on Tanga's direction.

During the night several flashes were noted followed by loud reports, and next day Red Cross flags were hoisted by the Germans over three houses. At 6 a.m. on Friday July 7 under ideal weather conditions *Severn* proceeded into the harbour, anchored, and sent ashore a naval party with native scouts, who scaled the low cliffs south of Ras Kasone, (see earlier map), without opposition, and hoisted the Union Jack, after which scouts advanced into Tanga town and rendezvoused near the hospital, whence *Severn* had been attacked on the previous August 19. Things were happening quickly today, the troops had swept over the ridge and by noon Tanga was occupied, with the British flag flying conspicuously over the town.

The next job was for whalers to sweep the entrance in search of mines, (none were found, and the enemy had never replaced those which *Severn* blew up eleven months previously); the squadron entered, anchored, and then *Talbot's* commanding officer, as well as Captain Fullerton with his signalman, went ashore to view the wreckage wrought by naval shells. The Germans had fled to Pangani, leaving behind the natives who welcomed their new masters with smiles and greetings.

Next day Admiral Charlton, as Commander-in-Chief, ceremoniously landed to make a tour of inspection. Remembering the hot time when monitors and whalers had come in to destroy *Markgraf*; recollecting, too, the disappointing failure of Indian troops on arriving at Tanga earlier in the war; there were those warriors who rejoiced with exceeding great delight that at last a new phase had commenced. A message came from General Edwards:

> I offer to the navy, to all officers, non-commissioned officers and men, my heartiest congratulations. It is a matter of the highest satisfaction to me that the former records of Tanga have been effaced.

Thousands of natives from outlying districts were now coming in, happy to regain their freedom of moving about and to resume their fishing. A certain amount of sniping from the enemy's outposts just outside the town went on vigorously against our patrols ashore, so that when the ship's band from *Vengeance* on Sunday afternoon went to play their music in Bismarck Square (as Germans previously had been wont), a change of site to the sea-front became necessary.

Not the least interesting feature, however, to the monitor's people was the sight of *Markgraf* lying painfully on her side, burnt right out, and a mere mass of rusty steel. Some even climbed aboard her to note the results of that bombardment which had been made under such distracting conditions, and now found that the conflagration had dominated the whole of her structure except the poop; but every item not already consumed the Germans had themselves removed. And also, was it learnt (as hinted in an earlier chapter) that the mines, which nearly a year ago *Severn* blew up on the raft, had been raised from the harbour only on August 18.

So, the monitor's crew on the first anniversary of *Königsberg's* defeat began relaying the moorings and navigation buoys, which the enemy had also taken up. The next duty took *Severn* gradually further south along the coast supporting the advancing army and bombarding the coast, trying to locate the enemy's camp, demolishing houses and factories. But sailors have the reputation for being handy men capable of tackling all sorts of queer jobs, and to *Severn's* seamen fell the task of erecting a new lighthouse on Ulenge Island which the enemy had pulled down. Assisted by natives as porters, the position was cleared, iron structures fetched off, the ruins demolished, and within a very few days a temporary light was working.

By wireless the good news was flashed on Sunday July 23 that, still further south, Pangani had been occupied this morn, following the bombardment and landing of Marines from *Talbot*. Only two days previously the morale of Dar-es-Salaam had been severely taxed when *Vengeance*, *Challenger*, and *Mersey* at 6.30 a.m. during five hours battered the capital severely. Ritter, who was serving there with some of the *Königsberg* remnant, refers in his diary to "the overwhelming shrapnel fire . . . the Englishman knows his goal perfectly well." And in the direction of Dar-es-Salaam the retreating enemy was gradually making.

On Monday *Severn* likewise proceeded to Pangani, carrying Captain Dickson with 100 of his native scouts and porters. A quaint crowd the latter presented on the monitor's spotless decks. Some wore as many as four hats, one was clad in a starched-front shirt, but on gaining the harbour entrance such a swell existed that entry could not be tackled. The gunboat thereupon showed her visitors how abominably she could roll at anchor, with a result that the unfortunate black men were lying prostrate everywhere and transforming the ship into such a state as to require disinfecting.

Next day ugly waves were still breaking over the bar and *Severn* waited till half-flood. Feeling her way cautiously through the surf, she found 11 feet, came past the narrow mouth and anchored off the town, putting ashore the dark-skinned passengers. The river was not 600 yards wide, the hill scenery on the south bank being magnificent, but the place had an evil reputation for fever, and one unfortunate

German officer suffering from the blackwater variety was fetched off to be accommodated in *Severn*. There were rubber plantations, and plenty of German gun emplacements met the eye, but lying on the beach was the gun-shield from one of *Königsberg's* 4.1. On this south side the ground seemed so suited for defence as to arouse wonder that the enemy did not remain.

Pangani was just another of those intricate places where only such units as a monitor or whaler could dare to pilot her way, and when *Severn* went out again over the bar she had to batten down till well past the surf. But conditions became far less pleasant as she let go anchor off Mkwadjie, where *Talbot's* marines were holding the village and keeping back a small force of the enemy not far distant. Here some more of Captain Dickson's scouts were landed, to aid the marines, but the weather was in a boisterous mood and the position off an open shore not suitable for small vessels even with both anchors down.

Just before six o'clock that evening a large crowd of natives. was sighted leaving their village in a hurry, carrying all their household goods and driving before them their cattle as if some force in the rear were impelling them to the shore. Next one black man from the beach began waving a red cloth, and a fire was also lighted: these were pre-arranged signals that the Germans now approached. *Severn* stood by, then five minutes later blazed away with her guns, firing rapidly for twenty-five minutes, and gave the enemy such a warm time that the threat vanished.

Next day (July 31) she was summoned across to Zanzibar for a naval conference, but came back to the continent the same night, arriving off Sadani and bringing up close to the beach. This was to be the first step in a series of operations along the coast that were to last six busy weeks and have the most important results. General Smuts had asked the navy to capture Sadani and hold it, so on August 1 the force had assembled off the place which lies facing the western side of Zanzibar Island. The bigger units as Outer Squadron comprised H.M.S. *Vengeance* and *Talbot*, the two monitors *Severn* and *Mersey* being inshore to cover with their guns the landing party.

All boats started for the beach about 6 a.m., naval ratings and marines being assisted by a detachment of Zanzibar Rifles. It was one of those picturesque affairs we used to see sketched in the weekly illustrated newspapers, and today occasionally are depicted on the films. Ships' boats were firing their machine-guns as they advanced, monitors were blasting the approaches, then as boats' keels touch the sand a mile north of the town out poured bluejackets making for the bush. From village they rushed into the town, and within less than an hour, trenches had been taken, the Union Jack was flying over old fort and castle; very slight opposition, and but three casualties being sustained.

This fort was found enclosed in a *"boma"*—an obstruction made originally for keeping out savages and leopards—surrounded by the native village and dense bush, which first had to be cleared. A German white officer, brought aboard as prisoner, had some interesting stories to relate. Herr Freyan before hostilities had been a merchant living at Tanga till joining up with the Defence Force.

This elderly man was a typical colonist, hard as nails, and caused some amusement when narrating that he had been dodging *Severn* ever since August 19, 1915 when she first went into Tanga to attack *Markgraf*, Freyan was in that port also when, seven months later, the Yambe Island adventure occurred: in fact he happened to be one of those who fired on the monitor's boats at the re-embarkation. Then he went to Ulenge Island, being the very fellow who laid the charge and lit the fuse which blew up Ulenge lighthouse. A few days ago, he was in Mkwadjie when *Talbot's* marines captured the village and nearly caught him, but he barely managed to escape. Then, coming on to Sadani, his luck failed and he found himself lodged aboard the *Severn*, where, having been made free in the Wardroom he chatted away with remarkable content.

"Everywhere I go", he remarked, "there is always this monitor."

The usual sniping continued ashore, a sergeant of the British troops being shot by a man hidden up a tree, and that night other snipers attacked the town from the north, but when searchlights were switched on from seaward and swept the coast no more of that trouble followed until daylight. Sadani having been taken, four days later the bluejackets were re-embarked when military forces came to relieve them.

Back again to Zanzibar went *Severn*, where another surprise awaited: for in steamed that ancient and obsolete sloop H.M.S. *Rinaldo* which monitors had last beheld whilst bombarding the Belgian shores. It was a curious war, anyway, that should require such an "old crock" to come all this way out to Africa's coral strand! But a sense of sadness pervaded *Severn* on August 10. Two years ago, Captain Fullerton had commissioned her at Barrow, he had since taken her in and out of countless tight corners, kept his men happy and fit, led them to victory, and won permanent renown for the *Königsberg* conquest. Through every kind of weather and temperature the ship had been steered and, in spite of her own difficult characteristics, she had been made to render exceptional service: yet now her commanding officer, having been marked out for a bigger vessel, was saying goodbye. After so many months of sharing experiences, the parting was not easy. As he went over the side for the last time, they gave him three rousing cheers, bidding farewell to "a good gentleman and a smart naval officer."

And that is about as high a regard as any seafarer can ever wish to be held in. He was succeeded by Commander W. B. C. Jones R.N., Gunnery Officer in the *Vengeance*, and not many days elapsed ere *Severn* was taking part amid a brilliant adventure.

CHAPTER 22

Bagamoyo and Dar-Es-Salaam

It was on August 12 that the British troops started their advance from Sadani in the direction of Bagamoyo, and next day a request from the military was wirelessed to Admiral Charlton that the navy would capture Bagamoyo as early as possible; adding that the enemy there were only about 10 whites and 49 *askaris* strong.

This German seaport was an important trading station which had always kept in close commercial touch with Zanzibar, the principal commodities being mangoes, oranges, lemons, and copra. The anchorage, however, was an open roadstead and large vessels found it impossible to get far in. During the night of August 14-15 *Severn* and *Mersey* steamed away, and let go anchor off the town just before 3 a.m. to await arrival of *Vengeance*, *Challenger*, and the aircraft carrier *Manica*, which was a converted merchant ship and had been on the station some weeks.

The plan was to employ the two monitors as inshore covering ships, whilst the heavier-draught vessels were to bombard from a distance. There was a slight swell, with little wind, and a bright moon when at 4.40 a.m. a landing party from *Vengeance* shoved off, but under such conditions complete surprise could scarce be expected. At 5.30 three tows of boats (numbering 10 in all) from *Mersey*, and three more tows (numbering 7 boats altogether) left *Severn*, and they made a magnificent sight rushing shorewards. Monitors then at once weighed and opened fire.

Until about now the enemy had been caught napping, but at 5.44 they began to concentrate against the boats a deadly repulse; for the military intelligence had not accurately appreciated the German strength, which actually included one *Königsberg* 4.1, one 5-barrelled pompom, 2 Maxims, and a total force more numerous than the naval landing party. Rifles, too, were firing from trenches along the beach so that it was only through the skill exercised by Commander R. J. N. Watson R.N. (of *Vengeance*) and Commander W. B. Wilkinson R.N. (of *Challenger*), who were in charge of the enterprise, that the enemy could be kept guessing; for, some little distance from the shore, the boats altered course and till the very last they deceived the Germans as to where disembarkation would take place.

The heavy fire from ships, and motorboats, and steamboats (towing the small craft), certainly saved invaders from quick death, though some men received wounds. Picture the boats grounding at 6.30 close under that *Königsberg* gun to the left of the town. This weapon had been part of the Tanga defences, whence the Germans sent it under haulage of 500 blacks and mounted it so recently as six days ago; but because they had chosen a position 30ft. back from a ridge, it was impossible for it to be depressed sufficiently.

Furthermore, a trio of very small vessels with their tiny guns now began to hit it as if three dwarfs were smiting a giant; and one of these three was having an opportunity for which she had waited a long, long while. She was none other than the armed tug *Helmuth*, which patrolled Zanzibar's South Channel that day when *Königsberg* sank *Pegasus*, but now from off the east of Bagamoyo beach her 3-pdr. made accurate aim which annoyed the German gunners intensely. Simultaneously a 3-pdr. mounted in *Vengeance's* steam barge, and another of the same calibre in that battleship's picket-boat, lopped shells round the same target; the range being only from 800 to 500 yards, this flotilla completely dominated the Germans' big hope. Certainly eleven 4.1 rounds had threatened the approaching tows and fallen unpleasantly close to monitors, but now the gun was abandoned to the onrushing shore party. Concerning this incident Admiral Charlton afterwards wrote:

> Its capture was, in my opinion, a most remarkable piece of work, reflecting the greatest credit on the boats and the attacking section.

Meanwhile *Manica* had got up her kite-balloon for spotting, but her seaplane (as so frequently in those early days of aviation) developed engine trouble and came down in the breakers at the mouth of Kingani River near the town, though luckily disaster was averted and she got back undamaged. The admiral then wirelessed the armed merchant cruiser *Himalaya*, and this ex-liner was just leaving Zanzibar: she arrived shortly with another seaplane, which at once dropped bombs on trenches and then began spotting. *Himalaya* also performed valuable work in the subsequent bombardment.

At 6.30 news came from kite-balloon, seaplane, and a portable wireless set ashore, that the enemy was retreating westward (between the sea and where the Roman Catholic French Mission buildings stood) to resist further landing. The German officer in charge was Captain von Bok, who was rushing his troops round to the opposite side of the town; but a 6-inch shell from *Severn* hit the five-barrelled pompom, destroying and almost pulverising it, killing another officer—Captain von Boedecke—and shortly afterwards Captain von Bok was slain too. With this the climax passed, all German initiative disappeared, and at 7 a.m. the Union Jack was flying over the governor's house, that is to say within half an hour of the first landing.

The British next established themselves firmly in a small, but important, quarter of the town whence they kept spreading all the time; gathering in Arabs, Indians, and native Africans. Now the capture of this place made a tremendous impression on the locals. Here was the former capital of the slave-trade, and starting place for the great caravan routes up-country. These simple-minded blacks had begun to inquire of their German masters in the Defence Force: "When are you going to let us go back to our homes?" And always the answer was: "When we have had a big fight with the English". Today the tussle had been witnessed, the black-skinned warriors became gradually demoralised, so that Mtoni Ferry, a strategic and strongly defended position on Kingani River some miles above the town, was evacuated, thereby flinging open wide the door to our troops coming south from Sadani towards Dar-es-Salaam.

No interference had been made with the French Mission, the Arabs' or Indians' quarters, but the 4.1 gun was afterwards removed to Zanzibar as a welcome trophy to remind all and sundry that, through gradual and persistent wearing down, a brave and enterprising enemy had been defeated by sea-power both within the delta and right along the coast. Having regard to the opposition and the difficulty of disembarkation, the British casualties turned out to be remarkably light. Captain F. H. Thomas of the Marine Light Infantry was killed as he reached an enemy trench. This gallant officer's loss caused a greater pang, not merely because of the promising career which seemed still before him, but for the reason that he had taken part in all the recent operations.

His body was afterwards committed to the deep by H.M.S. *Ven-*

geance. Two other marines, two seamen, two of the Zanzibar Rifles, also lost their lives, and of the latter regiment one was wounded. The enemy's casualties included the two German officers already mentioned, one German soldier, eight *askaris* —all killed; eight more *askaris* wounded; thirteen *askaris* and three Germans taken prisoners; among whom were three of the crew that had manned the 4.1.

Eventually 150 rounds of ammunition for this gun were discovered—evidently part of the cargo from *Kronborg* or *Marie*—and shipped to Zanzibar. It transpired that the enemy, accustomed to previous bombardments off the coast, had not expected such to culminate in anything more formidable.

But *Severn* slipped away secretly after dark for another nocturnal duty, and at 3 a.m. arrived in the neighbourhood of Dar-es-Salaam. It was known that one 4.1 still remained there, and the monitor's presence had the purpose of making the enemy fire on her so that the gun's position might be noted. Sure enough, at the first gleam of daylight its flash revealed the desired information from a hill well back inland, and a regular duel went on for some time against the monitor's two 6-inch: it amounted to a contest as to which—British or German—crews could fire the quicker, and one projectile dropped barely clear of the monitor's stern.

Then arrived *Vengeance* with her earthquaking 12-in., which silenced the German for a long while. Evidently, however, this *Königsberg* relic had been mounted on wheels for, as *Severn* steamed seawards, it blasted forth again fiercely, and even straddled her.

Doubtless it will amaze the reader that, after all these intensely active weeks, the crew of *Severn* were still able to carry on with the minimum of rest or recreation. Tonnage for tonnage, she was probably the hardest-worked unit, and most frequently in action, of any warship flying the White Ensign. But, contrary to all experience, it was the vessel herself which now began to break down; the old trouble with decks and supports manifesting itself again after so much firing. Back to Bagamoyo she went for a day or two, all the same, and then did some more firing further south where the enemy were raiding and setting a village alight.

What with General Smuts' soldiers ashore, and ceaseless naval activities, the time fast approached when the Germans must make their last stand at Dar-es-Salaam, and by mid-August trains full of troops from the interior were being rushed into that capital. If the end were not quite attained, every British leader knew that it was almost within

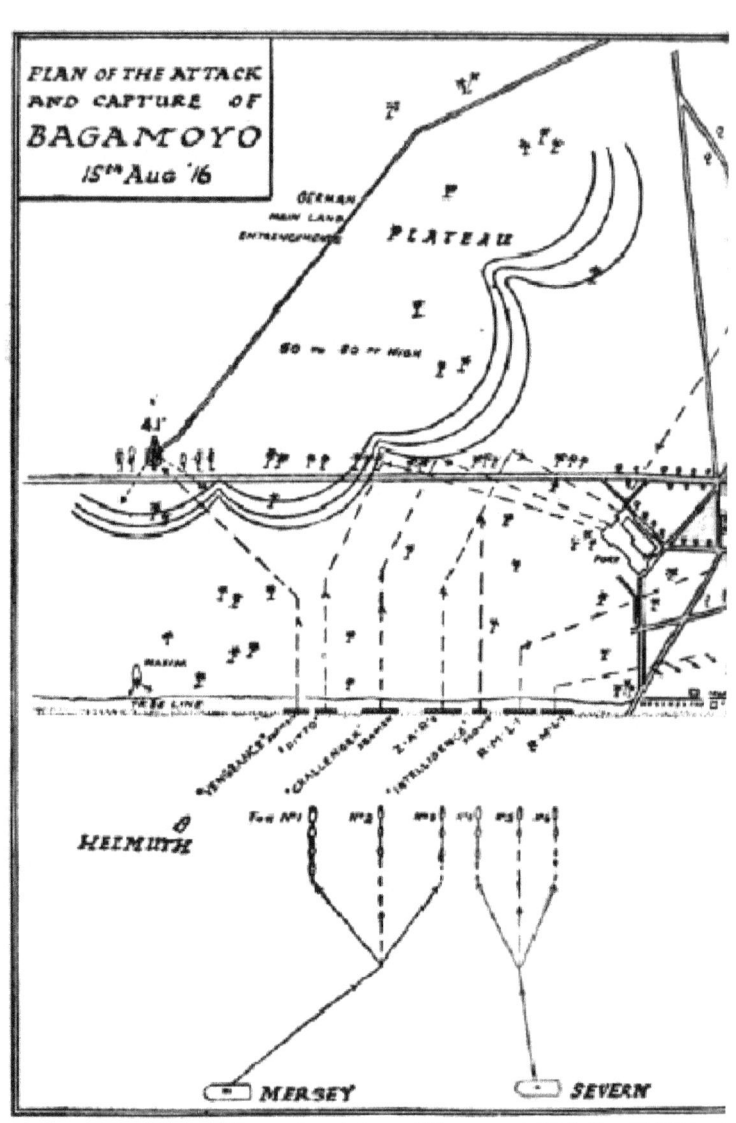

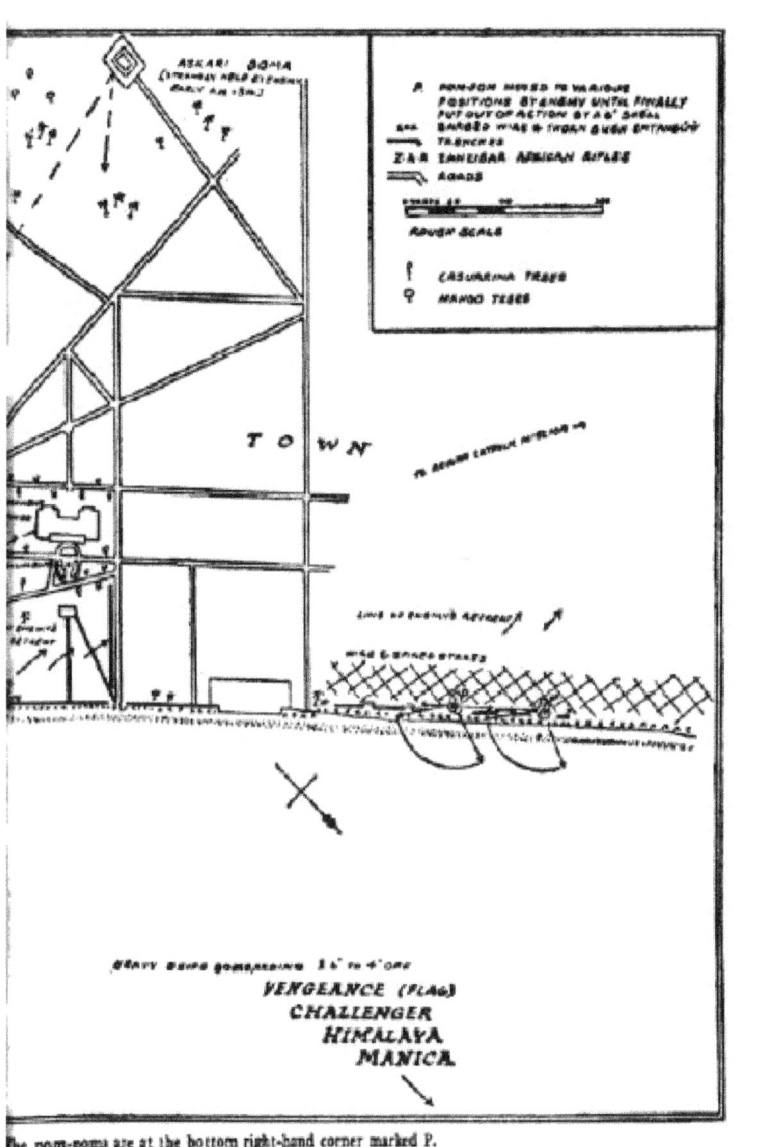

The pom-poms are at the bottom right-hand corner marked P.

sight, and the strategy next must be to keep on wearing the Germans down, harassing Dar-es-Salaam. That port was being bombarded now almost daily as a preliminary measure, and on August 26 when *Severn* came out of Zanzibar (after four short days to remedy defects) she took over the duties as guardship off Bagamoyo whence our troops would begin their final advance to effect Dar-es-Salaam's capture. A couple of *Severn's* Lewis guns, and crews, joined up with the military.

Never had Bagamoyo been so busy. Transports were arriving and emptying detachments, a landing-stage was being built of rough timber, stores were dumped ashore, mules brought, and all manner of gear; native porters by the thousand were being collected unloading lighters and carrying great packages into buildings. For this newly acquired Army Base, with its temporary aerodrome, was the final kicking-off place, and on the last day of August the troops marched out together with the store-bearing porters.

At 2.30 p.m. of August 31, *Severn, Mersey, Thistle* weighed and as a separate squadron were to steam on the army's left flank with whom they would keep in touch during the advance. The wind had risen, churning up a choppy white sea, which contrasted with the long straight khaki line swinging along the green coastal road. The objective was a spot named Mssasani quite close to Dar-es-Salaam, to capture a couple of hills overlooking the latter, after which more transports with heavy howitzers would be ordered from Zanzibar. It was known that there might be some trouble with a German big gun, also that the enemy had created a network of barbed wire, pits, and other defences; but these would all have to be surmounted. Then, at the right development, a man-of-war would be sent into Dar-es-Salaam with a joint note from the naval commander-in-chief and general demanding surrender of the town; but should that be refused, there would be no hesitation in destroying it.

Having anchored the first night at 5.30 p.m., the combined advance went on next day till reaching Konduchi, *Thistle* towing a large water-lighter for the troops. One of the two hills having been occupied, transports came with still more soldiers and Marines, the marching having made fast progress with negligble opposition.

At 6.30 on Sunday morning, September 3 (after the whalers *Pickle, Fly, Childers* and *Echo*—all under Commander R. O. B. Bridgeman—had simulated a landing at Upanga), all ships opened fire against Mssasani with terrific salvoes for half an hour directed on the gun positions north of Dar-es-Salaam, following which the troops came along and advanced to the capital's outskirts. Into Mssasani Bay now poured *Vengeance, Hyacinth*, transports, and the smaller vessels, where they remained anchored during the night. All day long transports were unloading, and suspense was something almost tangible. From the masthead were visible the spires and tops of Dar-es-Salaam's highest buildings, so that conclusion must follow one way or the other very speedily.

There might, after all, be whole batteries large and small keeping silence only till now, concealed torpedo-tubes, and so many magazines under bomb-proof shelters; that the Germans would not think of surrender.

So dawned Monday, and quite early H.M.S. *Challenger*, flying a white flag, entered with the demand note and hoveto off Dar-es-Salaam boom, whence a boat brought the joint message ashore. Nor was a reply long delayed. By 8 a.m. the deputy-*burgomaster*, together with the bank manager and interpreter, came off and agreed to surrender, giving all the required guarantees. This was the day for which so many hearts had hoped and longed during two years, and the occasion would be unforgettable.

The larger warships had sailed from Mssasani Bay at 5-30 a.m. and at 9 o'clock monitors were ordered to weigh. They had only one hour and a half's steaming before *Vengeance, Hyacinth, Challenger, Talbot,* and *Manica* were found anchored with whalers in the outer harbour. An impressive sight with white flags flying from every ship of the squadron. And now *Mersey* was sent inside to clear the boom-defence, which had been laid so long ago against British surprises.

It seemed a pretty stout affair, and needed plenty of the monitor's gun-cotton for destruction. The reader will not have forgotten that the Germans had placed their sunken dock across this entrance early in the war thereby shutting in the three steamers *Tabora, König,* and *Feldmarschall,* but apparently the door had been only partly shut. A British officer who served with the marines and became well acquainted with Dar-es-Salaam writes me to say:

> The entrance was only partially obstructed, and ships up to about 10,000 tons could always pass to the north of the obstruction. The Germans realised this and tried to complete the blocking by sinking the *König* in the passage-way. But they miscalculated the tide, and she swung harmlessly up on to the beach. . . . The *Challenger* (she was of 5,915 tons, and drew

21 ft), however, could pass freely in and out, and so could the other light cruisers and the monitors, as well as the smallest troopships. The *Feldmarschall* was salved soon afterwards and brought out, but the *König* and *Tabora* were lying on their sides, complete wrecks. The dock was not raised, though great efforts were made to do so.

So, *Mersey* had to sever the heavy chain cables, which stretched from *König* to large lighters across harbour, and it was such a formidable business that it required over five hours. But the German flags were hauled down ashore, during the afternoon the victorious troops marched in, admiral and commanding officers with a party from each ship landed, the naval band played, and up went the Union Jack once more. A 4 p.m. *Mersey*, followed later by *Severn*, went in past the sunken dock (noticeably awash) and brought up off the Government House. During this passage, eyes were regarding critically the position of a 4.1-in. gun on some low land, but after closer investigation it proved to be a very clever dummy fashioned out of a palm-tree.

Ashore were many other items of special interest: the plotting-tables and instruments lying about, the gun-mountings and shields intact, but the guns gone; the foundry which had recently been making shells, but had also repaired one of *Königsberg's* cylinders whilst she lay in the Rufiji for its return.

So, the whole of East Africa as to its northern half had been taken away from Germany within the first two years of hostilities, and the Admiralty were not slow in telegraphing their appreciation of the navy's share. Curiously for some weeks later the *Kaiser's* imperial arms still remained over the high altar in the local cathedral, so that as late as October 3 we find Admiral Charlton (himself a practising Roman Catholic) forbidding any Roman Catholics of His Majesty's Ships from attending service therein till such devices should have been removed.

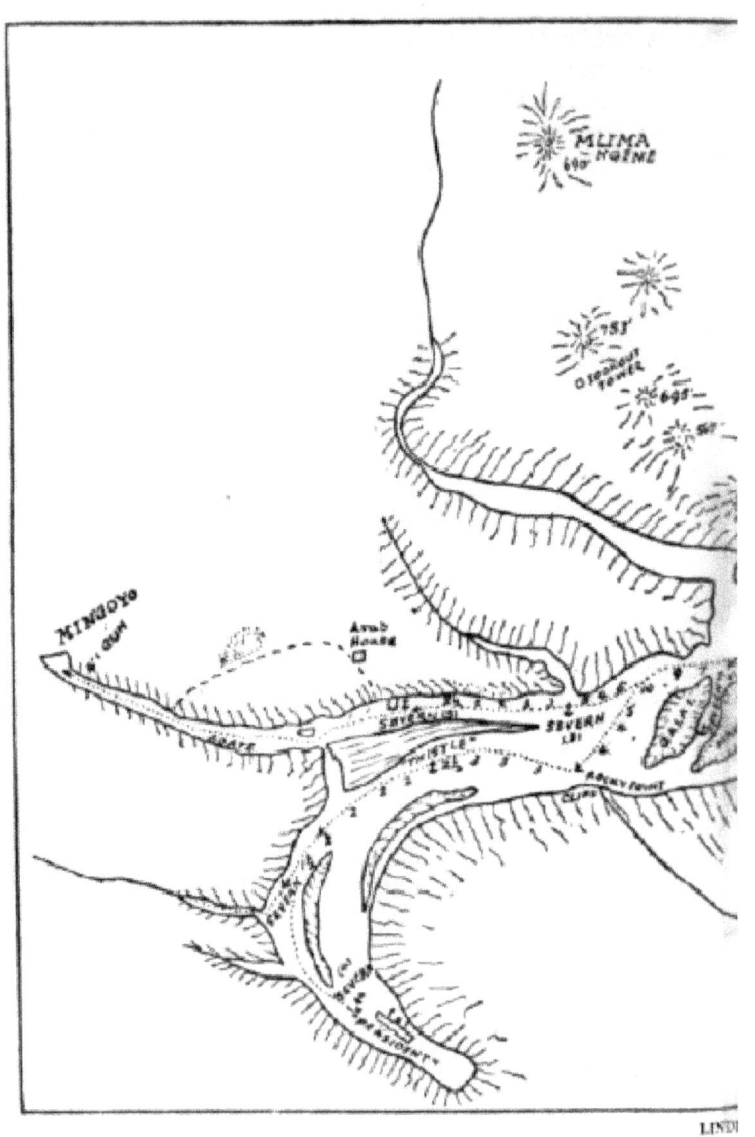

This plan (not drawn to scale) shows the five different positions

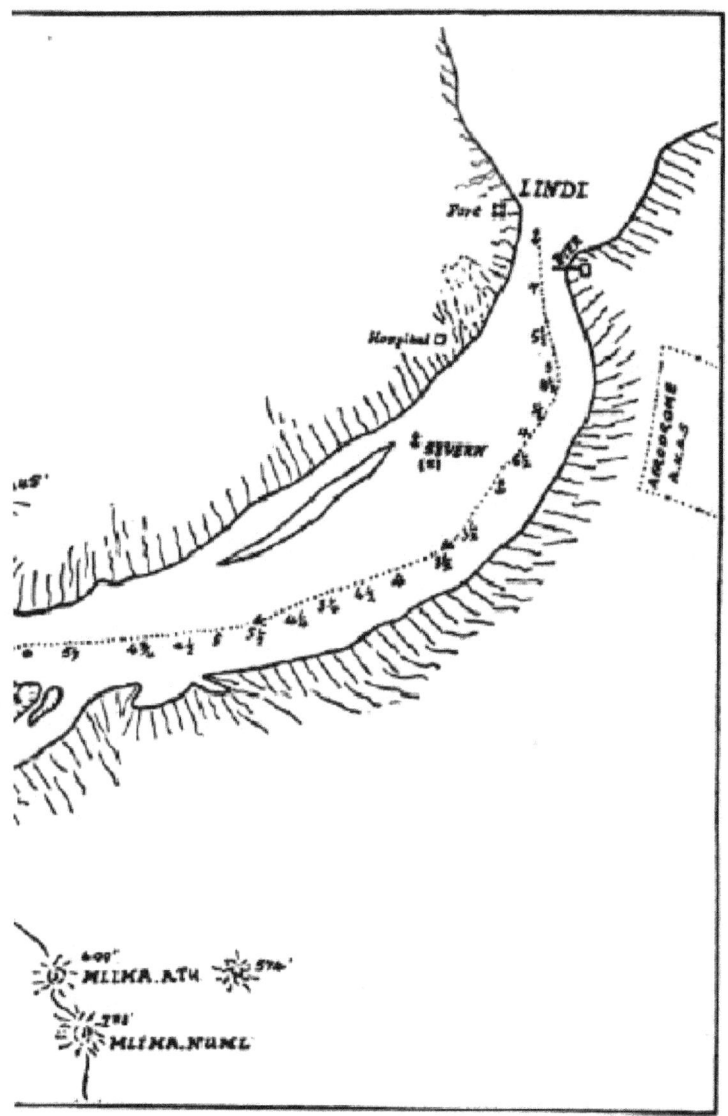

"Severn" brought up during the operations of June 1917.

CHAPTER 23

Down South

The next naval duty was to seize other coast towns further south, in order to hinder the enemy's retreat in that direction. Therefore, on September 7 a simultaneous attack was made on Kilwa Kivinje and Kilwa Kisiwani, for the purpose of possessing towns and holding the commanding hills. Both these attacks succeeded, Kivinje surrendering to *Vengeance*—town and hill being occupied—and Kisiwani similarly yielded to *Talbot*, who sent a party ashore to hold the place. Six days later operations began also against the remaining southern towns: Minkindani, Sudi, and Lindi. Thus, by the 18th the entire coast that once was German, extending right away from north of Tanga down to Kiswere and the Portuguese border, was now in British hands; though the Rufiji delta, if conquered, was not being held.

To that district, accordingly, was *Severn* sent at midnight on September 13-14 to observe if any towers or lookout stations still remained. Next day she entered the Kikunja mouth (for the first time since defeating *Königsberg*), and fired a couple of rounds at Pemba Hill. On the 16th she went up the Simba Urange again so far as Salale and noted the destruction she had rendered on a previous visit to the village. Now that the river no longer presented opposition, the trip seemed singularly pleasant, the scenery nice and green. Interesting, too, appeared those bushes abreast of *Newbridge*, where Allert had done his sniping.

It is a truth that, after the Dar-es-Salaam evacuation, Captain Looff, having recovered from his wounds, proceeded south and came first to the Rufiji area; thence to the Lindi district where he entrenched himself in front of the British positions, having with him three recently raised companies of *askaris* together with one 4.1-in. gun. Now when *Severn* was still about the delta this month, airmen were sent up from the *Manica* who reported the following items: two black masts—prob-

UP THE RUFIJI AT KIKALE
(Top) In the hole, where the man is standing, was found a spare propeller blade which the Germans buried after abandoning "Könisberg".

(Middle) Wreck of "Könisberg", looking forward. Notice both cables. The Germans landed on the steep-to bank here shown.

(Bottom) Wreck of "Könisberg" as she still lies up the Rufiji. View looking aft along port side.

ably for wireless—at Nyamsati, (off which monitors anchored in July 1915 when shelling *Königsberg*), up Kikunja River; a camp in Kikale at the head of the Simba Urange branch; trenches southeast of Kiomboni Point, where the river of that name empties itself through yet another of these Rufiji mouths; and new huts being erected at the Masala mouth, which lay still further south.

Photographs were taken from the air, and at first consideration it looked as if the enemy after all would now use every advantage of this difficult delta to start a minor campaign. The matter must be looked into immediately: wherefore *Severn* sent a boat with native spies to see what was happening up the Kikunja, and monitors themselves on September 20 entered the Simba Urange at 7a.m. This time *Severn* noticed the *Somali*, which had once been *Königsberg's* tender but now lay beached on the northern side near Salale, listing to port, her hull gutted and rusting away. The steamer's boilers, however, had been fixed up on the shore for the purpose of condensing water. *Severn* let go anchor just after 8 a.m., whilst *Mersey*, (see chart), went about 2 miles further up river with caution. The former's two motorboats in charge of Commander R. O. B. Bridgeman worked their way along till they came even to the *Königsberg* wreck, opposite which a concrete pier had been built; a wide area of trees had been cleared away, and many of the huts with camping places once used by her crew after the disaster were still visible.

Today's visit, however, established little further information and shortly after 2 p.m. both monitors were again out at sea. Nor was there justifiable enough intelligence for bombarding Kikale. Weeks passed and on December 10, having erected protective plates round her 6-in. gun aft, as well as splinter mats, *Severn* once more steamed into the Simba Urange anchoring well above Salale, after which her two armed motorboats set off to bring back any craft that might be sighted. For men who had assisted in the engagements of July 1915, this became a fascinating trip through impressive savage scenery and narrow winding creeks till the boats made fast along *Königsberg's* starboard side.

She was listing that way, as men were allowed to climb aboard and behold for themselves the large holes where 6-inch shells from monitors had entered decks before bursting inside. Splinter depredations were manifest every few feet; forebridge, chart-house totally wrecked from bursting shell; her middle funnel—see photograph—lying between the other two; fore-and-aft bridge knocked away, and charred

UP THE RUFIJI AT KIKALE

(Top) The place where "Könisberg's" crew camped near to the river after abandoning ship on July 11, 1915.

(Middle) Fifteen years after! Admiral Fullerton (with hat off) aboard "Könisberg".

(Bottom) "Könisberg" as she remains today, lying on her starboard side.

wood below indicating the terrible conflagration which had waged within. It was nearly high water so that the river filled her internals, yet though stripped bare of most things, including mountings for her guns, she still provided a few souvenirs for the British sailors.

The well-prepared landing placed on the bank abreast her port side only twenty yards away, together with the camping ground, did not fail to be noted, but the general impression of this curious naval picture was its incongruity: the strange setting of a wrecked man-of-war among the mangroves, miles inland from the sea. That a ship of this size should have worked herself through such intricate and narrow channels, gave these seafarers plenty of matter for discussion.

Christmas Day once more found *Severn* off the coast, but it was slightly less irksome than last year. At least they spent it anchored near Mafia, where some of the crew had landed to obtain evergreens for festooning masthead and yards in the traditional manner of the sea. Mess tables, too, were decorated though not so lavishly as aboard ships lucky enough to be serving in more civilised waters. The local fowl was better than tinned beef, anyway, and every man received a bottle of beer from the captain: yet at the back of all this modest festivity there hung a big element of suspense, and the ship was kept always ready for any sudden surprise.

Then an immense joy concluded this eventful year. Incredible news! *Severn* was actually to have her refit! On the last day of 1916 she came up to Zanzibar, went alongside *Trent*, and right away started to dismantle for another towing voyage. 'These preparations took some days, but on January 11 the intricate details—fixing up wooden breakwater, filling her with 30,000 kerosene tins, battening her down tight—were completed; so *Trent* took a strain on the tow-ropes, led her outside, worked up to 9 knots, and after a week's successful progress brought the monitor safe into Durban.

Both men and ship had more than deserved this change of existence; the return for a while to civilisation, with its kindliness and recreations, was welcome contrast after war and Rufiji weariness. But only four days before quitting Zanzibar a real tragedy had happened amid that dread delta. In spite of the monitors' upriver trips without obtaining information of enemy movements, a rumour reached Zanzibar that a German steam craft was still within one of the branches and likely to break out. Only one British aeroplane—long past its state of airworthiness—was immediately available, but efforts to find an observer failed, until finally Flight-Lieut. E. R. Moon found the gallant

Commander Bridgeman willing to accompany him in that capacity, though the hard-worked naval officer was not recovered from a bout of fever.

Alas! whilst hovering above the delta this aeroplane's magneto gave out, the machine crashed down to earth, hit the mangroves, capsized, yet neither occupant was killed; but during the next three days they suffered the worst privations. Without food or water, bitten by mosquitoes, stricken with fever, driven nearly mad by the thirsty heat, they made a raft from the wood of a German hut abreast of *Newbridge* and floated down Simba Urange with the ebb, and next the flood tide brought them back to the mud beach. Bridgeman succumbed, Moon almost collapsed but was taken prisoner and led to a lookout post, where German sailors treated him kindly. Bridgeman's body was found and buried at the Simba Urange entrance that had become, by so many incidents hereabouts, one of Africa's historic corners. At a later date, this brave and self-sacrificing officer's remains were exhumed when his sister the Countess of Sefton came out from England, and a reburial was made at Zanzibar.

It was the end of April 1917 by the time *Severn* had passed out of dockyard hands and arrived back on the station. Simba Urange still called her, but the district had at last been occupied by British forces; natives and fishermen being now given freedom to get on with their work. As the monitor on May 10 steamed up to Salale, she found the small S.S. *Mafia* waiting off the village with 100 prisoners aboard including 40 white Germans from an upcountry hospital; for British troops were not far off, and along this waterway their stores travelled by lighter. But it was a sign of the changed times that the monitor kept coming in and out of the river with impunity; that stores and coal were available at Salale; where also *Severn's* carpenters began to repair boats.

The beginning of June saw her so far south as Kilwa Kisiwani, a nearly-landlocked harbour that was being used as a base for the army's supplies; but at once she moved on to Lindi where it will be remembered that the S.S. *Präsident* had been rendered useless. The gunboat *Thistle* was now lying inside this river, for the purpose of protecting the British camp; but her artillery were not powerful enough to deal with an ex-*Königsberg* gun mounted on the hills which the Germans kept using, so *Severn* had come. Here, again, have we plain instance of the multifarious jobs for which monitors proved themselves ideal. *Severn* was precisely the kind of vessel which should be employed up this winding river, yet what a strange war, that all the way down East Africa from Tanga to Lindi she was ever meeting the live guns of Looff's dead ship!

Reference to the accompanying sketch-plan of Lindi River (not drawn to scale) will afford some idea concerning its situation between lofty hills; where the night hours were not without anxiety and guns' crews slept close up alongside the 6-in.; special lookout men with rifles and ammunition being posted as guard against any boats which might approach the vessel. The military could be seen busily preparing for an advance, and transports steamed in with more troops: yet the enemy had no intention of standing idly by.

When *Severn's* motorboat by night went some distance inland sounding the reaches, she was fired upon to the west of Gala Island by Germans who were placed north of "Arab House" (marked on the plan), a rocket and alarm signal being likewise set off: to which the motorboat replied, though over 1,000 yards distant.

Then came Sunday, June 10, with great bustle everywhere. Armed boats were testing their machine-guns, monitors had erected protective plates and were getting ready for going into action, bushes being brought aboard to disguise the masthead, officers holding a final conference: for tonight a surprise landing was to be attempted. Commander Jones having impressed on his men the absolute necessity for showing no lights or even the glimmer of a cigarette; at 7 p.m. the tows consisting of motorboats, steamboats, and pulling boats, set out from Lindi Pier with the 1,400 soldiers, porters and stores.

Simultaneously the *Thistle* shifted further up to cover these boats at which the enemy soon began to snipe, and by 8 p.m. *Severn* had brought up behind Gala Island, mooring head and stern in the manner she had been accustomed nearly two years ago up the Kikunja. In fact she was to employ those self-same tactics which had been used off Nyamsati against *Königsberg*, the range now being 10,000 yards. Midnight passed, and at 1.30 a.m. gun-firing could be heard echoing between the hills, but the boat-flotilla had gone by "Arab House" Creek and thoroughly surprised the enemy, so that a landing was made with great success. After firing several volleys, the German forces retired and our troops made quick work of occupying the surrounding villages.

This sudden booming of a big gun was from the *Königsberg* 4.1, mounted above the top of the creek at Mingoyo. Its wrath was being vented against *Thistle*—luckily unhit —but she and the steamboats were aground most of the night because the tide had ebbed. At 3 a m. *Severn* despatched her motor-boats to complete the landing and did some shooting at snipers, but with the dawn followed keener activity: for *Thistle* could be seen afloat again, and *Königsberg's* gun was concentrating against her at short range. Hits began to be registered, her engine-room received a shell, steam-pipes were damaged, and one man was killed. Compelled to retreat, she slowly made her way out of the river.

Now at 8.40 a.m. up rose a seaplane, which began wirelessing to *Severn*, telling her where to fire. The monitor's gunners lost no time in getting on to the target and so continued till 10.40 a.m. when the enemy were reported to be withdrawing from one position to another: but at 2.50 p.m. a 4.1 shell fell on Gala Island in the proximity of *Severn*, which indicated that the German gun had been shifted to another spot. The enemy had at last discovered this monitor's concealment. The third shell came nearer still, and for half an hour *Severn* was straddled, exactly as she had experienced in July 1915.

So hot did her anchorage develop that before 3.30 p.m. she cleared out, and brought up again at a spot near the mouth where also H.M.S. *Hyacinth* had been bombarding enemy positions all day, though at such extreme range that she must heel ship over till full elevation was obtained. But by now the exciting hours had won through to entire success, and the country round Lindi was cleared of Germans for a distance over 12 miles, though a certain amount of sniping persisted. The shooting of ships' guns had been excellent, but yet again *Severn's* structure was badly damaged by her own firing, the captain's cabin being wrecked entirely.

On Tuesday morning *Severn* proceeded up river trying to draw attention towards herself, but the 4.1 had been moved away by the defenders retiring south. Next day *Severn* was ordered to nose her way up to the top of Lukuledi Creek and, finding only 12 feet of water in places, at last came to the *Präsident* which had been the indirect means of revealing *Königsberg's* hiding-place in the Rufiji delta. Not unnaturally, therefore, the sight of this commercial, single-funnelled, steamer aroused an attention comparable with that which *Markgraf's* impotence had created.

At low tide *Präsident* was sitting tight on the creek's mud amid beautiful scenery, and almost enclosed by the hills. Several parties went aboard to remove any perishable stores, though little enough remained; after which the monitor steamed away along the "Arab House" Creek towards Mingoyo, surveying and laying down buoys for the traffic that was going on by motorboats, fetching munitions to the troops. Empty 4.1 cylinders were picked up, and proved beyond doubt what had been confidently supposed, and now was it learnt that during Tuesday night this heavy gun had been removed by locomotive on a light railway. We had captured 51 rounds of her ammunition, which was a serious matter to the Germans already running short and with no hope for another supply-ship to arrive; whereas such was the sea's freedom for the conquerors that *Trent* now came into Lindi with fresh supplies of shells, beef, and other stores, followed by a collier with more fuel.

But the notorious German gun next commenced shelling Mingoyo, so that *Severn* went into "Arab House" Creek to deal with the nuisance. She anchored bow and stern athwart the narrow passage, almost touching either bank and finding not more than 12 feet at low water. With extreme elevation she bombarded the enemy's trenches, scoring ten useful hits, thanks to aeroplane spotting, after which another aircraft bombed the German camp. A naval lull set in for a brief period, concerts and football matches recreated minds and bodies, but not for long was there respite.

It is thus that we approach the last of *Severn's* many adventures.

She was required to co-operate with the Army in what would be almost the final effort for rounding up the Germans that remained on African soil, and fittingly enough her old comrade *Mersey* would share the duties. During August 4 and 5 the British troops suffered a definite set-back, and an Indian regiment had some 700 casualties; for the Germans, who had been strengthened by reinforcements from Kilwa district, and strongly entrenched on a hill, were more powerful than had been supposed.

Additional transports bringing other British troops into Lindi had therefore to be awaited until the advance could be essayed on August 10. Just after 5 a.m. both monitors proceeded, *Severn* bringing up off the mouth of the Lukuledi River, *Mersey* anchoring above "Arab House". When the aeroplane arrived, *Severn* fired sixty rounds "rapid" against the enemy's positions on Tandamuti Hill most effectively, the enemy seeking cover among the trees and bush, but *Mersey's* shells soon were hammering that very clump. She then from noon fired slowly just in front of our advancing troops, and *Severn* blasted away setting on fire German positions beyond Tandamuti Hill further southwest, nor did the conflagrations die down till midnight. The nett result of this naval bombardment, which inflicted great losses, was to force withdrawal on the Germans who could not tolerate remaining on the hill any longer. And no one appreciated this valuable assistance more thoroughly than General O'Grady, who now wirelessed his thanks.

There was nothing more for the monitors to perform, and East African land warfare was rapidly ending. At any rate the Admiralty realised that all who had served more than eighteen months in these two units should be sent home; even if they had to be relieved, and the ships themselves should remain a few weeks longer on the station. This news affected the war-weary crews as a mighty tonic, and, whilst the change scarcely followed immediately so that men were not allowed to reach England in time for Christmas—though Admiral Charlton had sought otherwise—yet anticipation brought no little pleasure.

During November more and more German white prisoners surrendered, and simultaneously two British flying-officers were given their freedom: one was Flight-Lieut. Moon (whom we mentioned just now in connection with Commander Bridgeman), the other being Lieut. Cutler who had been captured in December 1914 when his aircraft crashed near Simba Urange mouth. But it was whilst *Severn* happened to be at Kilwa Kisiwani that Sub-Lieut. W. Price (who commanded the tug *Adjutant* at the time the latter fell into German hands) stepped aboard the monitor to have tea with her Captain. And before that month was out came news that a force of German whites and *askaris* had surrendered near the Portuguese border. This announcement created additional pleasure because it was learned that among them were Captain Looff and a good number of *Königsberg's* crew; but General von Lettow-Vorbeck had taken himself into the Portuguese colony.

Thus, by the first week of December 1917 the whole of German East Africa had been conquered, and hostilities ceased. On the 9th *Severn* hoisted her paying-off pennant, and her boilers were in such a condition that she could not steam even to Zanzibar; so, after Christmas at Lindi, she went back to Kilwa Kisiwani, where she was paid off on December 31, and the old crew went home. It had been a long and eventful commission ever since August 9, 1914.

But the ship herself was not yet due to leave till the following March, when she went up to Zanzibar and prepared for the return long tow through the Red Sea. By May 26, 1918, she had passed through the Suez Canal and reached Alexandria, where she had a lengthy but by no means premature refit. She left there on October

8, went up the Aegean to Mudros, though on October 30 the Dardanelles campaign ended there in the signing of armistice with Turkey. Yet, if she was just too late for participation in that war, she still voyaged onward, crossed the Marmara Sea into Constantinople, thence into the Black Sea, and so up the River Danube to Galatz.

There she spent the winter of 1918-1919, nor she could get down till the river became clear of ice in the first week of March. A couple of months at Malta, and early in June she arrived at Devonport. That was the very end of her short, but adventurous, career; for the Navy had not any further use for her, and they sent her to be broken up. No one who has been entertained by these chapters will deny that *Severn* deserves to be remembered among those famous ship-names which have helped to mould maritime history. In many ways—whether off the boisterous Belgian coast, or the torrid shores of Central Africa—she was by no imagination the most suitable vessel for the job: yet, by a strange set of circumstances, *Severn* with her sister *Mersey* achieved fame in shallow places where scarcely any other warship could have succeeded. For, if *Thistle* had the right draught, she was too lightly armed against *Königsberg*.

Eleven more years passed, Captain Fullerton pursuing his brilliant progress rose to flag-rank and during 1930 was Commander-in-Chief of the East Indies station, which stretches westward across the Ocean to East Africa. The time came on July 30 of that year when he anchored his cruiser a dozen miles from Simba Urange mouth, and went off by motorboat to revisit scenes of olden days. He brought with him a cement cenotaph to be erected just above high-water mark on the Simba Urange point, as a memorial to his friend Commander Bridgeman; whose life and death, energies and planning, had been bound up with the delta.

It was getting on towards the top of flood tide this July morning as Admiral Fullerton's boat passed the *Newbridge*: she had evidently sunk more deeply into the mud, since little but her masts, funnel, and tops of cowls were showing. Salale had become quite a promising village, and presently the old *Königsberg* revealed herself. By now it was half-ebb, which permitted most of her hull to be seen. Still lying on her starboard side, and all ironwork rapidly deteriorating, she had been purchased by Mr Nicols, a Roumanian, who was both professional diver and seaman. Having removed all the brass and metal that could be extracted, he was salving the 50 tons of Welsh coal which remained in good condition notwithstanding immersion for fifteen years.

Much had happened in the trend of cruiser design since *Königsberg* was built twenty-three years earlier, and that which especially struck Admiral Fullerton was the smallness of this 3,400 tons ship.

She looked minute compared with what cruisers are like today, and after all this time I wonder more than ever that we hit her at all.

Lying in the concave side of a sharp bend, her desolate appearance is shewn by the accompanying photograph. A 5-knot current sweeps past which has scooped out a deep channel between her and the steep-to bank on her port side.

From *Königsberg* a visit was next paid to the place where survivors had their temporary camp: the spot used for Captain Looff's tent under two trees was still outlined, and such articles as odd locks were lying about. This piece of low land was situated one quarter of a mile away from the wreck, and Mr Nicols had among the tree-clumps unearthed various items as awning-stanchions, pots of paint, pieces of searchlight; some of them doubtless having been put ashore after the first engagement. But a spare propeller-blade, buried in a hole, had also been discovered.

Who can say whether, in the years to come, other dumps will reveal more valuable items that once belonged to the smart S.M.S. *Königsberg*, which lost her freedom on that fatal day when she came up here to escape British guns?

The Royal Marines in the East African Campaign

by General Sir H.E Blumberg

COASTAL OPERATIONS IN EAST AFRICA

In the first six months of 1916, the campaign on shore in East Africa had made considerable progress, and by June the British forces had advanced as far as Kondea Irangi, whilst another German force had been driven from the hills on the east side of the Ruwu River to the Pangani River. It was therefore necessary to open up communication to the coast, and to establish new bases for the troops.

Tanga, Pangani, Sadani, and Dar es Salaam on the coast of German East Africa, were still in the hands of the Germans, whilst the navy were blockading the coast. Further there was the danger that the enemy on the coast might strike westward and make a flank attack on the British forces working south. The navy was therefore asked to assist the army in the capture of these towns.

On 7th June, 1916, under cover of the fire of H.M.S. *Talbot* and *Severn*, with the *Vengeance* (Flag of Rear-Admiral Charlton, the Commander-in-Chief), and the kite balloon ship *Manica* standing by, the army occupied Tanga, the scene of the disastrous reverse in the early days of the war. Captain F. H. Thomas, D.S.C., R.M.L.I., and his detachment with two machine-guns landed from the *Talbot* at Ulenge Island, which he held whilst the troops landed at Kwale Island and marched on Tanga. After the occupation, the *Talbot's* detachment was landed daily up to 21st July, in case of emergencies.

On 2lst July, as reports had been received that the enemy had mounted a gun at the mouth of the Pangani River, the *Talbot* (Captain R. Lambert) arrived off the Pangani just before dark on 22nd, and bombarded the Bweni Bluff. At daylight the next morning white flags were seen to be flying and Captain Thomas was sent in under a flag of truce, and was informed by the natives that the Germans had evacuated the place at 3 a.m. Seamen and marines were then landed; the Royal Marines occupying the hill on the south side of the river to hold the abandoned defensive position, whilst the seamen took over the town. The 57th Native Infantry, who had thus been enabled to cross the river, marched in from the north side, and the Royal Marines were embarked the next day. On 25th the R.M.L.I, took over the town until the 57th Native Infantry had crossed to the south bank and ascertained that the enemy had left the immediate vicinity. The *Talbot* proceeded 20 miles down the coast to Kipombwe, and shelled the village and a few of the enemy who were seen, and again on 26th the *Talbot* shelled Mkwadja, and the *Mersey* shelled Sadani.

It became evident that the Germans from Tanga and Pangani were moving on Sadani, therefore on 27th July, as there was no satisfactory report from Mkwadja seamen and marines from the *Talbot* were landed under Captain Thomas to take the village. The *Thistle* arrived at the same time and took up a position to cover the landing, which was effected without opposition. Shortly after the village was occupied, about 50 of the enemy were reported to be about a mile outside.

Captain Thomas at once advanced with the Royal Marines detachment and engaged the enemy who retired into the bush. He then cut the Pangani-Sadani telegraph line and withdrew again to the village. The Royal Marines were re-embarked on 29th July. Captain Thomas, Lance-Sergeant Perry and Privates W. Cooper and F. Galloway (all Plymouth R.M.L.I.), were brought to notice for these operations.

On 1st August, the squadron occupied Sadani, the place was important as a base of supplies for Andeni and Morogoro. The town was secured by a force of 250 seamen and marines (the marines being under Major C. Hall of the *Challenger*), with 50 Zanzibar Rifles, after a very feeble opposition. The naval party held it until relieved by the army on 7th August. Major Hall, and Captain Thomas and Colour-Sergeant P. E. Smith (Plymouth), were noted for good service.

CAPTURE OF BAGAMOYO, 15TH AUGUST, 1916.

On 13th August, Lieutenant-Colonel Price, commanding at Sadani, asked the naval commander-in-chief if he would take and occupy Bagamoyo, because it was essential that it should be occupied at the earliest possible moment, and all the available military forces were engaged at Mandera; the army, however, would relieve the navy at Bagamoyo as soon as the Mandera operations were completed. The

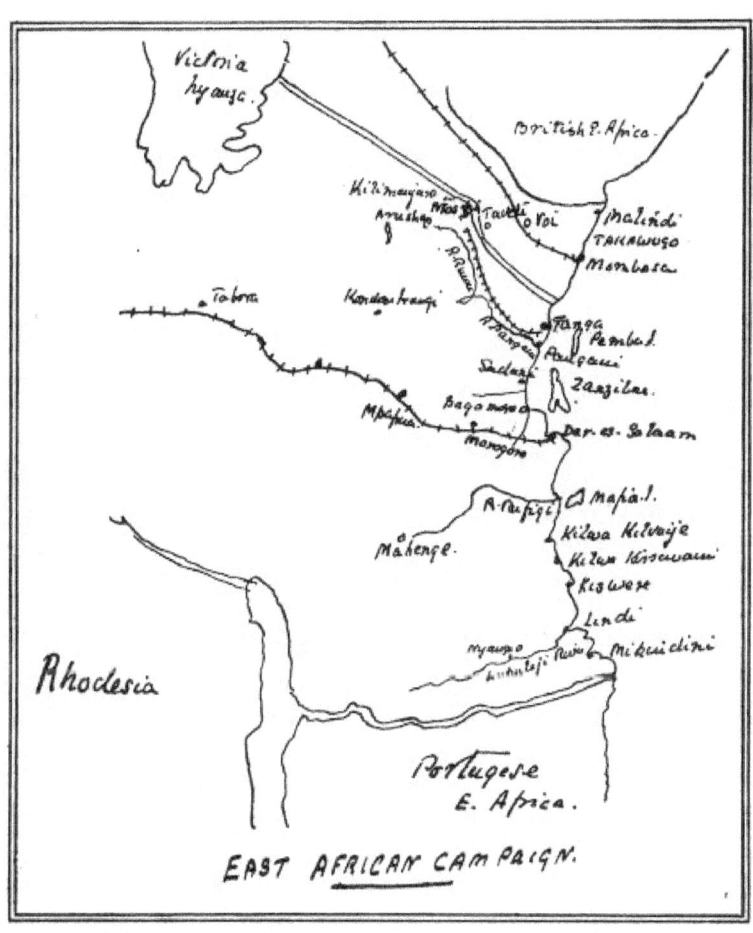

commander-in-chief replied "This will be arranged." He also asked that the R.M.L.I. detachment of the *Talbot* under Captain Thomas, which had been left at Sadani to supplement the army garrison, together with a detachment of the Zanzibar Rifles might be sent to him.

At Bagamoyo, therefore, the navy acted alone, and it was here that the stiffest fight was experienced. The intelligence officer had reported that it was held by only 10 whites and 400 *askaris*, but as a matter of fact they were stronger than the landing party, being composed of 60 whites and 350 *askaris*. The *askari* is a good soldier and a great bayonet fighter but an indifferent shot.

On 15th August, the *Vengeance*, *Challenger*, *Mersey* and *Severn*, with the kite balloon ship *Manica*, and the tug *Helmuth* anchored off Bagamoyo, at 3-30 a.m. At 4-30 a.m., the landing party went ashore in bright moonlight, the surprise was therefore not complete; the boats proceeded in a straight course towards the governor's house, and then turned six points to port and steered a zig-zag course, so that the Germans were deceived as to the actual landing place, and kept their men in the wrong place.

The boats actually ran ashore where a thick belt of trees ran down the slope almost to the water's edge. At the top of the slope, the Germans had mounted a 4-l-inch gun, which however, could not be depressed sufficiently to fire into the boats, but engaged the *Mersey* and *Severn*, which had closed in to bombard. The boats, however, came under fire from machine-guns, rifles and pom-poms, on their starboard side. The *Helmuth* and a picket boat with a three-pounder closed in and plastered the 4-1-inch gun at 500 yards range. Sub-Lieutenant Manning, Royal Naval Reserve, with a machine-gun section rushed and captured the gun.

The kite balloon and aeroplanes which were observing the fire reported at 6-30 that the Germans were abandoning their trenches, and falling back towards the French Mission buildings, behind the town. The enemy tried to take advantage of the natural reluctance to shell the Mission buildings and the Catholic Cathedral, by taking shelter there, but the French Fathers objected and the Germans did not actually enter the buildings; unfortunately, the buildings were hit by a 12-inch shell from the *Vengeance*.

In the meantime, the Royal Marines of the *Talbot*, *Vengeance*, and *Challenger* (60 all told), under Captain Thomas to whom were attached the Lewis gun parties of the *Mersey* and *Severn*, landed in the motor boats of the monitors, directed by Lieutenant Chapman, Royal

Capture of Bagamoyo.

Navy, under a heavy fire from pom-poms, machine-guns and rifles. They then advanced and captured the governor's house, and being joined by a party of the Zanzibar Rifles, advanced in a westerly direction. Parties of the enemy had concealed themselves in the long grass, and the Royal Marines came under a heavy fire.

Then gallantly led by Captain Thomas, they proceeded to clear the grass in front of the house, and came under fire from cleverly concealed trenches and dug-outs, during which movement Captain Thomas was killed, Private Dennis, his servant, immediately bayonetted the man who had fired the shot. His death was a great loss to the corps as he had shown himself both at the Dardanelles and in Africa, as a most gallant and skilful officer.

The seamen had simultaneously pressed forward, and charging across the front of the Boma, captured the enemy trenches, whilst another party worked round the governor's house, cutting the line of retreat. This charge was ordered on information brought by Lance-Corporal E.V. Deane (Plymouth R.M.L.I), who very. bravely rushed across to the commanding officer, under heavy fire, to point out the situation, and then opened fire himself to cover the seamen's advance; for this service he was awarded the Conspicuous Gallantry Medal.

The enemy fled in confusion, and lost maxims and two light guns, whilst the two German officers were killed and many of the enemy were captured in the dug-outs.

Arrangements were then made to meet a counter-attack; picquets were posted and defences strengthened. Commander Watson, Royal Navy, being placed in charge.

There was another strongly fortified post at Mtoni Ferry, about six miles up the Kigaki River, but the enemy were badly shaken and a large number of *askari* deserters came in.

Bagamoyo was regarded by the natives as a place of importance, as it was formerly the terminus of the slave caravans. Owing to Commander Watson's tact and diplomacy, the natives became friendly and gave useful information, and the capture of the place greatly enhanced the British prestige. The Germans had, among other things, forbidden the natives to fish, permission to do so was at once restored, which made them very contented, and many other similar acts were done. There was no doubt that the natives were greatly struck by the difference between the British and German methods of treating them.

On 18th August, the troops from Sadani arrived and took over on 19th.

Acting Company-Sergeant-Major P. E. Smith, Lance-Corporal W. Bradley, and Private W. Dennis (all Plymouth), were awarded the D.S.M., whilst Captain Thomas, Colour-Sergeant W. J. Fouracre (Plymouth), and Sergeant Harry Carter (Portsmouth), were mentioned in dispatches.

On 20th August, the Royal Marines of the *Vengeance*, *Challenger*, and *Talbot*, were re-embarked and replaced by Lieutenant T. F. Connew and 24 Royal Marine Artillery, but this party returned to the *Vengeance* on 26th.

★★★★★★★★★★

Note.—This officer and 24 R.M.A. (Short Service Gunners) had been sent out to reinforce the batteries, but as they were not at that moment required by the army they were utilised by the commander-in-chief to replace the detachment of the *Vengeance* which had been landed in February for service with the batteries. A second draft under 2nd Lieutenant H. Gardner of the same strength arrived on 30th September and were embarked similarly in the *Challenger*.

★★★★★★★★★★

On 21st August, the naval squadron commenced the bombardment of Dar es salaam, which was the principal enemy port, and on 29th, Lieutenant Connew and the Royal Marines of the ships present were sent to the *Trent* to organise for coastal landings.

On 2nd September, the Royal Marines under Lieutenant Connew landed at Kondechi, north of Dar es Salaam, and the next day the troops from Bagamoyo approached and the bombardment was resumed. On the 4th the *Challenger* was sent in with a flag of truce to demand the surrender of the town. The German governor surrendered on that day, and the place was occupied. Lieutenant Connew and his detachment returned to the *Trent* on 5th.

On 7th September, the Royal Marines were again landed at Kilwa Kivinte, which surrendered to the *Vengeance*, and Kilwa Kisiwane to the *Talbot* and *Challenger*.

On 9th September, the Royal Marines Force embarked in H.M.S. *Himalaya*, and landed on 13th September, with the army troops at Mikindani, without opposition, and on 16th the troops occupied Sudi. The squadron proceeded to Lindi and found the place deserted, the Royal Marine force landed, but re-embarked on 17th.

On 18th, the *Challenger* and a transport were sent to occupy Kiswere. The whole coast was now in British hands, so on 27th, the *Vengeance* left the station for Bombay, and returned home shortly after,

Lieutenant Connew and his party returning with her.

Following on these successes and to shorten the lines of communication, the base of the Expeditionary Force was first moved to Tanga from Mombasa, in July, 1916. In September, it was moved to Dar es Salaam, and in October, it was proposed to move to Kilwa, but in January, 1917, the base was moved to Lindi.

On 5th January, Lieutenant Gardner and his Royal Marine Artillery were landed from the *Challenger* and joined the batteries, being replaced afloat by Lieutenant Weir, and a full R.M.L.I. detachment from England.

The ships on the station *Hyacinth*, (Flag), *Minerva*, *Challenger*, and *Talbot* with *Rinaldo*, and *Thistle* sloops, and two monitors, with an armed merchant cruiser, were now fully occupied in blockading the coast and preventing stores being landed for the German Forces.

In June-July, 1917, a portion of Von Lettow's forces were reported to be making for Port Amelia, in Portuguese East Africa, where there was a considerable supply of stores and ammunition, quite unguarded. The *Talbot* embarked two companies of a West African Regiment, and these together with 40 R.M.L.I. and three machine-guns under Captain A. P. Dawson, R.M.L.I., were landed and put the town in a state of defence.

The Germans approached within three miles of the place, but fearing a trap, they turned back. The British forces were too weak to pursue, so the enemy escaped. After six weeks ashore, the Royal Marines were relieved by a battalion of the King's African Rifles, and a Baluchi Battalion; this place afterwards became one of the British bases.

Patrol of the coast was resumed until June, 1918, by which time *Minerva*, and *Rinaldo* had left the station. The *Talbot*, and *Thistle* were ordered in June to Quilimane, at one of the mouths of the Zambesi River. Every available man was ordered to land, seamen, stokers, and Royal Marines, to put the town in a state of defence against the Germans, who were advancing. About 180 men were landed (80 seamen, 60 stokers, 40 Royal Marines), under Captain Dawson, R.M.L.I.; there were also about 200 Portuguese troops in the town, who were doing nothing.

The force was ordered not to go more than five miles from the town, they therefore dug trenches, and put houses into a state of defence. The enemy approached one morning at daylight, and came into contact with the patrols, but after a few shots had been fired, the Germans who were about 500 strong retired, two *askaris* being captured. The force was ashore for about three weeks and was not again interfered with.

During 1917-1918, patrols from the ships were landed at various places such as Lindi, Mikindani, Kilwa, etc., to round up Germans, but as the commander-in-chief's orders were that they were to remain in sight of the ship, only occasionally did they succeed in making any captures.

ROYAL MARINE BATTERIES IN EAST AFRICA.

No units of the corps were employed in the land campaign in East Africa until early in 1916, when it was decided to send out General Sir H. Smith-Dorrien to clear up the campaign. There were, however, some representatives with the local forces, as several officers and men who had settled in the country were retained for service with the local units. They included Major N. A. W. Scott, Captains E. H. Pardoe, A. J. H. Smith and Lieutenants R. M. Bradshaw and L. J. Innes all of the R.M.L.I., some of whom rose to the command of Battalions of the King's African Rifles.

Early in 1916 as there was a shortage of heavy artillery, the Admiralty agreed to send out four 4-inch Mark VII. B.L. and four 12-pounder 18 cwt. guns on field mountings. Major and Brevet Lieut.-Colonel P. Phillipps, M.V.O., Captain G.Y. Russell, Lieutenants J. C. Guy, E. Morres and Act. Sergeant-Major W. H. C. Rogers, all R.M.A. embarked in S.S. *Saxon* for passage, whilst Major F. J. French, Captain H. R. Purser, 2nd Lieutenants B. S. Hawes and C. A. Stock with 19 specialist N.C.O.s and men, R.M.A. with the 12 pounders took passage in the Durham Castle. At the same time H.M.S. *Vengeance* was commissioned to join the station with a detachment composed of 50 *per cent*. R.M.A. and 50 *per cent*. R.M.L.I.

On 31st January, 1916, Colonel Phillipps and his staff landed at Kilindini and on 14th February the Royal Marine Detachments of the East African Squadron were landed to form the batteries.

The numbers landed were:—

H.M.S. *Vengeance*—Captain H. C. Atkinson ; Lieutenant J. F. Ellison, D.C.M., R.M.L.I.				
	2 sergts.	1 bugler	- corps.	27 gunners, R.M.A.
	4 sergts.	—	3 corpls.	31 privates, R.M.L.I.
H.M.S. *Hyacinth*—Captain R. C. A. Glunicke, R.M.L.I.				
	2 sergts.	1 bugler	- corps.	23 privates, R.M.L.I.
H.M.S. *Challenger*	—	—	2 corpls.	24 privates, R.M.L.I.
H.M.S. *Armadale Castle*	1 sergt.	—	—	7 privates, R.M.L.I.
H.M.S. *Orbita*	—	—	1 corpl.	10 privates, R.M.L.I.
H.M.S. *Lanconia*				
H.M.S. *Mersey*	—	—	2 corpls.	20 privates, R.M.L.I.
H.M.S. *Severn*				

On 3rd March Battery S.M. J. Bach, six N.C.O.s and 11 gunners, R.M.A., three privates, R.M.L.I. and the 4inch guns were landed from the *Armadale Castle*.

Khaki clothing, etc. had been sent out from England in the S.S. *Trent* so that the men could be equipped.

On 14th February, Colonel Phillipps and the personnel with the 12-pounder guns entrained for the base camp at Maktau, which was an entrenched camp with a shelter trench all round, outside of which was a deep belt of cut thorn bushes called a '*Boma*.'

Captain Glunicke was appointed Adjutant and the brigade was organised as follows. The 12-pounders were formed into No. 9 Battery under Captain Russell with Lieutenants Ellison, Guy and Morres and Lieutenant Helyar, R.F.A. attached, B.S.M. V. C. Willcox. The 4-inch guns which arrived on 8th March were formed into a battery under Major French with Captains Atkinson and Purser, 2nd Lieutenants Hawes and Stock and B.S.M. Bach—this battery had no number. Surgeon Wollaston, R.N. was medical officer and served throughout with one or the other of the Royal Marine units with whom he was most popular.

Except the R.M.A. specialists most of the men were quite untrained in land artillery, especially as there was such a large proportion of R.M.L.I.; training was therefore commenced at once and made good progress.

With the force was another battery of two 4-inch naval guns from H.M.S. *Pegasus*, numbered No. 10 manned by seamen and marines drawn from the fleet on 10th February and commanded by Captain Orde-Browne, late Royal Artillery; this battery was christened "H.M.S. Peggy" and the guns were drawn by lorries. Nos. 9 and 10 Batteries were brigaded under Colonel Phillipps and attached to army troops.

There were also two Naval 12-pounder 8-cwt. guns manned by men of the 1st Bn. Loyal North Lancashire-Regiment.

The guns of the 4-inch Battery weighed 4½ tons on their carriages and had to be provided with wheels suitable to the country before they were fit to operate in the field; the original wheels sent out were not adapted to the dust and mud of the bush tracks and the battery was finally not formed until May, when it was numbered No. 15.

The General Officer Commanding, Royal Artillery (General Crowe) in his book gives an interesting description of the heterogeneous collection of guns provided; except the Mountain Batteries from India and the Field Batteries from South Africa, there was nothing but out-of-date guns. Colonel Phillipps relates that though he picked up a few directors and other instruments he was never given a range-finder.

No. 9 Battery (12-pounders) was at once provided with oxen as transport animals and put through a course of instruction in land artillery warfare and gunnery practice.

General Sir H. Smith-Dorrien having been invalided, General Sir J. C. Smuts assumed command and carried out a most successful campaign.

When the advance commenced, the advanced guard was furnished by the 2nd Division (Gen. Malleson), touch was soon gained with the enemy who were in position at Salaita and on 8th March a reconnaissance was made of the position. With other batteries No. 10 Battery was in position behind a low ridge to the south of the road about eight miles east of the drift over the Ngoro River; with some field batteries No. 9 Battery was to the north of the road in a position screened by bush: fire was kept up all day, but at dusk the guns returned to Serengeti Camp, and an infantry screen remained in position. On the 9th the force again advanced, No. 10 Battery to its previous position, No. 9 to the north of the road under cover of a low ridge about one mile west of Ngoro Drift; the guns kept up a heavy bombardment and at 2 p.m. the infantry advanced and by 4 p.m. they had occupied the position.

On 10th March the force advanced to Taveta, an important post and township, where information was obtained that the enemy had retired to the position of Latema-Reata, two hills connected by a *nek*, to the south-east of the town. No. 10 Battery had been left behind and Colonel Phillipps and his staff accompanied No. 9. The 2nd Division was detailed to attack the position, and on 11th March at 4-30 p.m. No. 9 Battery crossed the river and was brought into action on the south side of the village and was joined by the 5th S.A. Field Battery and 2nd S.A. Infantry Brigade from Chala.

Parties of the 2nd Rhodesians and King's African Rifles gained a footing on Latema Hill where they held on all night, but the attack on Reata was not successful; the attack was renewed on the morning of the 12th when information was received that the enemy were retiring on Kahe; No. 9 Battery and No. 5 S.A. Field Artillery were then pushed up to the *nek*, the commander-in-chief accompanying them. No. 9 opened fire on the enemy column, and from the disappearance of the dust clouds the enemy had evidently dispersed into the bush. The battery was then ordered back to Taveta.

On 17/18th March, the advance was continued southwards and at 8-30 a.m. on the 18th the 1st East African Brigade supported by No. 9 Battery from Latema Nek was ordered to co-operate in the attack on Unterer Himo on the River Himo ; the East African Brigade advanced and occupied the hills which lie behind Unterer Himo and Mokinni and No. 9 Battery returned to Latema; but later in the day it was brought forward to the river arriving about 5 p.m.; the result of the day's fighting was very satisfactory.

On 19th an attack was made on the Rasthaus position, covering the River Ruwu, from Unterer Himo and Euphorbien Hill; the attack failed and under cover of the guns the infantry withdrew, but the 21st Indian Cavalry swam the river and reached Kahe Hill, and in spite of counterattacks held on so that General Deventer was able to occupy the station during the night; the Germans blew up their 4.1 inch gun and withdrew from the Rasthaus position leaving the waggon bridge over the River Ruwu intact; this action gave the force a hold on the railway, also on Moschi and all the country north of the River Ruwu. Posts were established along the river from L. Jippe to Kahe.

On 17th March, Colonel Phillipps and his staff were sent to Maktau to train the 4-inch battery, but on 23rd as no transport animals were available for the battery the guns were returned to the Ordnance Store at Voi and the personnel were employed on outpost duty at Maktau for about six weeks. Whilst entraining these guns Colonel Phillipps got sunstroke and was sent to hospital in Nairobi whence he was invalided home. Major French and Sergeant-Major Rogers were also returned to England in April, 1916 and Captain Atkinson, R.M.L.I. to H.M.S. *Hyacinth*. The R.M.A. Brigade staff was broken up and on 11th April Captain Glunicke became Adjutant of the 3rd Division Artillery Group, taking with him seven of the Royal Marine Headquarter details; Colonel Forestier-Walker, R.A. was in command of this group.

When the column advanced down the Pangani River, as all the oxen were required for supply duties, No. 9 Battery was left behind at Himo at the foot of Kilimanjaro and later moved to Mbyuni near Taveta. At the same time the right flank column under General Deventer also advanced to Kondoa Irangi.

On May 9th the enemy made four determined assaults on Deventer's Force, which were beaten off and the enemy withdrew; fighting on this flank was then confined to long range artillery and General Deventer was reinforced by No. 10 Battery.

Captain Glunicke and his detachment accompanied the 3rd Division from Mbyuni on 17th June in the advance down the Pangani; they were attached to a mounted brigade and known as the "Horse Marines" in the division, with which they underwent great hardships. They also accompanied the advance of the troops through the Nguru Hills to Morogoro and suffered greatly from fever, want of water and food added to the difficulties of transport, but earned the respect of the troops for the way in which they stuck to their unaccustomed duties and they shared in all the actions during the advance. Owing to the want of transport animals this column had no heavy artillery to reply to the German 4.1-inch guns near the Nguru Hills.

On 12th September, 1916, Captain Glunicke was appointed Staff Captain to Brigadier-General Crowe, commanding R.A. at General Headquarters, taking Bombr. Lawson and his attendant with him; as there was no brigade major, he combined the two duties until he was invalided on 30th June, 1917.

At the beginning of May, the 4-inch battery was ordered to be re-formed as No. 15. Captain Purser was appointed to command with 2nd Lieutenants Hawes and Stock and B.S.M. Bach. Only two of the guns were taken into use, the guns and stores were drawn from store and training commenced afresh; a lot of the men had been drafted off to other units and the best had to be made of what remained; although nominally an R.M.A. Battery most of the men were R.M.L.I. who had had no previous training in land artillery. In 10 days', time they were licked into shape by their most efficient B.S.M. Bach sufficiently to be complimented on their smartness and the efficiency of the specialists by the Colonel Commanding the R.A. (Forestier-Walker) when he came to see the battery shoot.

No. 15 Battery moved forward to Mbyuni, there to complete their training in readiness to move off with one of the mounted brigades, but still no transport was available. Eventually they were moved forward by rail as far as possible and arrived at railhead 220 miles distant without mishap; the railway running alongside the Pangani River for some distance amidst typical African scenery. The battery was then completed with transport, the guns being drawn by powerful motors and the waggons by oxen. Roads were deep in sand and the men had a lot of hard work, hauling the guns through particularly bad places; water was very scarce, whilst the country was infested with the *tsetse* fly which killed a number of the oxen; the men also suffered greatly from fever.

After a week's hard trekking the battery arrived at the advanced base at Msiha on 11th August in time for the advance to Morogoro. General Smuts inspected the battery and they then advanced south with the main column, the enemy retreating rapidly; eventually the battery reached the Central Railway. They found that the Germans had evacuated Morogoro, after destroying the bridges, ammunition and stores and had left the place to the mercy of the British who occupied the town on 26th August.

Here the battery remained halted until December; this trek was over 215 miles of bad roads, but all kept remarkably well and cheerful despite the fact that they were on half rations for some time.

In September, 1916, No. 9 Battery had been sent by rail to Tanga where the 12-pounder 18-cwt. guns were returned to store; Major Russell, Captain Ellison, Lieutenant Guy and B.S.M. Willcox with the personnel proceeded by sea to Dar es Salaam, and the battery was re-armed with the 12-pounder Horse Artillery guns, formerly belonging to the Calcutta battery and was renumbered No. 16 Battery. Mules were supplied for transport and leaving Dar es Salaam on 2nd December, it took part in the advance on the Rufigi River; it formed part of the Myanna Column under Colonel Burne, South African Forces, and it was in action several times. On 21st January, Major Russell went sick and Captain Ellison took command. On the commencement of the rains it returned to Dar es Salaam, arriving there on 1st March, 1917 and returned its guns to store.

Meanwhile a reinforcing draft consisting of Lieutenant Connew and 25 R.M.A. which had arrived at the Base Camp but was not required for the batteries, was appropriated by the naval commander-in-chief in August, 1916 as a detachment for H.M.S. *Vengeance* whose Royal Marines had been landed in February and was utilised for the Coastal Operations subsequent to the Capture of Bagamoyo (see above) and returned to England in the *Vengeance* in October, 1916. A second reinforcement consisting of 2nd Lieutenant H. Gardner and 25 R.M.A. who arrived in September, were also embarked in the *Challenger* to replace the detachment, where they remained until relieved by R.M.L.I. from England, when they were sent to the Base Detail Camp on 5th January, 1917 for instruction in order to form the nucleus of a Stokes Mortar Battery at Dar es Salaam; at this place they suffered a good deal from fever and eventually joined No. 16 Battery on 1st March.

No. 15 Battery took part in the advance to the Rufigi River and left Morogoro on 21st December, 1916 and crossed the Uluguru Mountains by way of "Shepherd's Pass" and reached Duthumi on 24th after a very exhausting four days march, first over mountain tracks and then through low and swampy country in the Rufigi River Valley. Kitoho was occupied as an artillery observation post and the map was marked out in squares. The battery took part in the action on January 1st and 2nd in support of the attack by the Nigerian Brigade from Mkessas on Mgeta, and on 8th January advanced to the Rufigi; on 10th January the battery reached Kimbambwe after another very trying march; (on one day, marching from 6-0 a.m. to 7-0 p.m., they only covered three miles). This battery was in action on the 12th to 15th. and 20th January, 1917.

As the heavy rains were now imminent, half the personnel under Lieutenant Hawes were sent to Msiha (the highest point in the Uluguru Mountains) whilst Captain Purser, B.S.M. Bach and the other half remained in the Rufigi Valley, which is most unhealthy; Lieutenant Stock had already been invalided. The party on the return to Msiha had a very difficult march owing to the rains, most of the men were sent to hospital by the way; they were therefore sent on to Morogoro where all the artillery were concentrated during the rainy season. No. 15 Battery, now consisting of Captain Purser, B.S.M. Bach and 13 other ranks with two guns, was the only unit remaining at Kimbambwe Crossing, all other troops having gone to New Crossing about five miles upstream. Captain Purser was taken ill, and on 23rd February was sent to hospital by Surgeon Wollaston; on the 28th he was sent on to Morogoro where he died on 17th March, 1917.

****

NOTE—Captain Purser, who joined the corps as a temporary officer in September, 1914, had seen a great deal of active service, having served in the Matabele War, and the South African War. He served with the R.M.A. contingent in German South-West Africa, and on his return to England, was appointed to the Royal Marine batteries in East Africa.

****

He was buried there, and the graves of several marines are close together, among them Private "Jock" White, the well-known footballer of the Forton Division and Gunner Bolton, R.M.A. The 26th Squadron R.A.F. made a wrought iron cross for each grave.

On 28th February, General Beves ordered Sergeant-Major Bach to move No. 15 Battery, which had now moved to New Crossing, across the Rufigi River and to take part in the advance to the south. The river, which here is twice as wide as the Thames at London Bridge, was crossed on a pontoon made by the Indian sappers and miners. Only one gun was taken across, as the only men available were Sergeant-Major Bach, one acting sergeant (a private of Plymouth Division) one acting bombardier, and six men with about 300 native porters to haul the gun and carry ammunition.

The native gun porters are a semi-military force, and not to be confused with ordinary carriers.

The objective was Niakasika, a fairly strong German position on the farm of Pretorious, who held the rank of Major as he was the Chief Scout of the British Expeditionary Force with which he gained the D.S.O. and the M.C. The gun could only be brought to an escarpment which was 15,000 yards from the objective. Trees were felled to make a platform and to clear an arc of fire, and a wire was run out to the F.O.O. (Captain Floyd, R.A.) this advance of 14 miles had been made through dense bush in two days. No sooner were they ready for action than the enemy evacuated their position and the gun was moved back to the south bank of the river; practically everyone was sent to hospital.

Owing to the rains the river was now rising rapidly so that the gun and party only just managed to recross in time; the Nigerian Brigade being the only troops left on the south bank. The guns and remnants of the personnel remained at the New Crossing Camp until August, 1917, and like marines made the best of things in spite of the rains; they lived in '*Bandas*,' large airy huts made of grass, and were constantly improving their arrangements. The native gun porters were trained as gunners and the marines all became specialists, and quite expert at using the slide rule, etc. Game of all sorts abounded and as rations were short, shooting parties went out daily to augment them; unfortunately, there was no shot gun so that they were not able to get any game birds; as soon as the rains ceased, road gangs set to work and on 2l1st July, 1917, Major Russell arrived with the motor transport and after an arduous march across the Uluguru Mountains they returned to Morogoro.

Meanwhile all the other Royal Marines had been collected into one battery at Dar es Salaam which was organised in four sub-sections, each capable of acting independently. Some reinforcements had been sent to Lindi to receive one of the 4-inch guns which was sent there from Voi, and on 10th April, 1917 Captain Ellison and Lieutenant Guy with one sub-section and equipment left Dar es Salaam to join them. On their arrival they found that the gun had been fired with the tampion in, the muzzle was blown away and one man badly wounded. Ellison with great initiative got four inches cut off the muzzle and: brought the gun into action and the German 4.1-inch gun was silenced as soon as the British gun opened fire. This gun was fitted with narrow wheels, but Captain Ellison told the general officer commanding that he had seen two wheels at Zanzibar which would be very useful and these when proven over in H.M. 5. *Thistle* and fitted proved invaluable for the work.

Meanwhile Major Russell and the remainder of the battery proceeded to Morogoro on 11th April, where they remained until it was possible to bring in B. S. M. Bach and the details of No. 15 Battery as related above in August.

OPERATIONS IN THE KILWA AND LINDI AREAS.

On 1st July Lieutenant Gardner and a small draft left for Lindi to take over the damaged gun, arriving there on 18th.

From 26th April until the advance on Mingoyo on 11th June, Ellison's gun had been constantly in action against Mingoyo village, Schaeffer Farm, and the adjoining German Camps. Lieutenant Guy carrying out the duties of observer on Kitulo Hill.

When the push began, it was decided to leave the gun behind, Ellison was therefore made acting Major to command the 25th Royal Fusiliers, whilst Colonel O'Driscoll was away; Lieutenants Guy and Gardner with the remainder of the personnel were sent to form a section of a new Stokes mortar battery.

With a couple of Stokes mortars, they were in action on 3rd August on Tandamuti Hill, a very hot fight; the Germans were strongly dug in with machine-guns and the Stokes guns fired 70 rounds into them without much effect. The British Force, consisting principally of new levies was forced to retreat, and in retirement bumped into a German raiding party under Krant; the porters stampeded and there was a good deal of confusion. The battery remained at Ziwami until the next move.

The Germans who were very strongly entrenched at Narunyu with their 4.1-inch gun at Mtua now realised that the British had no long-range artillery so that their 4.1-inch gun became rather a nuisance. As the force was to remain stationary for some time in order to give the Kilwa column time to act, the 4 inch gun was ordered to be brought up from Lindi; Lieutenant Guy was sent on with a small party; the remainder to follow as soon as they could be relieved with the Stokes guns; in the meantime Lieutenant Gardner and his party was sent to man the right post of the strong point, established close in front of the German positions at Narunyu, where they remained for three days without fires, lights or talking above a whisper after dark, and so were present at the affair of Narunyu on 18th August.

On 25th August the reliefs arrived and also the information that Lieutenant Guy was very seriously ill after bringing the new gun by raft as far as Mingoyo. Lieutenant Gardner therefore returned to Mingoyo and secured some strong trolleys and mounted the gun on two of them and with the help of native porters pushed the gun along the trolley line until it was abreast of Tandamuti Hill, and there prepared a position and camp. From that day the German gun never fired again by night. From August 29th they were almost daily in action, with aeroplane observation, though on two occasions Lieutenant Gardner observed from neighbouring hills.

They were employed bombarding the area about Mtua; information as to vulnerable points was obtained from the natives, and the aeroplanes would then try and locate them, a very difficult task in that bush country. The Germans generally replied with a few rounds always aimed at the British gun and one day it was nearly hit, the shell dropping within 16 paces. The range was 14,000 yards and the Royal Marines made use of observation posts on both flanks, and obtained their revenge two days afterwards; the Germans did not reply and moved their gun out of range. Sergeant Allman, R.M.A. died of malaria about this time, he had kept at duty when unfit which was probably the cause of his final illness.

On 24th September, General O'Grady resumed the advance and on 29th the gun was moved by trolleys to Mtua, the end of the line in British hands. The gun was then mounted on a carriage with the big wheels and moved to a position between Nambalika and Nyenged. Captain Ellison resumed command on 2nd October and various targets in the Mtama area were bombarded; the infantry occupying Mtama on the 15th. On 17th and 18th, the battery heard in the distance the firing at Nyangao, the fiercest fight in the whole campaign where there were 1,700 British casualties, but the Royal Marine gun was out of range.

On 23rd October they started with 500 porters and marched all night; spending the day at Mtama they left again in the evening, reach-

4-INCH GUNS IN ACTION IN EAST AFRICA.

No. 15 BATTERY CROSSING THE RUFIGI RIVER IN EAST AFRICA.

ing Nynagao at midnight marching over a sandy road. There was very little firing from this position; Lieutenant Gardner on November 6th accompanied General O'Grady In case long range artillery co-operation was required, and though there was sharp fighting at Hatia the gun was not required.

On 17th November, Major Russell arrived with Battery Headquarters and Captain Ellison was sent to hospital. The Germans had now run out of 4.1-inch ammunition and therefore took their gun to pieces and buried it, but it was all disinterred except the sliding breech block.

On 3rd December the battery left for the coast, towing the gun behind F.W.D. lorries, two and sometimes three lorries being required to move it. Reaching the coast on 5th they went by water on 16th from Mingoyo to Lindi and thence to Dar es Salaam. The following embarked for Durban on 4th January, 1918; Major Russell, Captain Ellison, Lieutenant Gardner and 41 N.C.O.s and men and left for England on the 21st January.

The personnel of the batteries had suffered very much from fever and privations and though none were killed or wounded, one officer and 22 N.C.O.'s and men died of disease whilst considerable numbers were invalided.

Total originally landed 199, reinforcements 22	221
Invalided or rejoined the ships	177
Embarked for home	44

It is interesting to recall that Colonel Von Lettow-Vorbeck the German commanding officer, who as everyone agrees conducted his campaign in a very brilliant manner was also a sea soldier, being a member of the German Marine Corps. The following rewards were gazetted for service in this unit during the campaign.

Military Cross. Captain J. F. Ellison, D.C.M., R.M.L.I.   Lieutenant J. C. Guy, R.M.A.

Meritorious Service Medal. Battery Sergeant-Major V. C. Willcox, R.M.A.
Acting-Corporal W. O. Croft, R.M.A.   Corporal J. W. Lawson, R.M.A.

Legion of Honour (French). Captain R. C. A. Glunicke, R.M.L.I.

Mentioned in Dispatches.—

Captain R. C.A. Glunicke, R.M.L.I.
Battery Sergt-Major J. Bach, R.M.A.
Bombardier A. Simms, R.M.A. (twice)
Bombardier J. W. Lawson, R.M.A.
Private W. G. Mann (Portsmouth R.M.L.I.)
Captain J. F. Ellison, R.M.L.I.
Captain H. R. Purser, R.M.A. (died)
Corporal G. P. Branston (Ply. R.M.L.I.)
Sergeant J. Clark, R.M.A. (twice)
Bombardier W. O. Croft, R.M.A.

Sergeant K. McK. Johnson (Ply.) R.M.L.I.
Gunner T. C. Westall, R.M.A.
B.S.M. V. C. Willcox, R.M.A.
Lieutenant J. C. Guy, R.M.A.
Sergeant F. Allman, R.M.A. (died)
Private J.W. Fields (Portsmouth R.M.L.I.)
Sergeant W. H. Mills, R.M.A.
Lieutenant H. Gardner, R.M.A.
Gunner F. Ellis, R.M.A.
Sergeant M. Powers, R.M.A.

www.ingramcontent.com/pod-product-compliance
Lightning Source LLC
Chambersburg PA
CBHW031624160426
43196CB00006B/268